Working as Equals

Working as Equals

Relational Egalitarianism and the Workplace

Edited by
JULIAN DAVID JONKER AND GRANT J. ROZEBOOM

with a foreword by
ELIZABETH ANDERSON

OXFORD
UNIVERSITY PRESS

Oxford University Press is a department of the University of Oxford. It furthers
the University's objective of excellence in research, scholarship, and education
by publishing worldwide. Oxford is a registered trade mark of Oxford University
Press in the UK and certain other countries.

Published in the United States of America by Oxford University Press
198 Madison Avenue, New York, NY 10016, United States of America.

© Oxford University Press 2023

All rights reserved. No part of this publication may be reproduced, stored in
a retrieval system, or transmitted, in any form or by any means, without the
prior permission in writing of Oxford University Press, or as expressly permitted
by law, by license, or under terms agreed with the appropriate reproduction
rights organization. Inquiries concerning reproduction outside the scope of the
above should be sent to the Rights Department, Oxford University Press, at the
address above.

You must not circulate this work in any other form
and you must impose this same condition on any acquirer.

Library of Congress Cataloging-in-Publication Data
Names: Jonker, Julian David, editor. | Rozeboom, Grant J., editor. |
Anderson, Elizabeth, 1959– writer of foreword.
Title: Working as equals : relational egalitarianism and the workplace /
Julian David Jonker and Grant J. Rozeboom ; with a foreword by Elizabeth Anderson.
Description: New York, NY : Oxford University Press, [2023] |
Includes bibliographical references and index.
Identifiers: LCCN 2023005110 (print) | LCCN 2023005111 (ebook) |
ISBN 9780197634301 (paperback) | ISBN 9780197634295 (hardback) | ISBN 9780197634325 (epub)
Subjects: LCSH: Industrial relations. | Equality. | Organizational behavior—Moral and
ethical aspects. | Business ethics.
Classification: LCC HD6971.W8553 2023 (print) | LCC HD6971 (ebook) |
DDC 331—dc23/eng/20230302
LC record available at https://lccn.loc.gov/2023005110
LC ebook record available at https://lccn.loc.gov/2023005111

DOI: 10.1093/oso/9780197634295.001.0001

Contents

Foreword	vii
Elizabeth Anderson	
Acknowledgments	ix
Contributors	xi

1. Introduction   1
   Grant J. Rozeboom and Julian David Jonker

2. What Is Wrong with the Commodification of Human Labor Power: The Argument from "Democratic Character"   13
   Debra Satz

3. An Objection to Workplace Hierarchy Itself?   32
   Niko Kolodny

4. Seeing Like a Firm: Social Equality, Conservatism, and the Aesthetics of Inequality   53
   Pierre-Yves Néron

5. Self-Employment and Independence   73
   Iñigo González Ricoy

6. *Hobby Lobby* and the Moral Structure of the Employee-Employer Relationship   94
   David Silver

7. Justice in Human Capital   113
   Michael Cholbi

8. Can Employers Discriminate without Treating Some Employees Worse Than Others? Discrimination, the Comparative View, and Relational Equality   132
   Kasper Lippert-Rasmussen

9. A Cooperative Paradigm of Employment   153
   Sabine Tsuruda

vi CONTENTS

10. The Workplace as a Cooperative Institution 174
Julian David Jonker

11. Relational Egalitarianism, Institutionalism, and Workplace
Hierarchy 194
Brian Berkey

12. Good Enough for Equality 214
Grant J. Rozeboom

Index 235

Foreword

What demands does the ideal of a society of equals place on the ways we work? What kind of ethos should animate workplaces, so that we can relate to each other as equals, both within the workplace and beyond it? Is a society of equals compatible with hierarchy within the workplace? This rich volume of essays proposes diverse answers to these questions. It thereby advances the project of relational egalitarianism in one of the most important domains of society.

The ideal of a society of equals is sociologically complex. We can relate to each other as equals in authority (as decision-makers), in standing (as persons with interests to be considered of equal importance in the ways others make decisions and treat us), and in respect, esteem, or status (as persons regarded favorably in the eyes of others). Hence, the ideal of relational equality makes multifarious demands—on the constitution of governments, whether of the state or the firm; on the kinds of reasons that may justify institutional arrangements and inform the deliberations of decision-makers; on our interpersonal attitudes and the norms of social interaction that express them. It also constrains the distribution of the diverse benefits and burdens of social cooperation, both within social organizations such as the firm, and overall in the joint operations of the basic institutions of society.

Taken together, the chapters in *Working as Equals* attend to all of these dimensions of relational equality. This volume considers how relational equality makes demands on the distribution of the benefits and burdens of human capital development. It shows how antidiscrimination norms place demands not just on our treatment of coworkers but also on our attitudes toward them. It explores how equal respect for the workers' personal autonomy places constraints on the kinds of reasons managers may consider in exercising their workplace authority. It critically analyzes the ways firms "see" workers in hierarchical terms, and how this normative way of seeing has its own romantic aesthetic, casting top executives as heroes. It thereby prompts us to reflect on what modes of seeing and aesthetics of work might be fitting for an egalitarian workplace, and whether they could hold at least comparable appeal.

viii FOREWORD

Relational egalitarian ideals for the organization of work have often gravitated toward two very different models. One advocates universal self-employment, in which no one has or is a boss. The other promotes a fully democratic workplace, in which workers cooperate in production on a nonhierarchical basis, making critical decisions about their enterprise collectively. Both models have intuitive appeal for egalitarians. *Working as Equals* raises important concerns about each. While the principal justification for workplace hierarchy is productive efficiency, some of these concerns arise from an egalitarian point of view. Markets may subordinate even self-employed workers to those who contract for their labor. Various factors may render some forms of workplace hierarchy compatible with a society of equals. Workplace hierarchy is tempered by various factors not found at the state level. This weakens the argument that democracy is required for workplaces as it is for state governments. But the employment relation also includes factors that enhance the case for a democratic workplace. Relational equality demands that individuals adopt an egalitarian ethos. If this ethos is pervasive, it may enable a society of equals even if the workplace contains a hierarchy of offices. Perhaps also workplace hierarchy can be made compatible with a society of equals as long as the justifications for employer directives are constrained by reasons acceptable to all participants. However, other chapters in this volume make the case for more robust forms of worker participation in the firm governance, either via codetermination (joint government by employers and workers), or a more fully democratic constitution, as in workers' cooperatives. We must also tend to interactions between workplace organization and the state: stabilizing democracy at the state level may require workplace democracy, because the latter cultivates the capacities and dispositions needed for state-level democracy to work well.

By highlighting diverse normative and empirical considerations at play in the ideal of relational equality as it should be realized in the workplace, *Working as Equals* takes a significant step forward in social and political philosophy. In an age of rising inequality within the workplace and beyond, this volume helps us think about what a better and more just domain of work would look like.

Elizabeth Anderson
Ann Arbor, Michigan

Acknowledgments

We thank our editors at Oxford University Press, Lucy Randall and Lauralee Yeary, for their support and enthusiasm throughout this project. The contributions to the collection were discussed at a workshop held in June 2021. We'd hoped to have this workshop in person but the continuing pandemic necessitated holding the workshop online. We thank all involved for their engagement and enthusiasm despite the changing (and challenging) circumstances. The workshop was generously supported by Bill Laufer and the Carol and Lawrence Zicklin Center for Business Ethics Research at the Wharton School of the University of Pennsylvania, and the Elfenworks Center for Responsible Business at Saint Mary's College of California. We appreciate the helpful discussion and comments offered by all involved, including the authors and the following program participants: Erin Beeghly, Mitch Berman, Nicolas Cornell, Samuel Freeman, Lisa Herzog, Nien-hê Hsieh, Rahul Kumar, R. J. Leland, Jed Lewinsohn, Daniel Markovits, Alex Motchoulski, Véronique Munoz-Dardé, Andreas Schmidt, Amy Sepinwall, Gopal Sreenivasan, and Han van Wietmarschen. Mia Jimenez and Jocelyn Villalta Lua helped ensure that the workshop ran smoothly. Jocelyn ably set up the workshop website and helped with other online logistics. We obtained very helpful advice and encouragement at the proposal stage from Erin Beeghly, Manuel Vargas, and R. Jay Wallace. Swift and precise copy-editing was provided by S. C. "Kappie" Kaplan. Brian Berkey, Alex Motchoulski, and Han van Wietmarschen provided incisive comments on early drafts of the introduction. We thank our partners, Hilary and Leah, and our families for their patience and tireless encouragement.

Contributors

Brian Berkey: Associate Professor, Legal Studies and Business Ethics, The Wharton School of the University of Pennsylvania

Michael Cholbi: Professor of Philosophy, University of Edinburgh

Julian David Jonker: Assistant Professor, Legal Studies and Business Ethics, the Wharton School of the University of Pennsylvania

Niko Kolodny: Professor of Philosophy, University of California, Berkeley

Kasper Lippert-Rasmussen: Professor in Political Theory, University of Aarhus, and Professor II in Philosophy, University of Tromsø

Pierre-Yves Néron: Associate Professor of Social and Political Philosophy, Université Catholique de Lille, European School of Political and Social Sciences (ESPOL)

Iñigo González Ricoy: Associate Professor of Political Philosophy, University of Barcelona

Grant J. Rozeboom: Assistant Professor, Business Ethics and Social Responsibility, Saint Mary's College of California

Debra Satz: Vernon R. & Lysbeth Warren Anderson Dean of the School of Humanities and Sciences, Marta Sutton Weeks Professor of Ethics in Society, and Professor of Philosophy and, by courtesy, Political Science, Stanford University

David Silver: Associate Professor, Sustainability and Ethics Group, and Chair in Business and Professional Ethics, W. Maurice Young Centre for Applied Ethics, University of British Columbia

Sabine Tsuruda: Assistant Professor, Queen's University Faculty of Law

1

Introduction

Grant J. Rozeboom and Julian David Jonker

A commitment to the moral equality of persons is both commonplace and difficult to make articulate. Many of us hope that such a commitment can provide meaningful guidance for structuring our relationships, organizations, and institutions. But to provide such guidance, the ideal of equality must allow for some of the forms of inequality and hierarchy that seem endemic to contemporary human social life, without tolerating so much of the status quo that it is empty or platitudinous. It must be both tolerant and demanding. This is not to say that the requirements of equality should bend to our convenience. It is simply to point out that satisfying these requirements should allow for some institutionalized forms of social coordination, though not uncritically so.

Political philosophers who have focused on the distributive dimension of equality—i.e., on whether the distribution of certain resources realizes an ideal of equality—have struggled to manage this balancing act between tolerance and demandingness. On the side of tolerance, few have claimed that the ideal of equality requires strict equality of whatever the currency of distributive justice is (the *equalisandum*).[1] Yet spelling out a tolerant-but-demanding positive account of equality's distributive demands has proven immensely challenging. For instance, it is natural to think that equality demands that persons be insulated from some of the effects of bad luck.[2] But capturing this

---

[1] The problem with strict equality is that it forecloses the opportunity to make some better off—in that respect, the Difference Principle proposed by John Rawls in *A Theory of Justice*, rev. ed. (Cambridge, MA: Harvard University Press, 1999) is preferable. But strict distributive equality has at least one defender: Kai Nielsen, *Equality and Liberty: A Defense of Radical Egalitarianism* (Totowa, NJ: Rowman & Allanheld, 1985).

[2] The suggestion is made by Rawls, *A Theory of Justice*, 63. For discussion see Susan Hurley and Richard Arneson, "Luck and Equality," *Proceedings of the Aristotelian Society*, supplementary vol. 75 (2001): 51–90. The debate is relevant to another controversial question: what is the equalisandum to be equally distributed? See Ronald Dworkin's "What Is Equality? Part 1: Equality of Welfare," *Philosophy and Public Affairs* 10, no. 3 (1981): 185–246, and "What Is Equality? Part 2: Equality of Resources," *Philosophy and Public Affairs* 10, no. 4 (1981): 283–345. See also Amartya Sen, "Equality of What?," in *Choice, Welfare and Measurement* (Cambridge: Cambridge University Press, 1982), 353–369, and G. A. Cohen, "On the Currency of Egalitarian Justice," *Ethics* 99, no. 4 (1989): 906–944.

Grant J. Rozeboom and Julian David Jonker, *Introduction* In: *Working as Equals.* Edited by: Julian David Jonker and Grant J. Rozeboom, Oxford University Press. © Oxford University Press 2023.
DOI: 10.1093/oso/9780197634295.003.0001

2 WORKING AS EQUALS

thought in a distributive principle seems to become either too demanding (as we insulate persons from more forms of luck, we expose them to invasive, unwieldy forms of public scrutiny) or too tolerant (as we allow persons' choices to play a predominant role in determining their shares, we accept greater inequalities). It is also difficult to arrive at an account of the distributive equalisandum that does not focus too narrowly on income and wealth but still allows for substantive criticisms of the economic inequalities that trouble many communities.

This has led some philosophers to focus, instead, on the relational aspects of the ideal of equality—i.e., to take the "relational turn" in political philosophy.[3] A commitment to the equality of persons is most fundamentally a commitment to certain patterns of interpersonal relations, not to certain patterns of distribution of an equalisandum.[4] (Of course, this does not preclude being concerned about unequal distributions. It is just to claim that the ultimate point of distributive justice is to create a society in which people relate as equals.)[5] What claims to equal authority, status, esteem, and justification can persons make? How can these claims be asserted and recognized within our practices and institutions? An aspiration of the relational turn is that, by focusing on these aspects of interpersonal relations rather than distributive patterns, we can more easily explain how some unequal yet intuitively acceptable features of human society might align with a commitment to equality. At the same time, the relational turn places substantive demands on our practices (concerning authority, status, etc.) that tend to be underappreciated by distribution-focused theorists. It is worth noting that these relational aspects of our practices are particularly resonant with the civil rights struggles of the late twentieth century, such as those concerning race, gender, and sexuality.

Despite these high hopes, relational egalitarians still face serious difficulties in articulating an ideal of equality that is adequately tolerant and demanding. To see why, consider the target of relational egalitarian criticism on which we focus in this volume—the workplace. On the one hand, those

---

[3] Kasper Lippert-Rasmussen, *Relational Egalitarianism: Living as Equals* (Cambridge: Cambridge University Press, 2018), suggests that some think that relational egalitarianism can *evade* these disagreements, though he observes that similar questions, such as those about luck, currency, and the time frame of equality, can still be articulated within the relational egalitarian framework.

[4] The classic formulation in these terms is Elizabeth Anderson, "What Is the Point of Equality?," *Ethics* 109, no. 2 (1999): 287–337.

[5] Samuel Scheffler, "The Practice of Equality," in *Social Equality: On What It Means to Be Equals*, ed. Carina Fourie, Fabian Schuppert, and Ivo Walliman-Helmer (Oxford: Oxford University Press, 2015), 21–44.

who insist on such relational egalitarian staples as equal status, authority, esteem, and power may make clear, substantive demands of workplaces. But these are likely to be simplistic or very difficult to square with the realities of contemporary economic production. An example here may be egalitarian demands for workplace democracy.[6] Many scholars worry (perhaps unfairly) that such demands are not feasibly satisfied in modern economies, in which transaction costs and other obstacles to production are solved by firm hierarchies, which in turn expand in order to take advantage of economies of scale.[7] On the other hand, relational egalitarians may weaken their demands so that they accommodate the unequal status, authority, and power found within contemporary firms. But at this point the relational ideal of equality can appear so thin and platitudinous that it becomes "otiose," as J. R. Lucas puts it.[8] One illustration (which, as above, may be somewhat unfair) is the proposal that the ills of workplace hierarchy are adequately remedied by ensuring that employees are entitled to easily exit the employment relationship.[9] This proposal seems to leave the current landscape of work almost entirely undisturbed, making hardly any egalitarian demands of it.[10]

This problem of providing a tolerant-yet-demanding account of relational equality in the workplace is made even more pressing by the pervasiveness and relative necessity of participating in workplace relations. The amount of time that is ordinarily spent in the workplace, together with the fact that for most people it is necessary to work for another in order to survive, means that the experience of being subject to a boss is second only to that of being subject to the coercive power of the state in shaping our experience of our

---

[6] For a survey of the burgeoning literature on workplace democracy, see Roberto Frega, Lisa Herzog, and Christian Neuhäuser, "Workplace Democracy—the Recent Debate," *Philosophy Compass* 14, no. 4 (2019): e12574. Nicolas Vrousalis, "Workplace Democracy Implies Economic Democracy," *Journal of Social Philosophy* 50, no. 3 (2019): 259–279, argues that egalitarian arguments for workplace democracy are committed to socialism as well.

[7] For an example of such concern, see Tyler Cowen, "Work Isn't So Bad after All," in Elizabeth Anderson, *Private Government: How Employers Rule Our Lives (and Why We Don't Talk about It)* (Princeton, NJ: Princeton University Press, 2017), 108–116. The theory of the firm as a response to problems of production was inaugurated by R. H. Coase, "The Nature of the Firm," *Economica* 4 (1937): 386–405.

[8] J. R. Lucas, "Against Equality," *Philosophy* 40, no. 154 (1965): 296–308, at 298. For a similarly general concern about the language of equality, see Peter Westen, "The Empty Idea of Equality," *Harvard Law Review* 95, no. 3 (1982): 537–596.

[9] Robert S. Taylor, *Exit Left: Markets and Mobility in Republican Thought* (Oxford: Oxford University Press, 2017).

[10] Yet it may be optimistic to claim that a right to exit would demand little change of the labor market. José Azar et al., "Concentration in US Labor Markets: Evidence from Online Vacancy Data," *Labour Economics* 66, no. C (2020): 101866, show that employers have significant monopsony power across regions and occupations in the United States. Guaranteeing the right to exit under such circumstances may require fairly radical policy intervention.

4 WORKING AS EQUALS

social world. The question for relational egalitarians is how to square the pervasiveness of workplace hierarchy with the requirements that relational equality places on our interpersonal relationships.

What resources does relational egalitarianism have for addressing this question? That is, what normative resources does it contain for finding a satisfying position between the two poles of being tolerant and being demanding, especially when we focus on the pervasive social context of the workplace? To better excavate the content of the relational egalitarian ideal, it is useful to consider how it emerged in the European Enlightenment as a response to two inegalitarian social realities of the day: feudal social orders, which created entrenched social hierarchies, and sectarian political rule, which stifled moral disagreement and oppressed religious dissidents. What emerged was a vision of social equality that was opposed to both hierarchy and sectarianism. (This may seem like an unduly Eurocentric origin story, but note that these twin egalitarian traditions have resonated beyond Europe in the anticolonial and postcolonial literature.)[11] This vision of social equality as antihierarchical and antisectarian sheds light on the theoretical developments pursued in this volume and, we hope, shows the way toward future refinements and applications of relational egalitarianism.

To illustrate the first, antihierarchical aspect of equality, consider how Jean-Jacques Rousseau developed the idea of relational equality in his best-known works, the second *Discourse* and *Social Contract*. In both works—and to paint with some very broad strokes—a guiding thought is that we must avoid social and political arrangements that leave some persons as the social inferiors of others. This is because we must avoid arrangements that injure or inflame "amour-propre"—our desire to be valued by those on whose wills we depend—which is frustrated by being left at the mercy of others' command.[12] These ideas of Rousseau's echo in the work of other Enlightenment moral and political thinkers, such as Immanuel Kant.

This antihierarchical line of relational egalitarianism found some clear continuity with republicanism, which is generally defined in terms of

---

[11] Here we think of the egalitarian ideal's continued influence upon critiques of colonialism, including those inspired by Marxism. For example, it is easy to read some of Frantz Fanon's remarks in *Black Skin, White Masks*, trans. Charles Lam Markmann (London: Pluto Press, 2008), such as those about exploitation (a problem which involves "restoring man to his proper place," 69) or relations of dependence (169), in an egalitarian light.

[12] For helpful studies of this aspect of Rousseau's thought, see N. J. H. Dent, *Rousseau: An Introduction to His Psychological, Social, and Political Theory* (Oxford: Basil Blackwell, 1988), and Frederick Neuhouser, *Rousseau's Theodicy of Self-Love: Evil, Rationality, and the Drive for Recognition* (Oxford: Oxford University Press, 2008).

its opposition to relations of domination (between, e.g., lord and serf). Contemporary republican thinkers such as Quentin Skinner, Frank Lovett, and Philip Pettit have refined the ideal of nondomination to provide accounts of how political institutions must be structured to broadly insulate persons from dominating social influences. But despite these refinements, republicanism does not, by itself, provide the antihierarchical line of egalitarian thought with a full account of how our social relations must respond to the ideal of equality, as we discuss below. It thus remains an open question how well the idea of nondomination captures the commitment to equality.

To illustrate the second, antisectarian line of thought, consider John Stuart Mill's influential defense of the liberal ideal of pluralism—of allowing a diversity of religious and moral views to be held and expressed by free and equal members of society. This may initially appear to be grounded solely in an ideal of individual liberty. But Rawls's development of this antisectarian line of thought, particularly in his account of political liberalism and reasonable disagreement, makes its egalitarian credentials clearer. Rawls's egalitarianism is most commonly identified with the influential account of distributive justice in *A Theory of Justice*, which serves as both the backdrop and foil for the relational turn in twentieth-century political philosophy. This account (including the apparatus of the Original Position) rests on the requirement that social institutions must be justifiable to all their members. The egalitarian motivation of this requirement becomes vivid in Rawls's later account of political liberalism.[13] In the liberal society envisaged by Rawls, people are empowered to develop divergent conceptions of the good life. Doing so generates competing comprehensive moral views, in light of which the institutions of a just society may not appear optimally just. Rawls's central idea, that these institutions must still be justifiable to holders of such divergent views on the basis of reasons they all can accept, is naturally understood as articulating an egalitarian ideal (sometimes expressed in term of respect) of treating individuals as having the equal standing to come to their own conclusions about what is good.

The above two strands of thought, which we have cast as the antihierarchical and antisectarian aspects of social equality, help to give content to the ideal of relational equality. Yet they leave open many questions about relational equality and how it bears on the workplace. The antisectarian tradition, especially in its Rawlsian form, is the most wanting

---

[13] John Rawls, *Political Liberalism* (New York: Columbia University Press, 1993).

6 WORKING AS EQUALS

in terms of its engagement with the workplace because it has focused so heavily on the state.[14] The antihierarchical tradition has, especially in its Marxist moments, engaged with labor relations. But it has left the relational egalitarian ideal undertheorized by treating domination as the fundamental problem, rather than treating domination as a symptom of a deeper problem of social inequality. This may make it difficult to accommodate impersonal forms of power and authority—such as the power of the state—that seem both dominating and unobjectionable because of how they realize democratic, egalitarian forms of coordination and governance.[15] We could be left with an ideal of equality that, to return to our initial problem, is insufficiently tolerant.

It is worth noting here that the neglect of the workplace within normative philosophy is not the fault of liberal egalitarianism alone. Some of the contributors to this book (including ourselves) participate in the field of business ethics, whose scholarly focus has been shaped by the demand for the professional education of managers. This institutional mandate can too easily frame business ethics as a form of applied ethics that issues advice for managers, ignoring the demands of social and political justice. (It may also be worth noting that this managerial myopia has emerged contemporaneously with the general decline of labor as a powerful political force and political economy as a prominent academic field.) So business ethics has only recently seen discussion of relational equality in the workplace.[16] It faces the prospects of a political turn at more or less the same moment that discussions of relational equality and of workplace democracy have begun to pick up steam.[17]

What, then, are the most philosophically important open questions about the relational conception of equality and how it bears on the workplace? Our

---

[14] This is in contrast with Enlightenment-era thought that was concerned with social and economic relations more broadly, as illustrated by Adam Smith's hope that free markets would enable participants to relate as equals. For exploration of Smith's point, see Debra Satz, *Why Some Things Should Not Be for Sale* (Oxford: Oxford University Press, 2010), 40ff.

[15] On this point, see Niko Kolodny, "Being under the Power of Others," in *Republicanism and the Future of Democracy*, ed. Yiftah Elezar and Geneviève Rousselière (Cambridge: Cambridge University Press, 2019), 94–114. But, for a defense of the republican focus on domination rather than relational equality, see Andreas T. Schmidt, "Domination without Inequality? Mutual Domination, Republicanism, and Gun Control," *Philosophy & Public Affairs* 46, no. 2 (2018): 175–206.

[16] An example of this engagement is Pierre-Yves Néron, "Rethinking the Very Idea of Egalitarian Markets and Corporations," *Business Ethics Quarterly* 25, no. 1 (2015): 93–124.

[17] On the political turn in business ethics, see Joseph Heath, Jeff Moriarty, and Wayne Norman, "Business Ethics and (or as) Political Philosophy," *Business Ethics Quarterly* 20, no. 3 (2010): 427–572, and Jeffrey Smith, "Navigating Our Way between Market and State," *Business Ethics Quarterly* 29, no. 1 (2019): 127–141.

first question concerns the scope of the relational egalitarian ideal. Is it an ideal that directly concerns how individuals conduct their relations with one another and the social ethos that emerges from their relations? This is suggested by the antihierarchical strand of thought, which seeks to disrupt relations of social superiority and inferiority and establish patterns of interaction in which people regard one another as equals. Or is it rather an ideal that, as the antisectarian, Rawlsian notion of justifiability suggests, most directly concerns the general principles that determine the structure of just economic and political institutions, and not (directly) the conduct and character of individuals? Is relational equality most fundamentally about how we interact or, instead, the structure of the institutions and practices within which we interact? Our volume's focus on the workplace reveals that this distinction is ultimately difficult to sustain. Our answer to the question must be "Yes, to both." For, as a number of our contributors suggest, we cannot fully understand the demands that relational equality places on individual workplace participants, such as managers deciding whether to dictate the dress and appearance of employees, without consulting the broader structural constraints that it imposes on the workplace and markets. And, conversely, we cannot fully understand how relational equality constrains the institutional features of the workplace without recognizing the demands it makes of individuals.

To illustrate, consider first the chapters that highlight the importance of individual-directed demands of relational equality, including those by Brian Berkey, Kasper Lippert-Rasmussen, and Grant Rozeboom. Berkey argues that those who are committed to relational equality as a tenet of institutional justice must concede that, at least in the workplace, equality places direct demands on the actions of those (such as managers) who are in a position to abuse their discretionary organizational power. As Berkey characterizes it, this is a rejection of a purely "institutionalist" conception of relational equality. Lippert-Rasmussen aims to vindicate a commonsense comparative understanding of discrimination (a paradigmatic failure to relate as equals), on which discrimination involves treating individuals worse than some comparators. The revised account of discrimination that Lippert-Rasmussen develops entails that avoiding discrimination cannot be achieved merely by institutions that could ensure that no persons are treated worse than comparators on the basis of objectionable factors, but rather also requires individuals to avoid holding objectionable, equality-undermining attitudes toward others. Finally, Rozeboom argues that, in order for relational equality

8   WORKING AS EQUALS

to oppose social hierarchy through the creation of egalitarian social norms, it must place demands on individuals' character traits. In this way, a commitment to social structures of relational equality generates a virtue ethics—a theory of morally good character. All of these chapters, then, show how an account of the requirements of relational equality for individuals must be developed hand in hand with an account of the more structural, institutional aspects of relational equality.

Other chapters, such as those by Niko Kolodny, Michael Cholbi, and Julian Jonker, highlight the demands that relational equality places upon institutions, rather than individuals. Cholbi, focusing on a novel question about what justice requires of the acquisition and use of human capital, presents a principle for evaluating whether human capital ledgers (comprising the benefits and burdens of human capital) are justly distributed. Given the complicated metaphysics of human capital that Cholbi describes, it is doubtful that the attitudes and virtues of individuals can satisfy Cholbi's principle on their own. Instead, there is likely a need for institutional and political arrangements that will regulate the just distribution of human capital.

Kolodny and Jonker propose related approaches to apparently distinct problems. Kolodny is concerned with whether workplace authority can be made compatible with the egalitarian principle that nobody be treated as another's inferior. A central claim is that the principle requires that bosses exercise authority on the basis of reasons that are impartial and impersonal. But his focus is not entirely individual-directed, and he turns to the question of whether workplace democracy is required to ensure equal workplace relations (though he leaves the question open after setting out the considerations that bear upon it). Jonker's discussion moves in the opposite direction. He begins with the question of how workplace authority is to be made compatible with liberalism's aim of accommodating disagreement about the good, and his answer focuses on the importance of an institutional perspective, defined in terms of a cooperative conception of the workplace, that respects the equal standing of workplace participants. But this proposal ultimately places egalitarian demands directly upon the individuals who exercise authority in the workplace.

A second foundational question is about the content of the relational egalitarian ideal. Along what dimension or measure must people be related as equals? A natural thought for those who take the antihierarchical aspects of relational equality seriously is that people must have some sort of equal basic *status*. A different view, which naturally stems from the pluralistic origins

INTRODUCTION   9

of relational egalitarianism, is that people's interests must receive equal *consideration*. This interest-focused view is implicit in the ideal of mutual justifiability that looms large in the chapters by Kolodny and Jonker, and it also receives a distinctively republican treatment in Iñigo González Ricoy's chapter. González Ricoy argues that self-employment may not be the salve for avoiding inegalitarian forms of dependence at work that many assume it is. Indeed, managerial authority can be constrained to track workers' interests, whereas the market forces to which the self-employed are exposed are not so easily constrained.

A third option that derives support from both the antihierarchical and pluralistic strands of relational egalitarianism concerns *autonomy*: what it is for people to relate as equals is for them to respect, support, and perhaps co-realize each other's equal governance of their own lives.[18] In addition to the autonomy-focused view of relational egalitarian virtue defended in Rozeboom's chapter, David Silver provides a conception of relational equality in terms of "self-sovereignty," whose sphere he takes to be demarcated by the democratic process. Making use of this claim, he argues that the owners of the Hobby Lobby company cannot use their religious beliefs to shirk their egalitarian responsibility to support the autonomy of their employees.

Note that these three general options for understanding the content of the relational egalitarian ideal are not mutually exclusive (perhaps a pluralist view is called for, as Kasper Lippert-Rasmussen has argued in earlier work)[19] and, in fact, may be combined. Note also that our answer to the question of what dimension(s) along which people ought to be related as equals should also help us answer the further question of how, or in what sense, the ideal is distinctively relational. How does this ideal contrast with nonrelational ideals of equality? The above notions of status, interest-consideration, and respect for autonomy suggest some plausible answers: we enjoy a certain status only in being related to others in certain practices and institutions; our interests are given adequate consideration only when our interactions with others reflect such consideration; our autonomy is realized in the relevant sense only when our relations to others are structured by respect for it.

A third and final foundational question concerns the justification of the relational egalitarian ideal. Why is it morally important for people to relate as

---

[18] This is closely linked to the relational dimensions of interpersonal authority, as developed by Stephen Darwall's notion of "second-personal" authority in *The Second-Person Standpoint* (Cambridge, MA: Harvard University Press, 2007).

[19] Lippert-Rasmussen, *Relational Egalitarianism*.

each other's equals? This issue has been seriously neglected, and there are several, sometimes overlapping views suggested by the chapters in this volume that provide viable theoretical paths forward. A common assumption, made explicit in this volume by Jonker and Silver, is that relational equality reflects basic moral equality. We ought to relate as equals because we *are* each other's moral equals. But this assumption is controversial: as Rozeboom argues, it is not clear that basic moral equality can adequately ground the imperative to relate as equals, and an adequate explanation of our basic moral equality may need to appeal to the fact that we ought to relate as equals, given the difficulty of establishing the basis of persons' moral equality.[20]

A different, negative approach to justifying relational equality is to identify the clearly objectionable forms of social inequality that we must avoid. This negative approach has previously been developed by T. M. Scanlon and Andrea Sangiovanni.[21] In this volume, it is pushed in a novel direction by Pierre-Yves Néron. Néron thinks that relational egalitarians have thus far misidentified their theoretical enemy as a form of libertarianism that, to put it roughly, tolerates social inequality for the sake of preserving expansive forms of economic freedom. Néron thinks the real opponent is rather a kind of conservatism that appreciates social hierarchy for its own sake. This hierarchy-appreciation is challenging to confront, because it is distinctively aesthetic—a kind of admiration and attraction toward social hierarchy that Néron calls the "aesthetics of inequality." Néron's view suggests that relational egalitarians need to reorient their efforts to justify relational equality to address this conservative opponent.

A third approach to justifying relational equality appeals to democracy: relational equality is important as a linchpin of democratic social and political institutions. We find this view in Debra Satz's chapter about how workplaces must foster the capacities and dispositions that democratic citizens need to engage with one another as equals. For Satz, the democratic capacity cultivation required of workplaces places constraints on the extent to which labor can be "commodified"—treated merely as something to be bought or sold on an open market. This adds an important line of argument to her earlier,

---

[20] For some recent discussion, see Ian Carter, "Respect and the Basis of Equality," *Ethics* 121, no. 3 (2011): 538–571, and Richard Arneson, "Basic Equality: Neither Acceptable nor Rejectable," in *Do All Persons Have Equal Moral Worth? On "Basic Equality" and Equal Respect and Concern*, ed. Uwe Steinhoff (Oxford: Oxford University Press, 2014), 30–52.

[21] Thomas M. Scanlon, *Why Does Inequality Matter?* (Oxford: Oxford University Press, 2018), and Andrea Sangiovanni, *Humanity without Dignity: Moral Equality, Respect, and Human Rights* (Cambridge, MA: Harvard University Press, 2017).

INTRODUCTION   11

influential work on the moral limits of markets. In a different vein, Sabine Tsuruda argues that the normative precarity that workers face calls for a default of cooperative, democratic workplace relations rather than the current default of authoritarian workplace relations. (This is closely related to the ideal of a cooperative workplace that we find in Jonker's chapter.) Rather than thinking of democracy as justifying workplace relations of equality from the outside, as it were, Tsuruda finds that the value of democratic interaction justifies relations of equality from within the workplace.

While we have been mapping the contributions to this volume in terms of their philosophical development of the ideal of equality, an important part of the appeal of relational egalitarianism is that it promises to shed light on, and make more tractable, important applied issues about workplaces. For instance, Lippert-Rasmussen's chapter, taken alongside Sophia Moreau's recent work,[22] shows the great promise of using the ideal of relational equality to diagnose and demarcate objectionable forms of discrimination. Issues of workplace blame and moral responsibility, while currently underexplored in the normative business ethics literature, take center stage for relational egalitarians, given their concern with mutual accountability and reciprocity. We see this in Rozeboom's chapter, and also in Tsuruda's earlier work.[23] González Ricoy's chapter makes a strong case for thinking that the contemporary landscape of self-employment should be a more prominent issue for both liberal egalitarians and republicans. Cholbi's chapter raises a novel question about the significance of how the benefits and burdens of human capital are distributed. And throughout many of the chapters, several underexplored issues about the exercise of managerial discretion—over, e.g., dress codes and employee speech—are given careful, clarifying treatment. While expansive, this is far from an exhaustive list of workplace (and marketplace) issues that would benefit from relational egalitarian scrutiny.

But we have chosen a more theoretical focus in this introduction because we hope to show that illumination can be obtained in the converse direction, too—that considering the bearing of relational equality on questions about the structure and place of the workplace in our social lives can be a fruitful path to deepening and clarifying our understanding of relational egalitarianism. In particular, we believe that the chapters here show how to navigate

---

[22] Sophia Moreau, *Faces of Inequality: A Theory of Wrongful Discrimination* (Oxford: Oxford University Press, 2020).

[23] Sabine Tsuruda, "Working as Equal Moral Agents," *Legal Theory* 26, no. 4 (2020): 305–337.

12 WORKING AS EQUALS

a path (or several interesting paths) through the tension with which we opened. They illustrate how the ideal of equality can critically inform, rather than simply accept or overthrow, our everyday workplace practices.

Perhaps most importantly, our contributors are united in recognizing that the state is not the only site for applying the political ideal of equality. Indeed, if we are to understand and make good on a political commitment to relating as equals, we need to figure out how to enact this commitment in the work-place. Work's place in our lives, and its significance for our economic, social, and political institutions, is too great to ignore. A society of equals must be one in which we work as equals.

2

What Is Wrong with the Commodification of Human Labor Power

The Argument from "Democratic Character"

Debra Satz

Karl Marx claimed that the defining feature of capitalism is its commodification of human labor power. On Marx's view, neither the exchange of commodities nor the existence of money is a sufficient condition for capitalist production; indeed, both conditions were found in the ancient world.[1] Instead, capitalist production requires the *widespread buying and selling* of labor power within a system aimed at increasing exchange value; a system where few alternatives to selling one's labor power are available for attaining a livelihood. In Marx's own work, this claim undergirds his theory of alienation, his theory of surplus value and exploitation, and his discussion of the path through which formally free labor becomes substantively unfree.

To fix ideas, human labor power becomes a commodity when it is developed and allocated according to market considerations and aims. This means, among other things, that people are employed in order to make a profit and dispensed with if they cannot produce (through their labor) at a rate that satisfies market demand. They are also liable to be replaced when another means of producing that is more efficient becomes available. Willy Loman's dismissal by his employer, in Arthur Miller's *Death of a Salesman*, captures this logic well: "It's a business kid, and everybody's gotta pull his own weight.... Cause you gotta admit, business is business."[2]

The commodification of human labor power also means that work is structured so as to maximize output and not in the main as a vehicle for human

---

[1] Peter Brown, *Through the Eye of the Needle: Wealth, the Fall of Rome, and the Making of Christianity in the West, 350–550 AD* (Princeton, NJ: Princeton University Press, 2012).

[2] Quoted in G. A. Cohen, *If You're an Egalitarian, How Come You Are So Rich?* (Cambridge, MA: Harvard University Press, 2000), 181.

Debra Satz, *What Is Wrong with the Commodification of Human Labor Power* In: *Working as Equals*. Edited by: Julian David Jonker and Grant J. Rozeboom, Oxford University Press. © Oxford University Press 2023.
DOI: 10.1093/oso/9780197634295.003.0002

14 WORKING AS EQUALS

self-development (except insofar as that promotes efficient output). In traditional assembly lines, as well as in many other unskilled jobs, there is little need for worker judgment, reflection, imagination, or dexterity. Instead, unaccountable power over workers, exercised on behalf of producing commodities at the lowest possible cost, controls much of the labor process.[3]

Consider the conditions of work in the factories and offices of America's two largest employers: Amazon and Walmart. Amazon workers are timed to the second during ten-hour shifts. *London Financial Times* economics correspondent Sarah O'Connor describes how, at an Amazon center in Rugeley, England, Amazon tags its employees with personal satellite navigation computers that tell them the route they must travel to shelve consignments of goods, and also sets target times for their warehouse journeys and then measures whether these targets are met.[4] When you are clocked in, you have only seconds to pick an item and begin moving, shelving, or packing it. Workers are also timed for bathroom breaks and questioned if they do not use the nearest bathroom available. Those who fall short of their targets are fired.[5] It was only after journalists like Spencer Soper exposed working conditions at Amazon's Lehigh Valley Center, where the temperature reached 102 degrees Fahrenheit—so hot that the company had an ambulance on stand-by ready to take workers to the hospital, that Amazon installed air-conditioning.[6] Walmart has settled class action suits brought by workers who were forced to work off the clock, and suits have been brought against the company for repeatedly denying rest and lunch breaks to workers when demand is high. It is certainly true that Amazon and Walmart deliver goods efficiently and at a competitively low price. But the human price is high.

And these problems are not just found at these employers. Automated systems are now upending predictable work schedules and shifting the costs to workers where previously employers had absorbed fluctuations in demand; and panopticon-like systems of eyeball tracking and location tracing are also on the rise. This is Taylorism on steroids.

---

[3] To be sure, not all work that looks "mindless" really is. See Katherine Newman, *There's No Shame in My Game* (New York: Vintage and Russell Sage Foundation, 1999). And even bad work can be important to self-respect in ways that I will discuss later in this chapter.

[4] Sarah O'Conner, "Amazon Unpacked," *Financial Times Magazine*, February 8, 2013.

[5] Simon Head, *Mindless: Why Smarter Machines Are Making Dumber Humans* (New York: Basic Books, 2014).

[6] Spencer Soper and Scott Kraus, "Amazon Gets Heat over Warehouse," *Morning Call*, September 25, 2011.

THE COMMODIFICATION OF HUMAN LABOR POWER   15

A few caveats are in order. First, to say that capitalism treats human labor power as a commodity does not mean that *all* human labor power within a capitalist society is commodified. For example, the housework my husband performs and the dinners I cook for friends are not treated as commodities.

Second, the fact that at work, people are treated according to market norms does not mean that they are treated *only* according to market norms. Marx himself acknowledged that there were social and historical factors that influenced the price of labor power—and therefore differentiated its sale price from that of other commodities.[7] We could produce and make use of human labor power more cheaply than we do. Moreover, many capitalist societies have gone much further in buffering or restricting the effects of commodifying human labor power than did the nineteenth-century enterprises of Marx's time. Consider unemployment insurance, free public education, minimum wage laws, the eight-hour workday, social security, and guaranteed healthcare. Developed capitalist societies have adopted these and/or other measures, very often in response to worker organizing and struggle. These measures can be thought of as partially decommodifying human labor power.

Third, it is possible for people who are little more than cogs in a machine at work to find outlets for self-development outside of work. And, all things being equal, some people may prefer mind-numbing, repetitive work at a higher salary to interesting work at a lower salary because of the resources the former affords them to pursue and satisfy their interests outside of work.[8]

Fourth, there are forms of work where people do enjoy substantial control and discretion over their time and effort. Tenured academics, for example, enjoy an almost unprecedented level of autonomy, voice, due process rights, and job security (although perhaps this will not last).

Still, notwithstanding these caveats, the experiences of millions of people at work in the United States and hundreds of millions elsewhere is structured by the fact that labor is allocated by markets where the overriding aim is increasing profits spurred on by competition. This not only affects the nature and quality of work, but leaves those who sell their labor power vulnerable to losing work when employing them is no longer efficient.[9]

---

[7] Karl Marx, *Capital: A Critique of Political Economy*, vol. 1, trans. Ben Fowkes (New York: Vintage Books, 1977), 275.

[8] Although see section 2.1 for findings about interaction effects between work and leisure.

[9] As Joan Robinson is said to have remarked, "The misery of being exploited by capitalists is nothing compared to the misery of not being exploited at all."

16 WORKING AS EQUALS

Recent egalitarian thought has not focused so much on the negative effects of the *commodification of human labor power*, largely directing attention to distributional measures that can be taken outside of the labor market, such as taxation, universal basic income, or those measures pertaining to securing equality of opportunity. Some of these distributional measures can be understood, as mentioned, as partially decommodifying labor power. But they do not necessarily change the nature of the work people do, nor how they are treated at work.[10] And, most importantly for my purposes in this chapter, they do not address any downstream consequences of work and workplace organization for democratic citizenship.

There are some notable exceptions to this lack of attention on capitalist workplaces. A "parallel cases" argument popularized by Michael Walzer[11] and Robert Dahl[12] argues that the case for democracy in the political realm supports the case for democracy in the economic realm. Elizabeth Anderson has recently defended a different, but related, argument. She argues that there are forms of hierarchy in corporations and businesses that amount to "private government," exercising power and authority over their employees without their consent or any accountability.[13] This, on her view, makes the power exercised illegitimate.[14]

Without rejecting these important arguments, I want to note that neither is necessarily incompatible with a degree of commodification of human labor power that erodes important human capacities. It all depends on how democracy or legitimacy in the economy is understood. For example, in John Roemer's conception of socialism, there is broad democratic public control over the economy, but firms are internally hierarchical and work is geared to productive efficiency.[15] To the extent that there is a trade-off between efficiency and innovation and mind-numbing, deskilled work with little discretion on the job, Roemer—not implausibly—opts for efficiency and

---

[10] There is an important debate on the extent to which efficiency is the root cause of the undemocratic nature of work. See Stephen A. Marglin, "What Do Bosses Do: The Origins and Functions of Hierarchy in Capitalist Production. Part I," *Review of Radical Political Economics* 6, no. 2 (1974): 60–112, for an argument that a drive for power and control are also part of the explanation.

[11] Michael Walzer, "Town Meetings and Worker's Control: A Story for Socialists," in *Radical Principles: Reflections of an Unreconstructed Democrat* (New York: Basic Books, 1980), 273–290.

[12] Robert Dahl, *A Preface to Economic Democracy* (Berkeley: University of California Press, 1985).

[13] Elizabeth Anderson, *Private Government: How Employers Rule Our Lives (and Why We Don't Talk about It)* (Princeton, NJ: Princeton University Press, 2017).

[14] See also the work of Nien-hê Hsieh, "Rawlsian Justice and Workplace Democracy," *Social Theory and Practice* 31, no. 1 (2005): 115–142, and David Schweikart, *Capitalism or Worker Control? An Ethical and Economic Appraisal* (New York: Prager, 1980).

[15] John Roemer, *A Future for Socialism* (Cambridge, MA: Harvard University Press, 1994).

innovation. And if people like hierarchy and are conditioned to be controlled and used at work as if they were tools, then the commodification of labor power may be legitimate. Anderson herself is skeptical as to whether workplace democracy is necessary to realize legitimacy in firms or industries.[16]

I want to pursue a different argument as to why a more substantial decommodification of human labor power reaching into the structure of the workplace is important: what might be called the "democratic character" argument. According to that argument, first put forward by John Stuart Mill, the commodification of human labor power—where people are hired to produce goods and services in order to make a profit—undermines some of the human capacities, traits, and preferences that political democracy depends on.[17] For this reason, Mill endorses worker-owned and worker-managed firms.

One final caveat. While I will be arguing for the need to further decommodify work, I am not assuming that such "decommodification" requires the abolition of the use of markets. We still know of no other mechanism as powerful as markets for producing growth and aggregating information across millions of people; the existence of labor markets is also an important way of accommodating the value of occupational choice. But the use of markets is compatible with limiting their extent and regulating their internal character. I will argue that we have democratic reasons for limiting workplace hierarchy, attenuating the extent of the divide between mental and manual labor, and providing opportunities for people to develop the important capacities needed for democratic citizenship. By contrast, when we allow market considerations to largely dictate the organization of work, we will find significant sectors of the economy in which people function as little more than cogs in machines.

2.1. Differentiating Types of Commodities

In my 2010 book on the moral limits of markets, I argued that there is an important distinction between types of markets.[18] Some goods, when they

---

[16] Anderson, *Private Government*, 130–131.

[17] John S. Mill, *Principles of Political Economy: With Some of Their Applications to Social Philosophy*, ed. Donald Winch (London: Penguin Books, 1970), 118–143. Related versions of this argument are also found in Carole Pateman, *Participation and Democratic Theory* (Cambridge: Cambridge University Press, 1970), and Josh Cohen, "Democratic Equality," *Ethics* 99, no. 4 (1989): 727–751.

[18] Debra Satz, *Why Some Things Should Not Be for Sale: The Moral Limits of Markets* (Oxford: Oxford University Press, 2010).

18 WORKING AS EQUALS

become commodities—when they are produced to be sold on the market to make a profit—do not change their character. Think about an apple. Whether I grow apples for my own enjoyment or buy them in the grocery store that purchased them to sell them at profit, the good received—the apple—is pretty much the same. The way that the apple is produced—on large-scale farms or on small plots—does not really matter: the apple's basic characteristics are not sensitive to these differences in production.

By contrast, the labor market is *constitutive*: the structure of the work we are paid to do has significant influences on our own development—on our capacities and traits as well as on our preferences. The classical political economists recognized this. Adam Smith, for example, raised concerns about repetitive, simple factory work:

> But the understandings . . . of men are necessarily formed by their ordinary employments. The man whose whole life is spent in performing a few simple operations, of which the effects are perhaps always the same, or very nearly the same, has no occasion to exert his understanding or to exercise his invention in finding out expedients for removing difficulties which never occur. He naturally loses, therefore, the habit of such exertion and generally becomes as stupid and ignorant as it is possible for a human creature to become. . . . The torpor of his mind renders him not only incapable of relishing or bearing a part in any rational conversation, but of conceiving any generous, noble, or tender sentiment, and consequently of forming any just judgment concerning many even of the ordinary duties of private life. Of the great and extensive interests of his country, he is altogether incapable of judging.[19]

Smith held that the way people labor—the nature of their work, their relationship to their work, their relationship to others at work—shapes their capacities. Smith's pin factory is breathtaking in its ability to produce thousands of pins at low cost. At the same time, its organization affects the people that it employs in a profound and damaging way. In other passages of the *Wealth of Nations*, including a famous passage differentiating a philosopher from a street porter, Smith attributes respective differences between

---

[19] Adam Smith, *An Inquiry into the Nature and Causes of the Wealth of Nations*, ed. R. H. Campbell and A. S. Skinner, 2 vols. (Indianapolis: Liberty Classics, 1976), 2:781–782.

THE COMMODIFICATION OF HUMAN LABOR POWER   19

people largely to the social division of labor, itself spurred on by the extent of the market.[20]

Marx also underscored the "constitutive" aspect of labor markets. He argued that a drive for increasing efficiency through market competition cripples individual human potential. In fact, Marx's normative condemnation of capitalism is that it degrades human beings to "appendages to machines"—a result of treating human labor power as a commodity—and *not* that it unfairly distributes income and wealth.[21] Smith and Marx both argue that our capacities, traits, and motivations are shaped by the institutional settings in which we work. If that claim is right, this suggests that in designing economic institutions we should take into account not only these institutions' instrumental effects in achieving productivity goals, but also their constitutive effects in fostering desirable motivations and capacities, and shaping human character.[22]

Marx, of course, went further than Smith in his criticism of labor markets, arguing in *Capital* that the anarchy in the social division of labor—the result of competition—caused "despotism" in the workshop.[23] That is, for Marx, the more that market competition holds sway, the more that work is relentlessly structured to enhance productivity—for example, breaking tasks into simple parts, promoting specialization, and treating labor inputs as simply factors of production.

Marx was wrong to think that all forms of labor in a capitalist system would be organized in ways that cripple human potential. At least three further conditions are needed: first, the labor process involved must be subject to fragmentation and mechanization so that skill and knowledge play no critical role; second, competition must lead to the intensification of work and the introduction of machines which play a central role; and third, workers must not have effective exit options available or substantial bargaining power.[24] However, notwithstanding the overgeneralized nature of his claim, Marx was right insofar as some workplaces in capitalist societies fit this despotic form,

---

[20] Smith, *Wealth of Nations*, 1: ch. 2.

[21] See Karl Marx, "Economic and Philosophic Manuscripts of 1844," in *The Marx-Engels Reader*, ed. Robert Tucker (New York: Norton, 1978), 66–125.

[22] Sam Bowles takes up this argument in many of his writings. See, for example, *The Moral Economy: Why Good Incentives Are No Substitute for Good Citizens* (New Haven, CT: Yale University Press, 2016).

[23] Marx, *Capital*, ch. 14 generally.

[24] See Michael Burawoy, "Between the Labor Process and the State: The Changing Face of Factory Regimes under Late Capitalism," *American Sociological Review* 48, no. 5 (1983): 587–605 for discussion.

20   WORKING AS EQUALS

and fail to provide workers the opportunity to use and develop important capacities. As we shall see, the failure of workplaces to offer room for the development of self-governing capacities (discretion, deliberation, voice, participation) is likely to have negative consequences for democracy.

So-called neoclassical economics, which favored abstract and mathematical representations of markets, lost sight of the classical economists' distinctions in types of markets. But not all markets are the same. We now have a rich body of empirical work that supports the idea that there is an endogeneity in labor markets that is not present in apple markets. Ely Chinoy's important study of the auto factory provided a powerful account of how boring, repetitive work with low levels of personal discretion generated high levels of dissatisfaction and alienation.[25] More recent scholarship has probed the consequences of such work further and found other disturbing effects that are more relevant for my purposes. Social psychologist Melvin Kohn, writing in the 1980s, documents the ways that parents who are able to exercise considerable self-direction at work are also much more likely to value independence (rather than obedience) in their children. In one study, Kohn and Schooler find that "occupational experience has a real and substantial impact upon ... psychological functioning."[26] Among other findings from that study, these are salient:

1. Work with substantively complex job content and that offers discretion has a measured effect on cognitive complexity.
2. Work without complexity is associated with "feelings of alienation."
3. People who are able to be self-directed at work and given challenging tasks tend to engage in more intellectually demanding leisure activities than those who do rote repetitive work.
4. Work without complexity and the opportunity for discretion is associated with lower levels of self-confidence and self-esteem.

While two of these findings measure such work's effects (primarily) on well-being with findings similar to Chinoy (2 and 4), it is important for my purposes that Kohn and Schooler's findings relate primarily to human

---

[25] Eli Chinoy, *American Workers and the American Dream* (New York: Doubleday, 1955). Being ordered about with no consideration for one's thoughts and feelings, one's interests or perspective, has also been associated with higher levels of cortisol and stress and lower levels of health.

[26] Melvin Kohn and Carmi Schooler, *Work and Personality: An Inquiry into the Impact of Social Stratification* (Norwood, NJ: Ablex, 1983), 55.

THE COMMODIFICATION OF HUMAN LABOR POWER   21

capacities and their development as well as to orienting preferences (1 and 3, and to some extent 4). Their study concluded, "Occupational self-direction has the most potent and widespread psychological effects of all the occupational conditions we have examined."[27]

The sociologist Arlie Hochschild also found that work in certain service industries was associated with changes in important human capacities. Hochschild reports that flight attendants experienced a distortion in their normal emotional responses. Having to respond with a smile to overbearing and entitled travelers all day at work diminished the flight attendants' ability to feel anger, even when it was appropriate in nonwork situations.[28]

A substantial body of literature suggests that different ways of working are associated with differing general attitudes and capabilities, even cross-culturally. Kohn's collaborative study of the United States, Japan, and Poland yielded consistent results in these countries: people who exercise self-direction on the job also value self-direction more in other realms of life and are less likely to exhibit the complex of traits that leads people to blindly follow orders and to be uncomfortable with ambiguity and complexity.

Kohn's study found that no covarying traits have as much predictive power as occupational self-direction. Other studies have attempted to go further in unpacking the direction of causation, and in distinguishing causality from mere correlation. Robert Karasek studied the effects of changes in job structure using panel data on the Swedish labor force. This allowed him to probe whether these psychological results arise because self-directed people select in to jobs where self-direction is substantial. He found that "workers whose jobs had become more passive also became more passive in their leisure and workers with more active jobs became more active. These findings were significant in eight out of nine subpopulations controlled for education and family class background."[29]

Work, whatever else it is, seems to be a giant school. There is considerable truth in Adam Smith's and Karl Marx's insight that at work *we make ourselves*, in addition to the goods and services we produce. In fact, it is not very surprising that recent empirical studies have found such significant connections

[27] Kohn and Schooler, *Work and Personality*, 81.
[28] Arlie Hochschild, *The Managed Heart: The Commercialization of Human Feeling* (New York: Basic Books, 1983).
[29] Robert Karasek, "Job Socialization: A Longitudinal Study of Work, Political and Leisure Activity," Working Paper 59 (Stockholm: Institute for Social Research, 1978). Sam Bowles discusses some of this literature in "Endogenous Preferences: The Cultural Consequences of Markets and Other Economic Institutions," *Journal of Economic Literature* 36 (March 1998): 75–111.

22 WORKING AS EQUALS

between work and personality traits, capacities, and preferences. From the ages of twenty to seventy, most people spend an enormous amount of their time participating in the labor market. The incentives and opportunities offered by the labor market encourage the development of some traits and capacities while others lay dormant or atrophy. To be sure, there are many intentional forms of inculcation of capacities, traits, and preferences: schooling, religion, families, advertising, and so on. These are undoubtedly important. The empirical studies cited above show that work influences are *also* very important in shaping who we are as well as what we can be and do.

2.2. Capacities for Democracy

Discussion has so far largely focused on the consequences of labor markets for the capacities, traits, and preferences of *individuals*. But some of these changes—for example, passivity and cognitive atrophy—also have *social effects*. And some of these latter effects are arguably relevant to the future and fate of democracy.

Democratic citizenship is an achievement. It offers the most powerful way we have of integrating the demands of equality with membership in a community. More specifically, it links a commitment to treating diverse members as free and equal individuals with the idea of society as a fair system of cooperation. It thereby sharply breaks—at least in its aspirations and assumptions—with older ways of organizing societies, on the basis of social caste, privilege, dictatorship, or minority rule. Democratic societies build a form of equality—all members—regardless of identity, religion, and way of life—are equal citizens—into their very structure.

This form of society is under a great deal of strain right now, both in the United States and around the world. Survey data, for example, shows a marked decline in support for democracy in developed countries.[30] The rise of populist autocrats has helped to make clear that democracy depends not only on laws and institutions, but also on the attitudes and qualities of society's members. Democracy cannot be taken as a given.

If we place a value on democracy, then we will want to ensure that our institutions are arranged to foster the development of people who are likely

---

[30] R. S. Foa et al., *The Global Satisfaction with Democracy Report 2020* (Cambridge: Centre for the Future of Democracy, 2020).

THE COMMODIFICATION OF HUMAN LABOR POWER   23

to support democratic institutions and to be able to function effectively in a democratic environment. Reflecting on the importance of such matters, philosopher John Rawls asks about the workplace:

> Would worker-managed firms be more likely to encourage the democratic virtues needed for a constitutional regime to endure? If so, could greater democracy within capitalist firms achieve much the same result? I shall not pursue these questions. I have no idea of the answers, but certainly these questions call for careful examination. *The long-run prospects of a just constitutional regime may depend on them.*[31]

Here, Rawls notes that the stability of a democratic society may well depend on whether or not the economic institutions of society flow along with the current of democracy and not against it.[32] This is an especially important consideration given that we want democratic institutions to be stable over time and to generate their own support.

What, then, are the capacities, traits, and preferences that citizens need to stabilize democracy over time?

A. Among the capacities that are important for democratic citizens to have would surely be the following:
   1. The capacity to work cooperatively with a diverse set of people, who differ in their conceptions of life and value;
   2. The capacity to feel empathy for, and solidarity with, this diverse set of people;
   3. The capacities involved in understanding and communicating relevant complex information, including literacy and numeracy;
   4. The capacity to make collective decisions;
   5. The capacity for self-efficacy—which in turn depends on the beliefs that one's actions matter and that our social institutions can be changed through the collective action by people working together;[33]
   6. The capacity for a sense of justice.

---

[31] John Rawls, *Justice as Fairness: A Restatement,* ed. Erin Kelly (Cambridge, MA: Harvard University Press, 2001), 178–179; my emphasis.

[32] Feminists have also made this argument with respect to the family, arguing that the structure of the family has important effects on what boys and girls can do and be. See Susan Okin, *Justice, Gender, and the Family* (New York: Basic Books, 1989).

[33] See Cohen, "Democratic Equality."

24 WORKING AS EQUALS

B. In addition to this list of capacities, there are a number of dispositions connected to the capacity for a sense of justice that are important to a democratic society:

1. A willingness to abide by democratically chosen rules, even when those rules are not in one's own self-interest, assuming that others are willing to abide by the rules and that the rules are not manifestly unjust;
2. A willingness to enforce penalties on those who break these rules;
3. A commitment to reciprocity—a willingness to do one's fair share when others are willing as well, and not to coast on the efforts of others;
4. An unwillingness to blindly surrender to authority;
5. A disposition to treat others in society as one's social equals.

2.3. How Does the Commodification of Labor Power Affect These "Democratic" Capacities and Traits?

I have presented some of the evidence detailing how work that leaves little room for discretion and judgment fails to develop or tends to erode preferences to exercise discretion and judgment outside of work as well as failing to develop cognitive complexity. This suggests that such work affects what I have labeled above as A3, A5, and B4 above. Further evidence regarding A4 and A5 is provided by an important study by Gabriel Almond and Sidney Verba.[34] Almond and Verba found that, across occupational types in five different countries, those who were consulted about their opinions on the job scored significantly higher on a measure of subjective civic competence. Their study measured workers' sense of personal efficacy in dealing with government bodies. This study suggests, then, that the surrender of authority to employers at work is not good for civic engagement.

One other consequence of the widespread sale of human labor power in a capitalist economy is worth calling attention to, a consequence discussed by Mill in his 1848 *Principles of Political Economy*. Mill thought that the relationship between capitalists and workers in which the interests of the latter were *dependent* on the interests of the former—because if the capitalist did

---

[34] Gabriel Almond and Sidney Verba, *The Civic Culture: Political Attitudes and Democracy in Five Nations* (New York: Sage Publications, 1963).

THE COMMODIFICATION OF HUMAN LABOR POWER   25

not make a profit, the worker was out of a job—was incompatible with a sense of justice by *either* party. The employers, he wrote, regard their employees as their "dependents and servants"; the workers meanwhile regard the owners as "mere prey and pasture" who must be satisfied only in order to eat.[35] This conflictual relationship is relevant to A6, B3, B5, and possibly A1 and A2.[36]

Interestingly, there have been few studies of the effects of being an "overlord." Is having so much power over the lives of others compatible with democratic character? While discretion over one's own work has been shown to have important, pro-social psychological effects, what about exercising dictatorial discretion over the work of *others*? Mill had earlier argued that families were schools of despotism for young boys. In patriarchal families, he claimed, boys learn that their interests are more important than the interests of their sisters, as well as that their mothers' interests are less important than their fathers'. Is the employer who can fire an employee for not taking his clothes to the cleaners or because he takes bathroom breaks likely to feel empathy with his firms' workers (A2), or incline to reciprocity (B3), or respect the rules (B1) in contexts where his own interests lose out? Does such a person really view his workers as his social equals (B5)?[37]

To the extent that labor markets shape preferences and capacities in ways that are relevant to a democratic society, workplace organization cannot be treated as a matter of participating individuals' concern and nothing more. In the same ways that we must care about the level and nature of children's education—for the children themselves, but also for the nature and benefits of society—so too have we a public interest in workplace design for workers themselves, but also for the long-term stability of a democratic society.

2.4. Self-Respect

Self-respect grounds our sense of efficacy, our ability to see ourselves as an independent and legitimate source of rights entitled to make claims.

---

[35] Mill, *Principles of Political Economy*.

[36] The fact that the interests of worker and capitalist owners are *conflictual* may also play an important role in structuring workplaces. This is because, as economists have noted, labor markets are incompletely specified. While I can specify a contract for apples—three hundred golden delicious apples with no bruising—how much work I will get from you will be influenced by your work ethic or degree of alienation—and the degree of control I can exert over you.

[37] See R. H. Tawney, *Equality* (London: Unwin, 1952), on the deleterious effects of the British private school system on elite sensibilities.

26 WORKING AS EQUALS

Self-respect is important as well for relating to others as their social equal. In his own theory, Rawls singles out the "social bases of self-respect" as the most important primary good.[38] But some work may undermine self-respect. This is troubling for reasons that are closely related to, but conceptually distinct from, the democratic argument I make above. It is distinct because people can relate to one another as equals outside of a democratic context, as when members of two different nations interact. It is closely related because a democratic society requires that its members relate as social equals at least with regard to their collective decision-making and with respect to their shared institutions.[39]

How, exactly, are work and self-respect related? On the one hand, people often draw a sense of self-respect from their work, indeed from the very fact that they work. Jobs are not only a source of income for many workers, they are also a source of meaning, and often support a way of life. Undoubtedly, the ties between work and the feeling of self-respect are culturally influenced. But the existence of this tie is important, and part of the reason why having an income is not a full substitute for having a job.[40] Anne Case and Angus Deaton argue that the loss of jobs is part of the explanation for the rise of "deaths of despair" among white Americans without a college degree.[41]

On the other hand, dependency—the dependency of workers on owners and managers for the design, oversight, and control of their jobs and livelihoods—fails to treat workers with dignity and respect. It is hard to think and behave as an equal when you can be ordered around, provided with no voice or consideration as to your conditions of work, fired without explanation, and discarded with little support. The term "hired hands" captures the devaluation of human beings. How could it be the case that workers who are

---

[38] Rawls, *Justice as Fairness.*

[39] Thanks to the editors of this volume for pressing this distinction. Not all the capacities and traits I list are equally important with respect to these different implications of self-respect. For example, literacy and numeracy are critical for democratic decision-making, but less directly central (although still important) to treating others as social equals.

[40] The psychological returns to work tend to be greatest for those who have meaningful and high-status jobs, many of which are also quite well paid. But there is evidence of such returns even to relatively low-paid and low-status work and of psychic harms beyond the loss of income from being out of work. Many people would be better off with a job than an unconditional grant of money, even at the same income level, because of the psychological returns to the former. See Jennie E. Brand, "The Far-Reaching Impact of Job Loss and Unemployment," *Annual Review of Sociology* 41 (2015): 359–375; for a dissenting view, see David Graeber, "On the Phenomenon of Bullshit Jobs: A Work Rant," (2013) https://theanarchistlibrary.org/library/david-graeber-on-the-phenomenon-of-bullshit-jobs-a-work-rant.pdf.

[41] Anne Case and Angus Deaton, *Deaths of Despair and the Future of Capitalism* (Princeton, NJ: Princeton University Press, 2020).

THE COMMODIFICATION OF HUMAN LABOR POWER   27

treated as appendages to machines are provided with the "social bases of self-respect?" One of the interviewees in Studs Terkel's *Working* says of his job as a farm laborer:

> Working in the fields is not in itself a degrading job. It's hard, but if you're given regular hours, better pay, decent housing, unemployment and medical compensation plans—we have a very relaxed way of living. But the growers don't recognize us as persons. That's the worst thing, the way they treat you. Like we have no brains.[42]

While having the opportunity for work is important to people's sense of dignity, the nature of the work is also important. Since the 1970s, many jobs in the manufacturing sector have disappeared in both England and the United States—jobs that were well paid and had strong unions and in which people developed different competencies—and many of the jobs that have replaced them not only have lower wages, but also less autonomy, less opportunity for discretion and initiative, less interaction with other people, fewer benefits, and less protection.

The above discussion, I think, suggests the importance of, and the limits to, certain redistributive strategies. While proposals like the Earned Income Tax Credit or a universal basic income would change the fallback position of workers, and perhaps enhance their bargaining power, many of the psychological, democratic, and respect-based problems with highly commodified work geared to profit-making would remain. To tackle the problem of promoting and sustaining democratic character, and also dignity and self-respect, requires considering different ownership possibilities, enhancing worker voice, providing adequate retraining and employment opportunities, having areas of society where the market does not prevail, and modifying the stark division between mental and manual labor so that no one is treated merely as a fungible hired hand at work.[43]

---

[42] Studs Terkel, *Working* (New York: Pantheon Books, 1974), 13.

[43] The Rawlsian "Aristotelian Principle" also provides support for distinguishing access to employment from access to income. See Seana Shiffrin, "Race, Labor, and the Fair Equality of Opportunity Principle," *Fordham Law Review* 72 (2004): 1643–1676, 1668ff.

28 WORKING AS EQUALS

2.5. Qualifications and Objections

2.5.1. Counteracting Forces: Arenas for Voice

For those denied much say at work, labor unions have given workers a forum for exercising choice and collective decision-making. Even if one's work gave little room for voice or discretion, unions have played a role in developing a collective voice and have pushed back against the worst forms of employer abuse, limiting working hours and raising wages. But labor unions are waning in influence. According to the Bureau of Labor Statistics, the percentage of wage and salary workers who were members of unions in 2020 was 10.8 percent. If we look only at private sector workers, that percentage falls further, to 6.3 percent. The analysis here highlights that the fall in union membership may be important for other reasons than its effects on wages and hours: it deprives workers of an opportunity for developing collective voice and exercising agency that can drive workplace changes. (To be sure, some unions are hierarchical and undemocratically run.) Given the general decline in civic associations documented by political scientists like Robert Putnam,[44] there are fewer other opportunities for workers to develop and exercise their participatory muscles. A strong union movement would be a counteracting force to the erosion of democratic capacities.

2.5.2. Counteracting Tendencies: Enhancing Democratic Character

Workplaces remain some of the most diverse parts of society, and more than any other organization except the military, they can bring people together across racial, ethnic, religious, and political differences. Cynthia Estlund has argued that such diverse workplaces play an important role in a democratic society: they allow citizens to interact with one another, learn from one another, and break down ignorance and stereotyping.[45] Treating human labor power as a commodity has played a part—often in the context of struggle and protest movements—in breaking down some of the barriers that remain in the larger society. Much, although not all, racial and ethnic discrimination is

---

[44] Robert D. Putnam, *Bowling Alone* (New York: Simon & Schuster, 2000).
[45] Cynthia Estlund, *Working Together: How Workplace Bonds Strengthen a Diverse Society* (Oxford: Oxford University Press, 2003).

inefficient. In this sense, commodified labor offers some support for A1 and A2.[46] The analysis here suggests that we should seek to couple the integrative aspect of many workplaces with measures to increase worker voice and control over their working conditions.[47]

2.5.3. Does Hierarchical Domination in the Workplace— Being Treated as No More Than a "Hired Hand"—Really Undermine Self-Respect?

In *Anarchy, State, and Utopia*, Robert Nozick rejects the idea that those in a subordinate position and who are ordered about at work with no room for discretion necessarily suffer from low self-esteem:

> But members of a symphony orchestra constantly are ordered about by their conductor (often capriciously and arbitrarily and with temper flareups) and are not consulted about the overall interpretation of their works. Yet they retain high self-esteem and do not feel that they are inferior beings. Draftees in armies are constantly ordered about, told how to dress, what to keep in their lockers, and so on, and yet do not come to feel that they are inferior beings. . . . Persons on their way up organizational ladders spend much time taking orders without coming to feel inferior.[48]

Nozick may well be right that workplace subordination does not *always* lead to low self-esteem. Lawyers who are timed to the minute as far as their billing hours and ordered about by their firms partners are probably not emblematic candidates for low self-esteem, unlike the Amazon workers I described earlier. If a psychological connection between work with little self-discretion and low self-esteem does not generalize across *all* forms of commodified work, neither does Nozick's self-respecting but ordered-about clarinet player. In addition to the fact that orchestra workers get to deploy higher and a more complex set of skills than Amazon workers, members of orchestras and armies share aims and a common good in a way that Amazon workers and

---

[46] At the same time, within workplaces, there remain considerable racial and gender segmentation.

[47] A caveat here is probably in order. As traditional work shifts to "gig work," more work will not take place in hierarchical firms where individuals have little discretion over their time. The rise of such work is also a problem for Anderson's analysis of "private government."

[48] Robert Nozick, *Anarchy, State, and Utopia* (New York: Basic Books, 1973), 246.

30 WORKING AS EQUALS

their employers and managers do not. While there may be good reason to tolerate undemocratic hierarchy in orchestras (but not temper tantrums),[49] it does not follow from this that we should refrain from taking measures that would improve worker self-esteem.[50] At any rate, my focus has been on democratic capacities and the problems that emerge when work is not only hierarchical but also rote, mindless, and insecure. If work were not so wedded to increasing profit, we could have less of that kind of work.

2.6. Conclusion

What I have been calling the "commodification of human labor power" is an ideal type. Human labor power is not completely commodified in the contemporary United States or anywhere in the developed world. But a significant part of the labor market comes close. Low-paid, expendable, and disposable, mindless rote tasks without voice or discretion are the epitome of such work. While income is one dimension of this kind of work, it is not the main dimension I have singled out in this chapter. Instead I have focused on certain forms of work—those characterized by a pronounced division between mental and manual labor, where workers are largely treated as bits of machinery, and disposed of when they are no longer efficient. This, I have argued, is not only bad for these workers but bad for democracy.

This is a broader and more multivariable diagnosis than either the parallel cases argument given by Walzer and Dahl, or the legitimacy argument offered by Anderson.

With respect to Walzer and Dahl, control over the economy is not the only issue singled out by the argument from democratic character. Instead, a complex of issues ranging over the effects of work on important human capacities and inclinations is central. The extent that work has these effects depends on a number of factors—the complexity of the skills used in work, the opportunities for voice and for discretion, and the extent of a social safety net are relevant.

With respect to Anderson's argument, the problem that I diagnosis does not only pertain to work in places like Amazon and Walmart. What about the worker who is employed as an Uber driver? Some of today's gig workers have

---

[49] Although some orchestras are experimenting with conductor-less organizational forms.
[50] Sam Freeman noted in his comments that the Me Too movement has brought to light numerous claims of sexual harassment and assault by orchestra conductors and soldiers over the last decade.

discretion—they are often not under the direct eye of their employer and they are granted autonomy in whether to work certain hours or not and how to dress—but on the other hand, they have no voice in the firm's decisions, no safety net or benefits, and are valued only as a means of producing profit. These drivers count for little in Uber's eyes—witness the company's massive campaigns to deny these workers traditional benefits and protections by insisting that they are nothing but "independent contractors."

Admittedly, there may be trade-offs if enhancing worker discretion and voice leads to inefficiencies. I claim, however, that we have not fully accounted for the democratic benefits of such enhancement, and the costs of failing to treat workers with greater respect.

Karl Polanyi singled out human labor power as a "fictitious commodity," arguing that when it is treated as something for sale rather than as an aspect of human personality and a locus of rights and liberties, our social world is endangered.[51] Perhaps that is overstated: our social world has limped along in the face of even worse things. But democracy is a fragile achievement, and we need to take care in cultivating the psychological bases that are needed to support it. Workplaces are a good place to start.

Acknowledgments

Thanks to Sam Freeman, who delivered incisive comments on this chapter at the conference "Working as Equals," to Julian Jonker and Grant Rozeboom, who organized the conference and offered helpful suggestions, and to the other conference participants.

---

[51] Karl Polanyi, *The Great Transformation* (Boston: Deakin Press, 1957), 68–76.

3

An Objection to Workplace Hierarchy Itself?

Niko Kolodny

In *The Pecking Order: Social Hierarchy as a Philosophical Problem*, I consider a number of political-philosophical commonplaces of the liberal democratic tradition, such as the idea that the state must be justified or legitimated, in part by being democratic; that public officials should not be corrupt and should treat like cases alike; and that discrimination is wrong. Negatively, I observe that we cannot fully explain these commonplaces by appealing to what I call "interests in improvement": interests that we be provisioned with the means to lead a fulfilling life. Positively, I conjecture that these commonplaces must be explained instead by what I call "claims against inferiority": claims that we not be set beneath another natural person in a social hierarchy. In this chapter, I suggest that among these commonplaces are that workers have objections to certain kinds of treatment in the workplace. Negatively, I observe that these objections cannot be explained by interests in improvement. Positively, I conjecture that they are explained by claims against inferiority. This amounts to a kind of "parallel-case argument": that because the firm is relevantly like the state, what is required of the state is likewise required of the firm. In particular, because bosses are relevantly like state officials, wielding asymmetric power and authority over others, what is required of state officials is required of bosses: namely, that they wield their asymmetric power and authority noncorruptly and impartially. The chapter then turns to a more common parallel-case argument: namely, that because the firm is relevantly like the state, the firm, like the state, must be democratic. Whether this parallel-case argument succeeds depends on whether the same "tempering factors" that are absent from the state are also absent from the firm. Tempering factors are conditions that make asymmetries of power and authority less objectionable in general, such as the asymmetries being escapable. On the one hand, some tempering factors that are absent

Niko Kolodny, *An Objection to Workplace Hierarchy Itself?* In: *Working as Equals.* Edited by: Julian David Jonker and Grant J. Rozeboom, Oxford University Press. © Oxford University Press 2023.
DOI: 10.1093/oso/9780197634295.003.0003

from the state are, or could be, present in the firm, such as a higher court of appeal or another recognized relationship within which the asymmetrically situated stand as equals. On the other hand, other tempering factors that are often present in the state are generally absent from the firm, such as that the state's decisions tend to apply equally to its highest decision-makers and that the state's commands tend not to assign ends to those who are commanded. The answer to whether there is a parallel-case argument for workplace democracy is, accordingly, inconclusive.

3.1. Setting the Stage

I begin by setting the stage. Any given individual, Indy, has "interests in improvement": in being better situated to lead a fulfilling life by being given access to, among other things, clean drinking water, an education, and protection from violent harm. If a potential benefactor, Benny, can improve Indy's situation—can raise the chances that Indy leads a fulfilling life provided that Indy chooses appropriately—and if doing so would not cost Benny too much, then Indy may have an "improvement claim" on Benny to improve Indy's situation. If Benny does not fulfill this claim, then Benny wrongs Indy, giving Indy an "improvement complaint" against Benny.

Whether Indy has an improvement claim on Benny, however, depends on the improvements to others, such as Altra, that Benny must forgo to improve Indy's situation. If improving Indy's situation would prevent Benny from improving Altra's situation, in a way that trades off Altra's interests at an unfairly low rate against Indy's, then Indy may lack an improvement claim on Benny. In this way, Indy's claim to improvement on Benny will often be comparative, in the sense that whether Indy has such a claim depends on comparing the improvement to Indy with Benny's forgone improvement to Altra, and trading off their interests fairly. However, Indy's interest in improvement is not an interest in something comparative, such as getting from Benny what Altra got from Benny, or not being worse off than Altra. Indy's interest in improvement is simply an interest in Indy's situation being better in absolute terms. What happens with Altra is neither here nor there. As shorthand, let us define the "public interest," relative to a certain group, as a state of affairs in which the improvement claims of each person of some relevant group are met: in which everyone's situation is improved so long as this does not come unfairly at another's expense.

34 WORKING AS EQUALS

Many of the complaints that workers can have about their work are improvement complaints. Some change in the work available to them to choose would better serve their interests: shorter or more convenient hours of work, interspersed with longer or more frequent breaks; tasks at work that would be less boring, lonely, draining, stultifying, alienating, or uncomfortable; less risk from work of poor health, injury, or death; and, of course, better pay and benefits. And this change would not be unfair to the improvement interests of others, by leaving consumers with unfairly more expensive, or poorer quality, goods and services, or investors with unfairly lower returns on capital investments.

Such complaints are typically also "bossless complaints": that is, in principle, a worker without a boss could have the same complaint. Suppose, for example, that the complaint of a bossed worker, Fisher, is that their working conditions could be safer, without unfairly burdening anyone else. Boss orders Fisher, on pain of firing, to work in those unsafe conditions. If Fisher refuses, the need to make a living will compel him to work for another boss, who will order Fisher to work in equally unsafe conditions. In principle, the need to make a living might compel a bossless worker, Angler, to work in similarly unsafe conditions. Angler might be under competitive pressure from other bossless workers, who find themselves in an unhappy equilibrium where, if any of them takes greater precautions, they will be run out of business by the others. The improvement complaint of bossless Angler, that their work could be safer, is in relevant moral respects similar to the improvement complaint of the bossed Fisher.

There might seem to be a difference. One might claim that in Fisher's case, there is an agent, namely Boss, who could make the work safer and so to whom Fisher's complaint can be addressed. In Angler's case, there is no agent who could make the work safer and so to whom Angler's "complaint" can be addressed. This is doubly mistaken. First, the state might be an agent who can respond to Angler's claim to safer conditions. The state might require all bossless workers to follow safety standards, subsidize the necessary equipment, and monitor compliance. Second, Boss might face the same competitive pressures as Angler. Either Boss orders the unsafe work, or Boss goes out of business. In that case, Fisher's complaint seems better addressed not to Boss, but instead to whatever agent has the wherewithal to stabilize a system of improved safety standards.

3.2. Neither Improvement Nor Bossless Complaints

However, some of the valid complaints that workers can have about their work are neither improvement complaints nor bossless complaints. Consider, first, the case of Nepotistic Promotion. Boss passes over Worker for a promotion in order to give it to Boss's nephew, even though Worker would perform far better. At first glance, Worker may seem to have a valid improvement complaint against Boss. Worker's situation would have been improved by the promotion. And since Worker would perform better, this would not be unfair to others, who benefit from the work being done well. Boss has disserved the public interest.

So why does Worker not have an improvement complaint against Boss? The question is why does Boss have a duty to serve the public interest in this way? After all, individuals do not, in general, have a duty to serve the public interest no matter what. Instead, individuals have a duty to serve the public interest so long as this is not outweighed by their personal reasons such as their own interests, relationships, or projects, or those of people close to them. If serving the public interest, by doing Great rather than Good, would mean that Private Citizen's niece founders on the job market, because Private Citizen cannot spend the time to help his niece polish her resume, then Private Citizen does not have a duty to do Great rather than Good. So why can Boss not say something similar: that he has no duty to serve the public interest better to that extent by forgoing nepotism, which would require sacrificing the interests of Nephew?

The difference, one wants to say, is that Boss is a boss. When Boss makes decisions in the office of boss, he is under what we might call a "Duty to Execute," which, to a first approximation, requires him to make official decisions that serve the public interest, even if he has genuine personal reasons that would, if he were acting as a private citizen, allow him not to serve the public interest to the same extent.

Consider, next, Car Wash. In this case, Boss has sufficient business reason to fire Worker, but also sufficient reason to keep Worker on. As far as the public interest is concerned, the decision is underdetermined. Boss would not wrong Worker by firing him outright. Why then does Boss wrong Worker if he tells him, "Unless you wash my car, you're fired!"? Worker has no improvement complaint against Boss for making this offer. After all, the offer puts Worker in a better situation than being fired outright. At least now Worker has the option of keeping the job if he wants.

36 WORKING AS EQUALS

Again, the problem, one wants to say, has to do with how Boss uses his office. Boss violates what we might call the "Duty to Exclude": the duty to avoid using an office for personal reasons. Whereas the Duty to Execute is a matter of which decisions the objective situation permits the official to make, the Duty to Exclude is instead a matter of which reasons subjectively motivate the official's decision. Breaking a tie cannot violate the Duty to Execute, since the objective situation permits both options. But breaking a tie for personal reasons can still violate the Duty to Exclude. The question is, then, what justifies the Duties to Execute and to Exclude, if not, as we have seen, interests in improvement?

Finally, consider Favoritism. Suppose Boss faces a decision, underdetermined on business grounds, of whether to allocate up to two hours of overtime, which workers Dee and Dum, who in all relevant respects are the same, have reason to want. Suppose, first, that Boss decides that no overtime will be allocated to anyone. Now contrast this with a case in which Boss allocates one hour to Dee, but none to Dum. If the improvement interests of Dee and Dum were the only thing at issue, then what the Boss did in the second case would be *less* objectionable. At the very least Dee's improvement interest was satisfied, even if Dum's was not. But if anything, the second case seems *more* objectionable. Dum seems to have a distinct complaint in the second case, a complaint with a comparative character. It arises only because Dum was not given the overtime, whereas Dee was. Accordingly, it does not seem to be an improvement complaint. Dum's objection, it seems, is that Boss violates the "Duty to Treat Equally." If Boss provides a benefit to Dee, then—once again because of his office—Boss should provide the same benefit to Dum, unless there is some justifying difference between them.

So why do bosses wrong workers when they violate the Duties to Execute, Exclude, and Treat Equally, if not because they fail to meet improvement claims? Because bosses thereby treat workers "arbitrarily"? First, there is no prohibition on "arbitrary treatment" in general. Favoritism, for example, is not wrong in general, not even among strangers. In general, if you do something supererogatory for one person, such as pick up one hitchhiker, you do not have to do it for everyone, even if there is no justifying difference. "Random acts of kindness" are permissible (at least so long as differential treatment does not contribute to a pattern of discrimination against race, religion, and suchlike). Second, why should anyone care about arbitrary treatment? What is at stake? Perhaps Boss is being inconsistent in allocating overtime to Dee but not to Dum, when there is no justifying difference

AN OBJECTION TO WORKPLACE HIERARCHY ITSELF? 37

between them. But that seems more like assigning a poor grade to Boss's rationality than lodging a moral grievance against Boss's conduct.

3.3. Claims against Inferiority

I suggest turning our attention from claims to improvement toward "claims against inferiority." These are claims against standing in a "relation of inferiority" to another person: against being subordinated to another or set beneath them in a social hierarchy. I begin by describing three general characteristics of relations of inferiority. First, relations of inferiority involve ongoing relations. Merely episodic interactions do not make for relations of inferiority. Second, relations of inferiority involve an unequal ranking. There is one party who can be identified as higher in the hierarchy, the other as lower. Finally, relations of inferiority are relations between individual, natural persons. They are not relations between an individual, natural person and an artificial person, or collective, or force of nature.

The second point, that relations of inferiority involve unequal rankings, partly explains the third point, that they are not relations between individual natural persons and entities of an entirely different moral category, such as a force of nature, or a collective or artificial person. What would it even mean for you to have equal, inferior, or superior status with a collective or artificial agent, such as Indonesia, or the Roman Catholic Church, or Procter & Gamble? It seems a category mistake.

What, more specifically, do relations of inferiority consist in? First, Loman's standing in a relation of inferiority to Hyman can consist in an untempered "asymmetry of power": in the fact that Hyman has greater power over Loman than Loman has over Hyman. Second, Loman's standing in a relation of inferiority to Hyman can consist in an untempered "asymmetry of de facto authority": in the fact that Hyman has greater de facto authority over Loman than Loman has over Hyman. De facto authority consists, in turn, in the capacity to issue commands, as opposed to advice, that are generally, if not always and without exception, complied with. The authority is "de facto" in the sense that the commands need not create, or claim to create, or be believed to create, reasons, let alone moral reasons, for compliance. However, I will, for convenience, often drop the qualifier "de facto," taking it to be implied.

38 WORKING AS EQUALS

Observing bosses in the wild, we find that they have ongoing discretion to do some or all of the following with respect to their workers:

1. To hire, fire, promote, demote, and reassign workers;
2. To determine workers' compensation;
3. To issue directives about how, when, and where workers are to work, including, importantly, setting ends for workers to pursue;
4. To control working conditions, such as time, location, noise, temperature, and safety;
5. To monitor and review performance, including as a reference for other employment;
6. And to encroach on workers' privacy (e.g., reading emails, requiring drug tests) or workers' sphere of control over their own person and effects (e.g., hairstyle), when workers are working, using the employer's property, or otherwise representing the employer.

This means, first and perhaps most significantly, that bosses have de facto authority over workers. They boss workers. Indeed, the workplace is one of the few settings in modern society, outside of relations with the state itself, in which some adults give other adults, for most of their waking hours, orders that they are expected to obey. Second, bosses have superior, ongoing power over workers. This superior power may be the source of superior authority, as when the boss's power to fire or otherwise discipline workers induces workers to obey the boss's commands. However, the boss can have superior power that does not support authority. That is, it may be power over workers that is not deployed in order to get them to do anything. Examples are depriving workers of safe or sanitary working conditions, or snooping on their email, or firing them out of personal animosity.

Contrast one-off, quid pro quo, market exchanges of goods or services for which there is a sufficiently complete contract. Here, there are no ongoing relations of asymmetric power and authority. While there may be asymmetries of power, they are episodic, not ongoing.[1] Nor are there ongoing relations of asymmetric authority, or authority at all. Neither market participant submits to future direction by the other. This is an instance of a broader point, that in the wide genus of human interaction, one-off, quid pro quo, market exchange is a special and perhaps somewhat artificial species. Part of the function of

---

[1] Michael Walzer, *Spheres of Justice* (New York: Basic Books, 1983), 291–292.

such exchange is to *extinguish* further normative (or pseudo-normative) relations among the participants. Buyer and seller can go their separate ways, without further normative entanglements. Consider Jed Lewinsohn's insight that one-off, quid pro quo, market exchange (as opposed to, say, gift exchange) functions to preempt future obligations of gratitude.[2] Similarly, I am suggesting, one-off, quid pro quo, market exchange functions to preempt the future submission of one participant to the superior authority or ongoing superior power of the other. Seen in this light, the problem with the exchange of labor for a wage is not, as A. J. Julius argues, the strategic, quid pro quo character of the contractual exchange.[3] It is that, because the quid the worker is contracted to supply is submission to authority, it risks being a relation of subordination.

In short, insofar as workers are subjected to the superior power and authority of their bosses, they are at risk of standing in an objectionable relation of inferiority to them. Whether they do in fact stand in an objectionable relation of inferiority, however, depends on whether these asymmetries are, to turn to a term that has not yet been explained, "tempered." The thought is that certain "tempering factors" delimit, contextualize, or transform these asymmetries in such a way as to make the charge that they amount to objectionable relations of inferiority out of place, or at any rate weaker. The idea is not that these tempering factors somehow outweigh or compensate for the bad of inferiority, but instead that they make it less of a bad to begin with.

3.4. Impersonal Justification and Least Discretion

In particular, there are tempering factors that keep our subjection to superior power and authority from being the subjection to the superior power and authority of another natural individual, and so from being relations of inferiority at all. For the moment, I will discuss two of these tempering factors, "Impersonal Justification" and "Least Discretion," which in turn explain the Duties to Execute, to Exclude, and to Treat Equally. Later, I turn to the tempering factor of "Equal Influence," which explains democracy.

---

[2] Jed Lewinsohn, "Paid on Both Sides: Quid Pro Quo Exchange and the Doctrine of Consideration," *Yale Law Journal* 129 (2020): 690–772.

[3] A. J. Julius, "The Possibility of Exchange," *Politics, Philosophy, Economics* 12 (2013): 361–374.

The first of these tempering factors, Impersonal Justification, is that the relevant asymmetry of power and authority of Offe over Indy constitutes an impersonally justified office. To say that the asymmetry constitutes an "office" is, for our purposes, just to say that it consists in Offe's making certain decisions, by certain processes, which have certain implications for Indy. And to say that an office is "impersonally justified" is to say that its existence and operation—that Offe makes those decisions, by those processes, which have those effects—serve impersonal reasons, against the relevant background, at least as well as any alternative, and better than any alternative not marked by a similar asymmetry.

By "impersonal reasons," I mean either "globally impersonal" or "locally impersonal" reasons. Let us focus first on globally impersonal reasons. These are reasons that are simply not personal at all: not grounded in the agent's interests, projects, or relationships as such. What Impersonal Justification thus rules out is a justification of my asymmetric power or authority over you wherein the asymmetry would serve *my* interests, projects, or relationships, as opposed merely to *someone's* interests, projects, or relationships. The pronoun "my," as it were, can add no weight to the justification. To be sure, my personal reasons, where the pronoun "my" does add weight, are genuine reasons. More than that, they are reasons that can justify my acting in ways against which someone would otherwise have a complaint. For example, you might have no complaint about my passing up some opportunity to help your child, because my child needs my attention instead. However, according to Impersonal Justification, personal reasons of this kind—that my child would get attention, as opposed merely that some child would get attention—cannot justify my asymmetric power or authority over you. If my asymmetric power or authority over you is justified, the case must be made in terms of globally impersonal reasons. Among globally impersonal reasons are both reasons to promote the public interest—to improve the situation of each person, as far as is possible while also remaining fair to others—as well as reasons given by claims against inferiority.

What about locally impersonal reasons? These are reasons that, while personal, are nonetheless shared by everyone who is at one or the other end of the asymmetry. Perhaps Offe and Indy share personal reasons to aid their compatriots, as opposed merely to aiding people. Impersonal Justification allows such shared personal reasons to justify the asymmetry of power and authority between Offe and Indy.

The second, and closely related, tempering factor, Least Discretion, is that Offe, in holding the office, should exercise only so much discretion in using it as serves the impersonal reasons that justify it. If Offe could serve the impersonal reasons no less well without such and such discretion, then Offe should not exercise it.

How do Impersonal Justification and Least Discretion temper asymmetries of power and authority? The basic idea is that jointly they effect a separation of the office from the natural individual who occupies it, to the extent possible. Thus, you are not, or less, subject to him, the person occupying the office, and rather, or more, subject to the office alone. Insofar as Impersonal Justification is satisfied, the office, in the first place, serves reasons, as opposed to the arbitrary whims of the occupant. Moreover, the office serves only impersonal reasons, as opposed to the personal reasons of the occupant, such as that she is my daughter. And insofar as Least Discretion is satisfied, the official's decision-making is strictly limited to the service of those impersonal reasons. To be sure, you are subjected to the asymmetric power and authority of the office itself. However, whatever the office is, it is not another natural person. It is not the sort of entity to which relations of inferiority (or superiority or equality) are possible.

Impersonal Justification explains the Duty to Execute, which we can now define as a duty to make official decisions by processes that serve impersonal reasons, against the relevant background, at least as well as any alternative, and better than any alternative not marked by a similar asymmetry. So understood, the Duty to Execute follows from Impersonal Justification. If Offe violates the Duty to Execute, then the office is not operating in a way that satisfies Impersonal Justification.

Whereas Impersonal Justification explains the Duty to Execute, Least Discretion explains the Duty to Exclude. In violating the Duty to Exclude, in deciding for a personal reason, Offe violates Least Discretion. Even if, when breaking a tie for a personal reason, Offe does not serve the impersonal reasons that justify the office any worse, still Offe exercises excess discretion. Offe could serve the office just as well without being sensitive to that personal reason.

Violations of the Duty to Treat Equally violate Least Discretion in a different way. Suppose that Offe, exercising due discretion, has exempted Dee from some onerous rule. Dum now requests the same exemption, with a case that, as Offe acknowledges, is relevantly similar to Dee's. The question is then why Offe should not be bound to apply to Dum's case whatever judgment

42 WORKING AS EQUALS

Offe reached in Dee's case. Why should Offe retain the further discretion to deny Dum the exemption, assuming that there is no justifying difference between Dee and Dum? This seems like unjustified, excess discretion. This is not to deny that a decision-making process that leaves Offe with discretion may serve impersonal reasons. The point of offices is largely to reap the benefits of Offe's exercise of judgment about particular cases. But once it is settled that, exercising that judgment, Offe has reached a certain decision in Dee's case, nothing is lost if Offe henceforth applies the same judgment to every case that in all relevant respects, as Offe acknowledges, is the same as Dee's.

3.5. The Impersonal Reasons of Bosses

In order to apply Impersonal Justification and Least Discretion, and their derivative duties, to the office of boss, we need to know how the office of boss serves, against the background of other social institutions, impersonal reasons. The answer presumably lies in the theory of the firm, pioneered by R. H. Coase and developed by later economists.[4] The basic idea is that the high costs of market transactions make it inefficient to organize certain processes of production by market transactions among autonomous buyers and sellers of the relevant factors of production, including labor. Organizing those processes instead under the hierarchical direction of a boss (which, for Coase, defines the firm) lowers those transaction costs. The resulting improvements in efficiency stand to benefit everyone. Such is the argument for an office of boss with some or all of the discretionary capacities that we attributed to bosses earlier.

This suggests, to a first approximation, that the decision-making processes that bosses follow should be sensitive only to factors that promote efficient production by the firm. However, first, efficient production by the boss's firm matters only insofar as it ultimately contributes to the public interest. If the workers at a firm bear unfair costs, say in terms of risk of injury, for a given increase in productivity, then this increase in productivity may actually detract from the public interest. Second, there are other impersonal reasons besides

---

[4] R. H. Coase, "The Nature of the Firm," *Economica* 4 (1937): 386–405; Oliver Williamson, "Markets and Hierarchies: Some Elementary Considerations," *American Economic Review* 63 (1973): 316–325; and Oliver Williamson, "Transaction Cost Economics: The Natural Progression," *American Economic Review* 100 (2010): 673–690.

the public interest, such as reasons to avoid relations of inferiority, such as are constituted by patterns of discrimination. So, it may be that the decision-making processes that bosses follow should be sensitive to factors besides what will promote efficient production by the firm, such as respecting safety standards and avoiding discrimination.

Note also that there may be locally impersonal reasons within a firm: personal reasons shared by all of those "insiders" who wield or are subject to the asymmetric power and authority that define that particular firm, even if they are not shared by "outsiders" who are not so subject. These locally impersonal reasons might be the "local public interest": improvements to insiders' situations fairly distributed among them. Or these locally impersonal reasons might be a shared mission in which all members of the firm are invested. Such locally impersonal reasons can also bear on whether Impersonal Justification is satisfied.[5]

This finally gives us the resources to explain why Boss wrongs Worker in Nepotistic Promotion, Car Wash, and Favoritism. In Nepotistic Promotion, Boss violates the Duty to Execute. Boss's personal reasons to look out for Nephew may be valid in themselves. But these reasons have no weight in justifying Boss's exercise of the superior power and authority of his office. By hypothesis, promoting Nephew does not serve efficient production or the public interest. And it is hard to see what other relevant impersonal reasons it might serve.

In Car Wash, Boss violates the Duty to Exclude. He uses his office for a reason that does not serve efficient production or other relevant impersonal reasons, even though, by hypothesis, there is in fact a sufficient impersonal justification for that exercise of his office. Worker's washing Boss's car is not, in the main run of cases, a factor that serves efficient production by the firm. And again, it is hard to see what other relevant impersonal reasons it might serve.

---

[5] This raises difficult questions about how, when locally and globally impersonal reasons conflict, they are to be weighed against one another in determining whether Impersonal Justification is satisfied. Offhand, one expects that there will be cases of both kinds: cases in which the boss does not violate Impersonal Justification by favoring the local over the global, and cases in which the boss does not violate Impersonal Justification by favoring the global over the local. If readers have the intuition that the boss's privileging of the global over the local—what Grant Rozeboom and Julian Jonker described to me as "moral vigilantism"—will always give rise to a complaint against inferiority, it is important to keep in mind that there may be complaints against inferiority arising not from Impersonal Justification, but instead from Equal Influence. If workers have a right to workplace democracy, then they have an inferiority complaint against the boss's unilaterally disregarding their opposition to privileging the global over the local.

44 WORKING AS EQUALS

In Favoritism, Boss violates the Duty to Treat Equally. In refusing the over-time to Dum that Boss gives to Dee, Boss decides in one way a case that he acknowledges is relevantly similar to a case that Boss has already decided in a different way. Although the objective power or authority exercised in each instance may not violate Impersonal Justification, its inconsistent exercise across instances amounts to excess discretion and so violates Least Discretion.[6]

3.6. Not Enforcement but hierarchy

We have been pursuing what is often called a "parallel-case argument": that because the firm is relevantly like the state, what is required of the state is likewise required of the firm. In particular, we have been arguing, in effect, that because bosses are relevantly like state officials, what is required of state officials is required of bosses:[7] namely, Impersonal Justification and Least Discretion. More commonly, however, parallel-case arguments take a different form: because the firm is relevantly like the state, the argument goes, the firm, like the state, must be democratic.[8] I turn now to this sort of parallel-case argument, as well as to problems with parallel-case arguments that we have so far not mentioned.

---

[6] In the literature, it is often suggested that the objection to Boss's behavior in our three cases is best explained by republicanism of the sort mostly prominently espoused by Philip Pettit in *Republicanism: A Theory of Freedom and Government* (Oxford: Clarendon Press, 1997) and *On the People's Terms: A Republican Theory and Model of Democracy* (Cambridge: Cambridge University Press, 2012). All three cases, it is said, involve interference in choice by an arbitrary, alien will, the mere exposure to which counts as domination. This is perhaps Elizabeth Anderson's main objection to the "private government" of the firm: that it is "a state of republican unfreedom, of subjection to the arbitrary will of another" (*Private Government: How Employers Rule Our Lives (and Why We Don't Talk about It)* [Princeton, NJ: Princeton University Press, 2017], 64). See also Elizabeth Anderson, "Workplace Government and Republican Theory," in *Republicanism and the Future of Democracy*, ed. Yiftah Elazar and Geneviève Rousselière (Cambridge: Cambridge University Press, 2019), 189–206; Iñigo González-Ricoy, "Ownership and Control Rights in Democratic Firms: A Republican Approach," *Review of Social Economy* 78 (2020): 411–430; Nien-hê Hsieh, "Rawlsian Justice and Workplace Republicanism," *Social Theory and Practice* 31 (2005): 115–142; and Claudio López-Guerra, "Against the Parallel Case for Workplace Democracy," *Revue de Philosophie Économique* 9 (2008): 11–28. In *The Pecking Order*, I explain why I favor my analysis, where the fundamental disvalue is not domination, but instead inferiority.

[7] Compare Christopher McMahon, *Public Capitalism: The Political Authority of Corporate Executives* (Philadelphia: University of Pennsylvania Press, 2009), and R. H. Tawney, *R.H. Tawney's Commonplace Book*, ed. J. M. Winter and David Joslin (Cambridge: Cambridge University Press, 1972).

[8] Joshua Cohen, "The Economic Basis of Deliberative Democracy," *Social Philosophy & Policy* 6 (1989): 25–50, and Robert A. Dahl, *A Preface to Economic Democracy* (Berkeley: University of California Press, 1985).

The starting point of any parallel-case argument, it would seem, is the premise that those who are subject to the state have some objection to it, an objection that can be overcome only if the state is somehow "justified" or "legitimated," by satisfying some "legitimating condition," such as consent or public justification. Likewise, the parallel-case argument continues, since those subject to the firm have the same objection to the firm, the firm must satisfy the same legitimating condition.

To judge from the literature on legitimating the state, however, the objection to the state is its force, or its threat of violent force, or its coercion (even if it is never entirely clear what the notoriously supple term "coercion" is supposed to cover). The guiding image is that of the state or its officers laying hands on people and imprisoning them, or threatening to do so, for refusing to comply with the state's directives. The objection to the state is that it "Enforces" its directives, with a capital "E." If this is the objection to the state, then there is not, it seems, the same objection to the firm. The firm does not imprison or threaten imprisonment. It does not Enforce its directives. So, parallel-case arguments have no foundation. The legitimating condition required of the state to overcome the objection to its Enforcement is not similarly required of the firm, because the firm does not Enforce in the first place.[9]

As I argue in *The Pecking Order*, however, it is a mistake to think that the objection to the state is Enforcement. The objection is instead to the hierarchical structure of the state itself: to the fact that those who control the state wield asymmetric power and authority over those who are subject to it. Even if the state, for contingent reasons, must Enforce in order to wield asymmetric power and authority, the objection to the state is not to those acts of Enforcement themselves, but instead to the ongoing relations of asymmetric power and authority that those acts sustain. If this is the objection to the state, then it puts parallel-case arguments on a new foundation, for the firm, like the state, is open to the same objection. The firm, like the state, wields ongoing asymmetric power and authority over those subject to it.

Indeed, if the objection to the state is to the asymmetric power and authority of those who control the state, then there is a straightforward explanation of why democracy, in particular, should be a legitimating condition on the state. (By contrast, it is less clear why, if the objection to the state is to

---

[9] While many parallel-case arguments acknowledge that the firm does not Enforce, they pass over in silence that, at least in the view of most political philosophers, the objection that calls for the state to satisfy a legitimating condition is precisely that it Enforces. See Tawney, *Commonplace Book*, 34–35; Dahl, *Preface to Economic Democracy*, 113; and Anderson, *Private Government*, 38.

46 WORKING AS EQUALS

Enforcement, democracy should be thought to meet it.) In addition to the tempering factors of Impersonal Justification and Least Discretion, there is the tempering factor of Equal Influence, which is satisfied insofar as any individual who is subject to superior power and authority has as much opportunity as any other individual for informed, autonomous influence over decisions about how that power and authority are to be exercised or over the delegation of such decisions. The rationale is simple. If I have as much opportunity for informed, autonomous influence over the exercise of the power and authority as anyone else has, then there is no natural person to whom I can point and say that, because they had greater influence, I, in being subjected to that power and authority, am subordinated to their superior power and authority. Granted, I have far less influence than the collective or artificial will, if any, that wields the superior power and authority. I have far less influence than the "will of the People." But that collective or artificial will is not another natural person, with whom a question of equality arises.

3.7. Other Tempering Factors

Does it follow that democracy is likewise required of the firm, to temper the asymmetries of power and authority that the firm involves? Not necessarily. This is because there are other tempering factors that might be present in the firm, yet absent in the state. Perhaps these factors temper the asymmetries of the firm sufficiently even without Equal Influence. Note that we find asymmetries of power and authority even outside of the state and firm, such as in clubs, schools, mass transport, and houses of worship. We greet these asymmetries more or less with equanimity, even in the absence of Equal Influence. This is, I suggest, because other tempering factors are present.

One such tempering factor is "Context Limitation": that the asymmetries are limited in time, place, and context. Teachers might only be able to tell students what to do in class, and this extends only for a given semester or course of schooling. Flight attendants might be able to tell passengers what to do, but only for that interval between when they board and disembark the plane.

A second tempering factor, "Content Limitation," is that the asymmetric power or authority is limited in content: that is, in what can be done or commanded. Teachers might simply be ignored if they were to command students to perform tasks that had no bearing on their own or their fellow students' education, or flight attendants ignored if they were to command passengers to do things that have no bearing on a safe and decorous flight. (Lacking such authority, teachers and flight attendants would not have so much as the opportunity to violate Impersonal Justification by exercising it.) Another important form of Content Limitation is that the power and authority do not impose ends. Rather than setting ends for people to pursue, the power and authority regulate only the means that people take to their own ends. For example, sound traffic regulations do not command where motorists are to travel, let alone if they are to travel at all. Instead, they command certain means of travel, which facilitate the pursuit of each motorist's independent ends, by coordinating their pursuit of those ends with the like pursuits of other motorists. This example also illustrates another kind of Content Limitation: that activities are regulated only in a coarse-grained way, leaving much to agents' discretion. Traffic regulations do not command motorists to take the quickest or cheapest route to their destination, for example.

A third tempering factor is "Escapability": that the asymmetries may be escapable, at will, with little cost or difficulty. To take an extreme case, if one can exit a slave contract at will, then it is not clear in what sense one really is a slave. Another way of putting this is to say that what matters for relations of inferiority is not so much inequality in exercised power or authority, but instead inequality of opportunity for power and authority, where equality of opportunity is understood not as equal ex ante chances to end up on the winning side of the asymmetry, but instead as sustained freedom to exit the relations in which the asymmetry arises. The point is not that while being on the losing end of asymmetries is always a burden, one forfeits one's complaint when the burden is self-imposed—that one has no one to blame but oneself. It is rather that the freer one is to exit what would otherwise be an objectionable relation of inferiority, the less it seems an objectionable relation of inferiority to begin with. Importantly, what matters is freedom to exit an otherwise objectionable relation of inferiority of a given kind. It is not enough that one is free to exit a relation of that kind with one individual, if upon exiting that relation with that individual, one is constrained to enter into a relation of the same kind with another individual. We must keep in mind the Marxist insight that the proletarian's freedom from any given capitalist is compatible with subjection to (to put it somewhat misleadingly) the capitalist class.

A fourth tempering factor, "Higher-Level Equality," has two parts. To begin with, the asymmetry is first, not "final"; it is itself regulated by

48 WORKING AS EQUALS

higher-order decisions, such as a court of appeal, or a decision further up the chain of command. Second, these higher-order decisions are not themselves marked by the same asymmetry. What managers can ask of workers, for example, might itself be regulated by bargains struck at the start of each year. In brief, inequality at a lower level in a decision-making hierarchy is tempered by equality at a higher level. Whatever hierarchy there is regulated from a standpoint of equality.

A fifth tempering factor, "Egalitarian Relationship," is that the people in the relationship marked by the asymmetry also stand as equals in some other recognized relationship. Off campus, teacher and student are just equal citizens. Once all have deplaned, flight attendants are just other travelers searching for ground transportation.

These five tempering factors are absent in the case of the state. Regarding Context Limitation, the state has extensive reach. The classroom, as it were, reaches all the way to the national borders. Regarding Content Limitation, there are few limits on what the state can do to us, or command us to do. Regarding Escapability, it is costly and difficult to avoid relations to the state within whose jurisdiction one resides, and all but impossible to escape the jurisdiction of some state. Regarding Higher-Level Equality, the state's decisions are typically final: that is, they sit at the apex of the hierarchy, above which there is no further appeal. So there can be no recourse to a decision higher up the chain of command, with a different character. Regarding Egalitarian Relationship, one relation within which you might stand as an equal with others, whatever other asymmetries might mark your relations with them, is equality of citizenship: that you stand as an equal with them insofar as you and they interact with the state. If equality of citizenship with others is not available, because if, say, they but not you can influence the state's decisions, then it is not clear what other relation of equality with them will be available, at least in a society marked by cultural, religious, regional, and professional diversity. Little wonder, then, that with these five tempering factors absent, the state should so urgently need the tempering factors of Impersonal Justification, Least Discretion, and Equal Influence.

By contrast, these five tempering factors are, or could be, present to a greater degree in the case of the firm. Whether Context and Content Limitation are absent in the firm seems largely to depend on the economic and legal structure. Granted, "at will" employment, prevalent in the United States, undermines Context and Content Limitation. But there can be labor laws that ensure Context Limitation. Managers might be able to tell workers what to do only on the shop floor, when they are on the clock. Likewise, with sensible labor protections, there might be Content Limitation. Managers might be able to tell workers to perform only work-related tasks. They might be able to fire them only with cause. They might not be able to use their power and authority in the workplace as a lever to extract personal favors, or support for their political or religious aims.

Whether the firm is Escapable also largely depends on the broader economic and legal structure. With a generous social safety net, opportunities for worker retraining, support in searching for new employment, and the state as an employer of last resort, the asymmetries of subjection to a particular employer might be Escapable at will, with low cost or difficulty. Granted, one might doubt whether such opportunities for exit will be entirely sufficient. First, there is again the Marxist point that if all firms are alike, then although one can escape subjection to this boss, one cannot escape subjection to some boss. Second, there is reason to expect that exit will carry some cost or difficulty. For example, workers may lose their investment in firm-specific human capital when they move to a new firm. And efficiency wages may lead employers to pay higher wages than whatever fallback the welfare state provides.

Against a backdrop of democratic political institutions, Higher-Level Equality will be present in the case of the firm. The asymmetries within the firm will themselves be regulated by a higher court of appeal, or a decision further up the chain of command, which is not itself marked by that asymmetry. The firm itself will be regulated by a legal order that workers have equal opportunity to influence. The hierarchy of the firm will itself be controlled from a standpoint of equality.

Finally, against a backdrop of equal citizenship, Egalitarian Relationship will also be present in the case of the firm. The persons in the relationship marked by the asymmetry or disparity stand as equals in some other recognized relationship. Once the whistle blows, the manager is just another citizen.

3.8. Countervailing Considerations

The greater presence of these five tempering factors in the firm than in the state suggests that the case for the earlier tempering factors—Impersonal

50 WORKING AS EQUALS

Justification, Least Discretion, and Equal Influence—is weaker in the firm than in the state. This tends to undermine parallel-case arguments.

There are, however, three further considerations that tend in the opposite direction. First, there is the fact that, in certain ways, the asymmetries of authority in the workplace are less Content Limited than the asymmetries of authority in the state.[10] First, the boss's orders impose ends on the worker in which the worker has no independent investment; they do not simply regulate how workers pursue their own ends. Second, as Taylorism famously codified, the boss's orders are often exceedingly fine-grained. They significantly constrain how, when, and where those ends are to be achieved, leaving little to the worker's discretion. By contrast, much of a liberal state's orders, its laws, do not assign ends to citizens. Nor do they much constrain how, when, and where those ends are to be achieved. Rather, its laws are meant to facilitate the pursuit of citizens' own ends, in a fair way, with the main constraints deriving from the need to fairly provide like opportunity to others. Consider, for instance, the orders that a dispatcher gives to drivers, which give them specific destinations, routes, and arrival times. Contrast that with the state's traffic regulations, which simply set up a framework which allows citizen motorists to drive safely and efficiently, in a way that is fair to all, to whatever destinations, by whatever routes, at whatever times those citizens have chosen for themselves.[11] The law of contracts, likewise, leaves largely open what the content of those contracts are. The laws of incorporation leave largely open what the corporations are incorporated to do. The tax code leaves largely open how one goes about acquiring the funds that are to be sent to the treasury. Building codes (or, at least, sensible ones) leave largely open what structures are built and for which purposes.

Second, the further tempering factor of "Equal Application" seems more likely to obtain in the state than in the firm. Equal Application obtains just when exercises of asymmetric power and authority apply as much to those who wield them as to those who are simply subject to them. The commander addresses the same command to herself as she addresses to others and is just as inclined to follow it. The wielder of power exercises power in a way that affects him as much as it affects others. Put another way, the decision-maker is someone to whom her own decision applies. The highest officers of the state, such as legislators and chief executives, are themselves typically subject

[10] Compare Anderson, *Private Government*, 63.
[11] Compare Anderson, *Private Government*, 67.

to the laws and executive orders that they make. By contrast, bosses are not typically subject to their own orders. Issuing and monitoring compliance with workplace orders is a full-time job, with no time left over to fulfill the orders that one has issued.

Finally, the further tempering factor of "Upward Unaccountability" seems more likely to obtain in the state than in the firm. Upward Unaccountability obtains when, even though Hyman has superior authority over Loman, Loman is not accountable to Hyman for obedience Hyman's commands. By "accountability," I mean here not only moral facts, such as that is one person is entitled to resent another for what that person does, but also merely social facts, which depend entirely on actual attitudes and dispositions. That "Loman is accountable to Hyman for obedience to Hyman's commands" might mean that Loman is apt to be punished, at Hyman's discretion, for disobeying Hyman's commands; or that Loman is subject to Hyman's expressions of resentment for disobeying (or to others' expressions of indignation on Hyman's behalf); or that Loman is expected to justify to Hyman any failure to obey or any discretion exercised in obedience. In general (apart from, perhaps, findings of contempt of court or Congress), obedience to the commands of state officials is understood not to be owed to them even in their official capacities, but instead owed to other citizens. However, it is less clear that this is true in the case of bosses: that, say, working the night shift is understood as owed to fellow workers, let alone citizens as a whole.

3.9. An Inconclusive Conclusion

So, where does this leave us? Is what is required of the state—not only the tempering factors concerning offices, Impersonal Justification and Least Discretion, but also the tempering factor concerning democracy, Equal Influence—also required of the firm? Is the parallel-case argument to this conclusion sound? It is hard to say. In some ways, the case for these tempering factors seems stronger with respect to the state than the firm. In other ways, however, the case for these tempering factors seems stronger with respect to the firm than the state. So, we cannot claim to have proposed a resolution of pretheoretical controversy over workplace governance. But we have proposed a theory of the deeper sources of the controversy.

Acknowledgments

Thanks to discussants at the workshop, especially to Jed Lewinsohn, who gave prepared comments, as well as to Chris Havasy, Julian Jonker, Tom Parr, and Grant Rozeboom, who sent written comments after. Portions of the text were first published in *The Pecking Order* (Cambridge, MA: Harvard University Press, 2023).

4

Seeing Like a Firm

Social Equality, Conservatism, and the Aesthetics of Inequality

Pierre-Yves Néron

C'est cette démultiplication de la forme "entreprise" à l'intérieur de corps social qui constitue, je crois, l'enjeu de la politique néolibérale.
—Michel Foucault, *Naissance de la biopolitique*[1]

To think about the prospects for building more egalitarian relationships in the workplace, as advocates of relational egalitarianism do, we need to think in reverse. We need to take seriously conceptions of the corporation that tend to erase the importance of social equality and instead praise workplace hierarchies. Yet, from a normative perspective, the emphasis on hierarchies is usually justified on utilitarian or libertarian grounds. Moreover, and more generally, in our ways of thinking normatively about economic institutions, we tend to use libertarianism to make theoretical sense of right-wing intuitions, which goes with the use of a certain kind of normative vocabulary, centered on notions of private property, self-ownership, voluntariness, etc. I argue in this chapter that that is misleading. To put it plainly, the way that the corporation "sees" is probably more a conservative one than a libertarian one, strictly speaking. To normatively unveil what it means to "see" like a firm, we need to move from a focus on libertarianism to a focus on conservatism.

More generally, I argue that taking conservatism more seriously allows for a better understanding of what the proponents of relational egalitarianism are up against, their "enemy." In this sense, this chapter aims to

[1] Michel Foucault, *Naissance de la biopolitique* (Paris: Seuil, 2004), 154.

Pierre-Yves Néron, *Seeing Like a Firm* In: *Working as Equals*. Edited by: Julian David Jonker and Grant J. Rozeboom, Oxford University Press. © Oxford University Press 2023. DOI: 10.1093/oso/9780197634295.003.0004

54 WORKING AS EQUALS

provide a contribution that could be called "negative" to the relational theory of equality, and the way it can help us think critically about economic institutions.

4.1. Markets and Firms as Normative Orders

In a 1991 article, economist Herbert Simon invited his readers to imagine that an extraterrestrial from Mars could examine the earth with a very special telescope: it would allow the alien to see markets in red and firms in green. What would our mysterious visitor see, asks Simon? Tiny red spots combined with huge areas of green, says an ironic Simon.[2]

Playing off Simon's remark, I argue that we can benefit from a shift in theorizing that attempts to both *characterize* and *criticize* neoliberal societies as "market societies." This is not, of course, to deny the importance of the market, but rather to recognize that neoliberal societies are not only market societies, but also, and perhaps specifically, "corporate societies." It will then be a matter of thinking through the ramifications and implications of such an observation. If neoliberalism can be understood, according to Wendy Brown's own phrasing, as a "particular form of rationality that reconfigures all aspects of existence in economic terms,"[3] then we need to think not only about market rationality, but also about "corporate rationality" in its specificity. As we shall see, this fits well with conservatism.

Of course, what Simon had in mind in 1991 is more than fifty years of development of the economic theory of the firm. Indeed, this theory draws much of its inspiration from the analyses of Ronald Coase who, in 1937, asked a seemingly simple but fundamental question: why do these things called "firms" exist?[4]—a question that *The Economist*, in a tribute to Coase, described as the equivalent for economists of the question of Being for philosophers.[5] More precisely, Coase asked why, if markets are such powerful tools for allocating resources among economic agents, do we have these organizations within our economies, which in many respects are based on radically different operating mechanisms: hierarchical relations,

---

[2] Herbert A. Simon, "Organizations and Markets," *Journal of Economic Perspectives* 5, no. 2 (1991): 25–44.

[3] Wendy Brown, *Undoing the Demos: Neoliberalism's Stealth Revolution* (Princeton, NJ: Princeton University Press, 2015).

[4] Ronald Coase, "The Nature of the Firm," *Economica* 4, no. 16 (1937): 386–405.

[5] "Why Do Firms Exist?," *The Economist*, December 18, 2010.

bureaucratic operations, suppression of the price mechanism and of competition, etc.? Why, then, if decentralized markets are so efficient, do organizational hierarchies such as firms occupy such a large place in the modern capitalist economy?

From the point of view of the theory of the firm, the answer is that the corporation is itself a response to market failures. In short, the use of hierarchical structures makes it possible to reduce a certain number of transaction costs: costs linked to the accumulation of information, monitoring costs, residual losses, etc. Thus, from the point of view of efficiency, an alternative form of coordination of economic activities, the firm can be superior to the market, provided that it uses hierarchical, centralized structures whose main characteristic is the use of managerial authority. To use the expression of the business historian Alfred Chandler, the invisible hand of the market often needs to be replaced by the visible hand of management.[6]

For Oliver Williamson, whose analysis pursued Coase's project, this suggests a restructuring of economics around the opposition "market/firm," or "market/hierarchy," to use his words.[7] From this perspective, the main task of economists is to understand when, and under what conditions, markets or organizational hierarchies produce optimal outcomes.

It is worth taking a few steps back here. In historical/genealogical studies of neoliberalism, the role played since the 1930s by German ordo-liberalism, the Austrian school, and then the Chicago school—in the development of what Foucault called a "reprogrammed liberalism"[8] in reaction to collectivism, the New Deal, and all forms of state planning of the economy—has been amply emphasized. In this view, contemporary neoliberal societies are inheritors of this skepticism about the centralizing and planning state that threatens the ideal of a society based on the praise of individual freedom; a skepticism that is coupled with the affirmation of a new key role of the state, namely to organize generalized competition. However, this (dominant) account overlooks the fact that at the same time, a whole constellation of economists, businessmen, and management thinkers were praising hierarchical and centralized structures. Determined to finally "open the black box" of the firm, to use the well-known expression, they discovered the opposite

---

[6] Alfred D. Chandler, *The Visible Hand: The Managerial Revolution in American Business* (Cambridge, MA: Harvard University Press, 2002).

[7] Oliver E. Williamson, *Markets and Hierarchies: Analysis and Antitrust Implications* (New York: Macmillan, 1975).

[8] Foucault, *Naissance de la biopolitique*, esp. "La leçon du 14 février."

56 WORKING AS EQUALS

of markets: the power of hierarchy and managerial authority structures. Williamson emphasized this very well in his 2009 Nobel Prize in Economics acceptance speech.[9] While Hayek, as *the* theorist of "spontaneous orders," was impressed in 1945 by the marvels of markets that produce "autonomous" adaptations, theorists of the firm retained the lesson of Chester Barnard in his important and influential *The Function of the Executive*, published in 1938: the firm produces "coordinated adaptations" that are "conscious, deliberate and thoughtful."[10] Again, it is the magic of the visible hand of management at work. The good manager is essentially one who excels in the art of planning.

The Function of the Executive has had a resounding success and an incredible influence on economics, management, and the business community. Kenneth Arrow considers Barnard's intuition that the firm is a conscious, deliberate, and thoughtful creation of hierarchical structures to be an axiom of economics, while Williamson, in the above-mentioned speech, readily acknowledges his debt to Barnard in the articulation of transaction-costs theory.[11] In many respects, though, Barnard's thinking is Hayek's nightmare, at least theoretically. Indeed, although he softened his views following his reading of Polanyi and his correspondence with Hayek, the Barnard of *The Function* leaves us with a theory of the firm as a *planned* coordination centered on the crucial importance of "lines of authority." He constantly hammers home the idea of "deliberate," "thoughtful," and "conscious" cooperation—one would be tempted to add "rational" to scare Hayek even more—and maintains that "organizations are the result of modifications of the individual's action" and that "deliberate, thoughtful and specialized control is the essence of the manager's function."[12] Thus, some of Hayek's worst fears are realized through a certain institutional form, but this time the responsible one is not the socialist, Keynesian, or redistributive state, but the firm.[13]

Thus, a focus on the firm and its particular nature helps us to gain some distance from attempts to both *characterize* and *criticize* neoliberal societies

---

[9] Published as Oliver E. Williamson, "Transaction Cost Economics: The Natural Progression," *American Economic Review* 100, no. 3 (2010): 673–690.

[10] Chester I. Barnard, *The Function of the Executive* (Cambridge, MA: Harvard University Press, 1938), 17.

[11] According to Williamson, "Transaction Cost Economics."

[12] Barnard, *Function of the Executive*, 13.

[13] For similar remarks, see Benjamin L. McKean, *Disorienting Neoliberalism: Global Justice and the Outer Limit of Freedom* (Oxford: Oxford University Press, 2020).

as "market societies," in which we supposedly interact with independent producers and consumers linked only by the decentralized mechanism of price within networks of voluntary contracts. Such a conception may correspond to a normative wish, a kind of fantasy of spontaneous orders à la Hayek, but it only provides an erroneous empirical portrait of things, because it fails to underline the centrality of hierarchical economic organizations in contemporary capitalism. In contrast to the portrait of our economies as decentralized and uniquely competitive, we live instead, as David Ciepley writes, in deeply organizational societies that are "hierarchical, semicooperative, and structured by authority relations."[14] From this perspective, claiming, as neo-Foucauldians do, that neoliberalism is based on a "political rationality" modeled on the market will not be enough. Our goal should be to think not only about a "market rationality," but also about a "corporate rationality," with its own specificity.

From this perspective, the key task is to question the type of government and hierarchical order that the firm represents, and the kind of "corporate rationality" that underlies it.[15] It is also where the relational argument in favor of workplace democracy comes in. The features of contemporary business firms mentioned above—hierarchical structures of managerial authority—should be of particular interest to relational egalitarians and induce greater critical scrutiny. The pervasiveness of corporations in our organizational societies makes certain economic *relations* of authority and hierarchies predominant in the lives of a large number of citizens, which is crucial (because it is worrisome) from the point of view of social equality.[16]

Here, it is worth following Joseph Heath, who argues that the firm-market distinction informs us not only about the empirical realities of these institutions, but also about their "implicit normative logic."[17] In other words, to draw attention to these institutions—their modes of operation, policies, and expected outcomes—is also to draw attention to a certain "normative order," a set of values, norms, expectations, justifications, and moral

---

[14] David Ciepley, "Beyond Private and Public: Toward a Political Theory of the Corporation," *American Political Science Review* 107, no. 1 (2013): 139–158, at 140.

[15] See Elizabeth Anderson's important book, *Private Government: How Employers Rule Our Lives (and Why We Don't Talk about It)* (Princeton, NJ: Princeton University Press, 2017).

[16] I developed this line of argument in various papers. See my "Social Equality and Economic Institutions: Arguing for Workplace Democracy," in *The Equal Society: Essays on Equality in Theory and Practice*, ed. George Hull (Lanham, MD: Lexington Books, 2017), 311–332.

[17] Joseph Heath, *Morality, Competition and the Firm: The Market Failures Approach to Business Ethics* (Oxford: Oxford University Press, 2014).

58 WORKING AS EQUALS

imaginaries that underlie them.[18] Our task then is to draw the contours of these normative orders that are the market and the corporation. According to Heath, the normative order of the market is based on the value of *competition*, via the price mechanism, whereas that of the firm is based on the value of *cooperation*, via the hierarchy.

Note here, and it is a crucial point of this chapter, that Heath does an excellent job on one side of the equation, the market. Indeed, Heath proposes a very sophisticated and original theory of the implicit morality of competition and adversarial relationships. However, his theorization of the other side, the firm, is less sophisticated. His approach combines transaction-costs economics, the nexus-of-contracts view of the firm, and game theory to make sense of cooperation via hierarchy. However, by doing so, he fails to excavate the implicit morality of hierarchy, its valuation, its moral imaginaries, and its immense appeal. As we shall see, it fits well with conservatism.

In some sense, and taking some cues from the work of James C. Scott, Heath invites us to imagine how these institutions "see" the world normatively.[19] Indeed, in his seminal book *Seeing Like a State*, Scott asks what it means to "see with the eyes of a state."[20] He argues that the state tends to adopt "tunneled" visions that are necessarily *narrow* and force us to use *simplifying lens*.[21] Similarly, in a recent paper, Marion Fourcade and Kieran Healy invite us to think about the ways in which markets can "see" the world in radically new ways through what they call "the classificatory architecture of the digital economy."[22] They argue that in the era of big data, markets create "classificatory struggles" with important (and potentially worrisome) "stratification effects." As digital traces of consumer behaviors are aggregated, stored, and analyzed, "markets see people through a lens of deserving and undeservingness, and classification situations become moral projects."

---

[18] Heath is not using the notion of "normative orders." I am using it to broaden his approach in order to be more aware of the importance of the "moral imaginaries" that come with markets and firms.

[19] The distinction is not always so clear-cut in the complex reality of our economies. Firms of course evolve themselves within more or less competitive markets, ranging from extremely competitive to monopolistic. And such an account obviously draws on a highly idealized version of markets operating through the decentralized price mechanism and perfect competition. As many have recognized, there are also forms of power and authority in markets. See, for instance, Anne Phillips, "Egalitarians and the Market: Dangerous Ideals," *Social Theory and Practice* 34, no. 3 (2008): 439–462.

[20] James C. Scott, *Seeing Like a State: How Certain Schemes to Improve the Human Condition Have Failed* (New Haven: Yale University Press, 1998).

[21] Ibid.

[22] Marion Fourcade and Kieran Healy, "Seeing Like a Market," *Socio-economic Review* 15, no. 1 (2017): 9–29, citations here and below at 16.

SEEING LIKE A FIRM   59

Yet an often overlooked aspect of this approach (by Scott himself) is that the lenses used by an institution are largely normative. Empirically, the simplifying lens of an institution may be, well, . . . simplifying, but much of its power of attraction lies in its normative dimension. This allows institutions to identify the contours of a certain normative order, corresponding to a certain imaginary, a certain repertoire of normative resources that serve to evaluate, justify, or criticize certain attitudes and certain treatments for the agents attached to this institution. Thus, I suggest that we take inspiration from the spirit of Scott's project while adding a "normative twist" to it.[23] Hence, our task would be to understand what it means to "see like a corporation," to unveil how these radically simplified designs of economic organization, to paraphrase Scott, rely heavily on simplified but powerful normative views.[24]

Here, one could also say that this approach fits quite well with one of the fundamental components of the relational theory of equality, namely its capacity to draw attention not only to the distributive effects of our practices and institutions, but to their expressive dimensions. As some relational egalitarians argue, the relational approach aims to help us to think seriously about how our institutions, in addition to distributing resources, wages, esteem, power, etc., carry messages and meanings.[25] From such a perspective, we need to take note of how institutions express, reinforce, or legitimize certain attitudes and forms of treatment toward individuals and groups. Thus, the type of look that an institution casts on its agents also has a communicational content; it sends messages. One could therefore say that "seeing like a firm" is also "speaking like a firm."

Following on from this, and emphasizing the complex relationship between the two institutions, one could of course claim that the corporation is often seen as an entity driven solely by the pursuit of profit without regard for anything else, a view that led legal scholar Joel Balkan to argue in 2004 that it has the psychological profile of a psychopath.[26] One could thus say that the "tunnel vision" of the corporation is that of almost obsessive profit maximization.

---

[23] Therefore, I am not simply "applying" Scott's approach. For instance, I am not suggesting that the corporate optic relies on a "high modernist" ideology, which is a key component of Scott's approach.

[24] See Scott, *Seeing Like a State*, 7.

[25] See Pierre-Yves Néron, "Rethinking the Very Idea of Egalitarian Markets and Corporations: Why Relationships Might Matter More Than Distribution," *Business Ethics Quarterly* 25, no. 1 (2015): 93–124.

[26] See Joel Bakan's book, *The Corporation: The Pathological Pursuit of Profit and Power* (New York: Free Press, 2004), and the documentary based on the book.

60 WORKING AS EQUALS

While there is of course some truth in such a view, it nonetheless erases a huge part of the "normative vision" of the corporation, particularly the one which it casts on its employees. Using Heath's account, one could argue that it does not provide us an "inner" look at the firm, at its *internal* relations.[27] The business firm is not uniquely an ongoing project of profit maximization, to paraphrase Scott again. The "tunnel vision" of the corporation, which makes it clash with the ideal of a society of equals, is that of hierarchy, the "simplifying" corporate optic is profoundly antiegalitarian. If by "normative simplifications" we mean, in a similar way to Scott, mobilizing certain values and norms to develop "schematic thinking" while ignoring otherwise relevant features,[28] the great simplification of the firm is that of putting aside our status as equals. Indeed, the corporate optic is composed of hierarchical patterns of authority lines, superiors and inferiors, rankings, what Brown sees as an obsession with evaluation, and what Fourcade and Healy call "classificatory struggles."[29] As Richard Wilkinson and Kate Pickett note in their study of the many ways in which "inequalities get under your skin," the workplace is the place where we are "most explicitly placed in a rank-ordered hierarchy, superiors and inferiors, bosses and subordinates."[30]

From this point of view, the corporation is of course an institution that reinforces preexisting social hierarchies. It is a well-known and documented fact that the corporation contributes significantly to the reinforcement of preexisting inequalities and forms of subordination, which are embodied in many ways in its structures, operations, modes of governance, and management, as well as in its daily functioning. And if, as Scheffler notes, certain inequalities of rank, power, and status are endemic to social life, the firm undoubtedly contributes to their exacerbation.[31] However, the corporation does more than that. It *formalizes* these inequalities while promoting and validating them through a vast set of policies, lines of authority, and

---

[27] Heath's account relies heavily on a sharp distinction between "external," market-type relations, and internal, hierarchical, or cooperative, relations. See Heath, *Morality, Competition*.

[28] Scott, *Seeing Like a State*, 81.

[29] Fourcade and Healy, "Seeing Like a Market," 13.

[30] Richard G. Wilkinson and Kate Pickett, *The Spirit Level: Why Equality Is Better for Everyone* (London: Penguin Books, 2010), 250. See also Danièle Linhart's impressive work on worker subordination, *L'insoutenable subordination des salariés* (Paris: ERÈS, 2021) and her *La comédie humaine au travail: De la déshumanisation taylorienne à la sur-humanisation managériale* (Paris: ERÈS, 2016). For a fascinating study of the complex relations between the pervasiveness of workplace injustices and the crucial importance of demands for equal standing, see François Dubet's insightful book, *Injustices: L'expérience des inégalités au travail* (Paris: Seuil, 2006).

[31] Samuel Scheffler, *Equality and Tradition: Questions of Moral Value in Moral and Political Theory* (Oxford: Oxford University Press, 2010), 225.

managerial styles, but also various forms of discourses and "hierarchical myths," as the literature on the "romance of leadership" clearly shows.[32] The corporation is therefore not only the place where inequalities are reproduced, but also the place where the spectacle of inequality is performed on a daily basis.

It is at this point that the opposition between libertarianism and conservatism becomes crucial. Indeed, how do we make sense of the "hierarchical lens" of the firm from a normative point of view? Here, libertarians will provide us with a narrative that combines the theory of the firm as a nexus of contracts with transaction-costs economics. Hierarchical structures of managerial authority are justified for the sake of efficiency; the rest is individual interaction, notably between managers and employees, the latter being protected by their employment contract. This is the kind of view that led John Boatright to argue that managerial authority is a nonissue.[33] The normative story of libertarians will therefore focus on voluntary exchanges, self-ownership, and respect of contracts between free individuals. Conservatives, on the other hand, and this is the heart of my argument, will produce a very different narrative. To a certain extent, the corporation (and the business world in general) represents for them a perfect laboratory. To use Corey Robin's definition of conservatism, and we will go back to it later, the corporation acts as the private regime of power par excellence.[34] As a result, conservatives will offer us a different normative narrative, centered on stronger forms of authority, as they tend to be more enthusiastic about political and economic elites. Unlike egalitarians, who will look skeptically at the "self-made man" stories that business circles are so fond of, conservatives will have far less hesitation in telling such stories about economic elites. Unlike egalitarians again, who will attempt to constrain hierarchies and authority, they will see these structures as mirroring a social order that reflects so-called "natural" hierarchies and clearly sets limits on the pursuit of equality, limits that can be transgressed only through a guilty hubris.[35] Simply put, the emphasis on hierarchies, strong forms of authority, and leadership, combined with a form

---

[32] For a classical account see James R. Meindl, Sanford B. Ehrleich, and Janet M. Dukerich, "The Romance of Leadership," *Administrative Science Quarterly* 30, no. 1 (1985): 78–102.

[33] John Boatright, "Review of *Public Capitalism: The Political Authority of Corporate Executives*, by Christopher McMahon," *Business Ethics Quarterly* 23, no. 3 (2013): 477–480.

[34] Corey Robin, *The Reactionary Mind: Conservatism from Edmund Burke to Donald Trump* (New York: Oxford University Press, 2018), 15.

[35] See Russell Kirk's 1953 book and his famous "six canons" of conservatism in *The Conservative Mind* (New York: Gateway, 2016).

62   WORKING AS EQUALS

of elitism that is so common in the business world, reflects a social order that conservatives cherish.

4.2. The Aesthetics of Inequality

This chapter draws a lot on Robin's work in his important *The Reactionary Mind: Conservatism from Edmund Burke to Donald Trump*. One of the great advantages of Robin's approach is that it invites us to go beyond *formal* conceptions of conservatism to produce a *substantive* interpretation of it. For the simplest definition of conservatism is indeed purely formal in the sense that it does not link the conservative to a substantial political vision, but only to a certain attitude toward change, one mixing resistance, skepticism, and annoyance. Conservatism would then be rooted in a form of psychological ethos of aversion to change combined with acquiescence to the natural and well-founded character of what is and has been. We could thus rely on Michael Oakeshott's famous definition: "To be conservative is to prefer the familiar to the unknown, the tried to the untried."[36]

Indeed, if one adheres to this purely formal conception of conservatism, there seems to be no reason to deny the existence of a left-wing conservatism. It is a well-known refrain: the defense of the welfare state and its achievements is associated with a left-wing conservatism incapable of adapting to new realities. Beyond the rhetorical effects, however, the problem is that such definition is not only overinclusive but potentially meaningless, and makes the label lose its very meaning.

According to Robin, conservatism can be defined substantially in terms of the following three elements: first, the defense of a natural social order: conservatism consists of a desire, not simply to "preserve the existing," but to defend and maintain a "social order" that is interpreted as natural or spontaneous. Second, and corollary, is the valorization of hierarchies and inequalities. They are viewed as a reflection of what Kirk refers to as the conservative belief in the existence of natural distinctions extraneous to positive law. Policies aimed at equality are widely distrusted as both unfounded and utopian, based on a guilty faith in "political rationalism" and ultimately contrary to the natural order of things (a key theme in Hayek's thought).

---

[36] Michael Oakeshott, "On Being a Conservative," in *Rationalism in Politics and Other Essays* (London: Liberty Fund, 1958), 168–198, at 169.

SEEING LIKE A FIRM   63

Conservatives are regularly at pains to denounce, in a Tocquevillian vein, the dangers of the "passion for equality."[37] Third is the preservation of *private power regimes*, what Robin describes as "the private life of power."[38] In short: the family, the workplace, the army. This is illustrated by the persistent attachment to the authority figures of the paterfamilias or the heroic warriors.

Relying on Robin's approach, I focus here on the very particular relationship of conservatives to inequality. My argument is that this relationship is one of positive appreciation, not merely tolerance, which distinguishes conservatives from libertarians. While the latter seek to provide constraints on justifications for inequality (which nevertheless leads them to tolerate very high levels of it), conservatives seek to provide us with reasons to *value* inequality. While libertarians justify inequalities and hierarchies based on self-ownership and the voluntariness of interactions, conservatives offer various considerations of the value and beauty of inequalities. Inequalities are produced in the former case, but they have no normative value as such; whereas in the latter, they have a natural dimension and possess a normative force. For libertarians, inequalities can be justified and therefore tolerated. For conservatives, inequalities are good, even beautiful, and should therefore be valued. Hence, a libertarian approach gives us reasons to *tolerate* the hierarchical structure of the corporation, while a conservative approach invites us to *appreciate* the corporate spectacle of inequality I was referring to earlier.

Thus understood in its relation to inequality, conservatism is characterized by what I propose to refer to as an *aesthetics of inequality*, understood as a positive appreciation, perhaps more intuitive than principled, of inequality and its various manifestations. It is less "principled" than intuitive in the sense that it corresponds to the conservative "methodology." It is less an appreciation of inequalities that would result from a principle of justice than from an ethos, a complex set of attitudes, values, sensibilities, and relationships to the world. The aesthetics of inequality is, in short, the adoption of an ethos characterized by the positive appreciation of an unequal socioeconomic order. However, the key point is that this aesthetic of inequality is part of the repertoire of conservatism, not that of libertarianism. Conservatives are the true lovers of inequality. It is, I argue, this *aesthetic of inequality* that

---

[37] A denunciation that is often truncated because it is presented only in a negative light, even though Tocqueville recognized its ambivalence.

[38] Robin, *The Reactionary Mind*, esp. ch. 1.

64 WORKING AS EQUALS

represents the normative core of conservatism, and that should inform our analysis of the implicit morality of the firm.

The concept of *aesthetics of inequality*, I suggest, provides us a useful overarching interpretation of the above-mentioned features of conservatism. First, it clarifies the kind of social order that conservatives want to defend. Second, it clarifies the specific nature of the relationships conservatives entertain with hierarchy and inequality, one that is of appreciation, not merely toleration. Third, it shows why private regimes of power like the firm ought to be preserved, because they represent the theater in which inequality is being *exposed, performed, confirmed*, and *celebrated*.

From this point of view, the meritocratic ideology embodies one of the main expressions of the aesthetics of inequality.[39] In his *Capital in the Twenty-First Century*, Thomas Piketty has done us a favor by making us rediscover the words of Émile Boutmy, the founder of Sciences Po Paris,[40] a key institution of French meritocracy, who declared in 1871 that

> obliged to submit to the rule of the majority, the classes that call themselves the upper classes can preserve their political hegemony only by invoking the rights of the most capable. As traditional upper-class prerogatives crumble, the wave of democracy will encounter a second rampart, built on eminently useful talents, superiority that commands prestige, and abilities of which society cannot sanely deprive itself.[41]

These words, which Piketty describes as "an incredible statement,"[42] perfectly reflect the attitude of the elites of the time, who rejected republican equality not by resorting to blood, but by virtue of their extraordinary abilities. They therefore echo a change of register in the justification of inequalities, which can no longer be *explicitly* aristocratic; it must be based on merit. They also represent a beautiful expression of meritocracy as an ideology, serving as a discourse legitimizing social reproduction. However, let us also note the aesthetics of inequality that is at work, where the condemnation of an

---

[39] Here it should be obvious that I am relying on critical, if not negative, account of meritocracy, as being mainly an ideology for the justifications of inequalities, in a way that is similar to Michael Young's spirit when he coined the term, for satiric purposes. *The Rise of Meritocracy* (New York: Routledge, 2017).

[40] Called the École libre des sciences politiques, at the time.

[41] Thomas Piketty, *Capital in the Twenty-First Century*, trans. Arthur Goldhammer (Cambridge, MA: Harvard University Press, 2014), 487.

[42] Piketty, *Capital*, 487.

egalitarian hubris is suddenly replaced by the celebration of a meritocratic one. Inequality will henceforth be exposed, performed, confirmed, and celebrated via this spectacle of great men with dazzling abilities, and a failure to appreciate this beauty can only be madness. From Sciences Po to the contemporary corporation, the logic is the same.

Here one could raise doubts about the epistemic value of conservatism, and its "aesthetics of inequality," for rationally debating about justice, since I described it as a "sensibility" or an "ethos." Thus described, the argument goes, conservatism simply does not represent a valid option if we want to have rational debates about the meanings of justice.

In response to this, I would like to make two remarks. First, one could argue, following Joe Wolff, that egalitarians would gain by doing *precisely this*: to adopt a less principled view, maybe less "rational," and try to theoretically make sense of something like an egalitarian "ethos." Indeed, in a series of papers in which he attempts to articulate some of his own dissatisfactions with regard to recent egalitarianism, Wolff argues that describing the egalitarian doctrine as a simple set of principles that we can "apply" to various situations is misleading.[43] Egalitarianism, according to him, is better understood as an "egalitarian ethos," a complex but coherent collection of values and attitudes associated with a commitment to sustain equal relationships. In a similar vein, I suggest that such an approach would also need to make sense of the antiegalitarian passions that animate conservatism and its aesthetics of inequality.

Second, it is worth noting here that the "sovereign virtue" hypothesis, held by Ronald Dworkin, Amartya Sen, Will Kymlicka, and others, probably played a huge role in how philosophers ended up neglecting conservativism.[44] To recall, the key idea underlying this hypothesis was that moral equality, or the ideal of equal concern or respect for all, should be at the heart of *every* theory of justice worth discussing in democratic societies. Of course, the epistemic goal of the sovereign virtue hypothesis was precisely to help us have rational debates about the *best* way to interpret the *shared*

---

[43] See Jonathan Wolff, "Fairness, Respect and the Egalitarian *Ethos* Revisited," *Journal of Ethics* 14, no. 3 (2010): 335–350.

[44] See Ronald Dworkin, *The Sovereign Virtue: The Theory and Practice of Equality* (Cambridge, MA: Harvard University Press, 2002); Amartya Sen, *Inequality Reexamined* (Cambridge, MA: Harvard University Press, 1992); Will Kymlicka, *Contemporary Political Philosophy: An Introduction* (Oxford: Oxford University Press, 2002), 4.

66 WORKING AS EQUALS

ideal of equal respect.[45] The result? Libertarianism came to be viewed as *the* main model to make sense of right-wing intuitions. It is because, like egalitarians, socialists, feminists, cosmopolitans, etc., libertarians start with the ideal of equal respect. Or course, they move on to conclude that having free unregulated markets without redistributive policies is the best way to treat individuals with equal respect, by taking seriously their status as autonomous agents able to make economic decisions for themselves. Still, they are somehow "egalitarians" in the very abstract sense.

However, and this is crucial for my argument, from the point of view of the sovereign virtue hypothesis, we must admit that conservatism does not fit well. While conservatives do not necessarily totally reject the ideal of moral equality, their preference for hierarchy and inequality is strong enough to threaten it.[46] They are therefore excluded from "rational" debates about justice.

It is of course beyond the scope of this chapter to deal with all the epistemological issues that are at stake here. However, I would like to submit the following idea: this underlying hope for rational debates might be helpful for the quality of philosophical discussions, but it comes with a price. Indeed, the faith in the sovereign virtue hypothesis has deprived theorists of justice of the possibility of thinking seriously about a certain antiegalitarian passion that animates conservative thought and whose manifestations are multiple in the contemporary crisis of equality.[47] The argument articulated in this chapter suggests it was misleading. As I argue, we need to understand the aesthetics of inequality.

4.3. The Rise of Conservatism of Commerce

My argument also relies on the substantial transformation that contemporary conservatism has undergone. Indeed, there is a strong tendency to

---

[45] As Will Kymlicka puts it, if all theories share this point of departure, "We might be able to show that one theory does a better job at living up to the standard that they all recognize" (*Contemporary Political Philosophy*, 4).

[46] Interestingly, we find an explicit rejection of the assumption in Hayek. Citing Dworkin, he writes that "it is not by conceding 'a right to equal concern and respect' to those who break the code that civilization is maintained" (Friedrich A. von Hayek, *Law, Legislation and Liberty*, 3 vols, vol. 3, 171. [Chicago: University of Chicago Press, 2010], 172).

[47] For a powerful account of the contemporary crisis of equality, in terms of a vanishing of the ideal of a "society of equals," see Pierre Rosanvallon, *The Society of Equals*, trans. Arthur Goldhammer (Cambridge, MA: Harvard University Press, 2013).

reduce conservatism to a set of stances on "social" issues, and not to a position on social justice or political economy. From this point of view, the privileged arena of conservatism seems to be that of social values rather than economics as such. This is the "classical" way to interpret political divides.

This classical interpretation is also the one taken up by Wendy Brown in her germinal study of the relationships between neoliberalism and value conservatism, which she described as two "political rationalities" that are fundamentally different but that can converge on the rejection of the "social" and their antidemocratic aspects.[48] However, it seems to be misleading: once the normative core of conservatism has been identified, namely its aesthetics of inequality, this core is destined to be deployed as much on the moral side as on the economic side. And from this point of view, markets and firms are not innocent objects. They are not the simple locus of voluntary interactions in the Nozickian sense: first, because they remain very largely conceived as producing "natural" orders; second, because they both constitute paradigmatic sites of private regimes of power.

To grasp this, we must first understand an important transformation in contemporary conservatism. Historically, conservatism has been filled with thinkers who abhor the market. To the baseness and tediousness of commercial affairs, they preferred the grandeur and nobility of the high affairs of state. The figure of the great man was that of the head of state, the war hero. As an aging William F. Buckley, who is largely considered as the godfather of contemporary American conservatism, said at the turn of the twentieth century: "Capitalism is boring. To devote your life to it is terrifying, partly because it is so repetitive. You hear about it once and you get it. It's like sex."[49] Now, if Buckley makes such remarks, it is because he is well aware of the transformation that is at work, to which he has greatly contributed and which he partly regrets, namely the rise to power of a market conservatism. This opposition between value conservatism and market conservatism is, moreover, flagrant in Roger Scruton's thinking. While Buckley ultimately remains a great supporter of the market, which he sees as intrinsically linked to the individualism he cherishes and that allows great men to emerge,[50] Scruton

---

[48] See Wendy Brown, *In the Ruins of Neoliberalism: The Rise of Antidemocratic Politics in the West* (New York: Columbia University Press, 2019), esp. ch. 3. On the relationships between neoliberalism and social conservatism, see Melinda Cooper's groundbreaking book *Family Values: Between Neoliberalism and the New Social Conservatism* (New York: Zone Books, 2019).

[49] Quoted in Robin, *The Reactionary Mind*, 22.

[50] Concerning the exaltation of great men, William F. Buckley Jr.'s collection of speeches, *Let Us Talk of Many Things: The Collected Speeches* (New York: Basic Books, 2008), is telling.

68 WORKING AS EQUALS

is more explicit in his contempt, activating more willingly the conservative tradition of disgust with commerce. Indeed, in *The Meaning of Conservatism*, he addressed the architects of nascent Thatcherism in 1980, reminding them that there *is* such a thing as a society and that their market individualism failed to understand our status as inheritors of the past, of history and tradition.[51] He deplored the many ways in which economic considerations took precedence over all else, to the neglect of deeper moral and aesthetic values. Thus, Scruton contrasted a Thatcherism focused on economic matters with a conservatism focused on preserving what matters. And for him, the market is boring. His conservatism is based on a concern not so much for commercial life as for friendship, love, music, etc.

Scruton's defeat must be acknowledged, as his grievances have had very limited resonance. From Thatcher and Reagan to Trump, contemporary conservatism bears the mark of a powerful form of commerce conservatism. For Robin, understanding this transformation of contemporary conservatism now seems crucial. Indeed, in the first edition of his book, subtitled *Conservatism, from Edmund Burke to Sarah Palin*, Robin gave crucial importance to violence in his analysis, in order to make sense of the Bush-like, "war-mongering" neoconservatism that was easily discernible at the beginning of this century. In the second edition, this time subtitled *Conservatism, from Edmund Burke to Donald Trump*, Robin admits to having neglected issues related to political economy and thus the place of the market in conservative thinking, which turns out to be crucial to making sense of "Trumpism." The result of this admission is an important shift in focus, in which Robin invites us to think less about the links between Burke, Nietzsche, and Leo Strauss than about those between Burke, Nietzsche, and Hayek.[52] A fine reader of the contemporary Right, from Hayek to Trump's *The Art of the Deal*, Robin thus traces the lines of a conservative reading of neoliberalism, a conservatism that has of course passed, from Nietzsche via Hayek, through the type of transformations I am trying to articulate here.

Nietzsche wrote in *Ecce Homo* about his destiny that "one day the memory of something formidable will be attached to my name,—the memory of a

---

[51] Roger Scruton, *The Meaning of Conservatism* (London: Palgrave-Macmillan, 2001).

[52] Following Robin, I take for granted here that Hayek's self-description as nonconservative, in a famous article ("Why I Am Not a Conservative," reprinted in *Law, Legislation and Liberty*) does not hold water. The celebration of Burke's social philosophy, on which Hayek draws extensively, combined with his criticism of rationalism, his hatred of the French Revolution, his elitism, his praise of tradition, and his contempt for egalitarianism: much militates in favor of the thesis of a conservative Hayek.

SEEING LIKE A FIRM   69

crisis such as there has never been on earth, the memory of the deepest colli-
sion of consciences."[53] Robin expands on Nietzsche's famous remark:

> It's one of the great ironies of intellectual history that the terms of that col-
> lision can best be seen in the rise of a movement Nietzsche in all likeli-
> hood would have despised. The Nobel Prize–winning economist Friedrich
> Hayek is the leading theoretician of this movement, which is often called
> neoliberalism but can also be understood as the most genuinely political
> theory of capitalism the right has managed to produce. The theory does
> not imagine a shift from government to the individual, as is often claimed
> by conservatives; nor does it imagine a shift from the state to the market
> or from society to the atomized individuals, as it is often claimed on the
> left. Instead, the theory recasts our understanding of politics and where it
> might be found. It takes what Nietzsche called *grosse politik*—a conception
> of political life as the embodiment of ancient ideals of aristocratic action,
> aesthetic notions of artistic creation, and a rarified vision of the warrior—
> and locates that vision not in high affairs of state but in the operations and
> personnel of a capitalist economy.[54]

If we follow Robin, conservatives have been "reprogramming" their
doctrine, to use a vocabulary that would please the neo-Foucauldians, by
redefining the locus of aristocratic politics.[55] The result? A Nietzschean political economy animated by a romantic conception of economic activity,
in which it becomes more exciting than efficient, the new locus of expression of aristocratic excellence, artistic creativity, and warlike action, rather
than the mere repository of bourgeois selfishness.[56] This Nietzschean political economy is then characterized by a new mix that Nietzsche himself
would have hated: meritocratic ideals, commercial exaltation of creativity,
and a heroic vision of economic action. In short, Trump, Silicon Valley, and
the French so-called *startup nation*: the vulgar version of Nietzsche's neo-
aristocratic dreams.

---

[53] Quoted in Robin, *The Reactionary Mind*, 133.

[54] Robin, *The Reactionary Mind*, 133.

[55] One of the key themes of the neo-Foucauldian analysis of neoliberalism is that neoliberals did
not simply produce a reaffirmation of liberalism, but a significant *reprograming* of it, namely through
the affirmation of liberal interventionism. See Pierre Dardot and Christian Laval, *The New Way of the
World: On Neoliberal Society* (New York: Verso, 2014).

[56] Deidre McCloskey would argue that it became the repository of the bourgeois *virtue*. See her *The
Bourgeois Virtues: Ethics for an Age of Commerce* (Chicago: of Chicago University Press, 2006).

70 WORKING AS EQUALS

Here one could argue that it provides us a fruitful *conservative* reading of Hayek's assertion that "politics must be dethroned."[57] Less than the simple affirmation of individualism against collectivism, or the symbol of a colonizing political rationality based on the market (à la Brown), the dethronement of politics represents in fact an important turning point in conservative thought, marked by a double reallocation: first, the reallocation of the conservatives' contempt, which is no longer directed at low commerce but at the high affairs of the state; second, of the admiration of conservatives, which is redirected from the state and the army to the market and the firm, the new locus of emergence and discovery of great men. This reallocation completely alters the nature of the aristocracy of excellence, the enhancement of which motivates conservative thought.

We can thus better understand the enchantment of economic life that is at work in the conservatism of commerce. It is a reconfiguration of the types of private regimes of power that conservatives cherish and the hierarchical logic that presides over them. Devotees of inequality and partisans of a strong and unabashed moral perfectionism, conservatives can launch into the praise of the market and the firm as the true locus of the private life of power, that of the excellence of great men.

Thus, the contemporary history of conservatism, via neoliberalism, is that of the defeat of a certain type of conservatism, à la Scruton, supplanted by a form of *conservatism of commerce*. And the latter proceeds to a radical reconfiguration of our relationship to the market. It becomes the place where the action is, to the detriment of other places, such as the state or the army, which lose some of their luster to the benefit of economic life. Markets and firms are no longer "neutral," "amoral," or simply "boring" institutions; they become profoundly moral institutions, the ultimate places for the discovery and exhibition of great men, of "talents."[58] And, as I argue here, it is especially true for the firm. Through the immense appeal of the ideology of meritocracy, it becomes the moral and political theater where a battle between "winners and losers" is played out, to take up a theme beloved to Trumpism, between those who dare to "cross the street" to find a job against those "who are nothing," to draw from a few infamous words from French president Emmanuel Macron.[59] The institutions of commerce are no longer an object of contempt

---

[57] Hayek, *Law, Legislation and Liberty*. See Brown, *In the Ruins*, for a critical analysis.

[58] This fits well with Lindhart's account of what she refers to as the "managerial over-humanization" of the workplace. See her *La comédie humaine du travail*.

[59] For the reference to the need to cross the street to find a job, see "Emmanuel Macron à un chômeur: Je traverse la rue, je vous trouve du travail," *Le Figaro*, September 16, 2018. For "those who

for conservatives, but of glorification. Markets and firms are no longer what lead conservatives to boredom, but what excite them.

By adopting such a conception of conservatism, and of its recent transformations, it seems to me that we might be better equipped to understand some aspects of the "implicit morality" at work in the market/firm distinction, especially on the second side of the equation, which is a key goal of the burgeoning political theory of the firm. Indeed, following Heath, political theorists of the firm have for the moment mostly emphasized the *adversarial* dimensions of the market as well as the *cooperative* dimensions of the firm. In doing so, they have largely failed to think about the hierarchical aspects of economic life, particularly in the corporation. However, it seems to me urgent to excavate the "hierarchical vision" that is so prevalent in the business world, and not simply in terms of its links to efficient cooperation, but in terms of its imaginaries of inequality, its valorization of it, of what I have proposed to call its *aesthetics of inequality*. This chapter represents a contribution to such a project.

4.4. Conclusion

In this chapter, I have tried to take the market/firm distinction seriously, not so much to highlight its descriptive usefulness as to draw out the various "normative imaginaries" or orders at work in it. This, I argue, can help us to rethink certain key elements of our neoliberal societies. For example, Catherine Rottenberg, following Brown, argues that neoliberalism, as a political rationality, "has no political imaginary outside of the market and market metrics—these are colonizing all spheres of life."[60] However, from the point of view I am trying to develop here, this is partly misleading. The imaginary of neoliberalism is not only that of the market, with its obsession with generalized competition and entrepreneurship. It is also the imaginary of the corporation, with its celebration of hierarchy, authority, and subordination.

---

are nothing," see Emmanuel Macron's speech for the opening of the Station Fs a startup center in Paris, June 29, 2017. See Michael J. Sandel's latest book for both a critique of meritocracy and an analysis of its huge appeal: *The Tyranny of Merit: What's Become of the Common Good?* (New York: Farrar, Straus and Giroux, 2020).

[60] Catherine Rottenberg, *The Rise of Neoliberal Feminism* (Oxford: Oxford University Press, 2020), 16–17.

72　WORKING AS EQUALS

I have also tried to take seriously the claim that firms "see" in a conservative way. The normative tunnel vision of the corporation is that of hierarchy, and the great simplification of the corporate optic is to set aside the demands for equal standing. To make sense of this conclusion, two things are necessary. First, we must clarify the relationship conservatives have with inequality, which is one of approval, appreciation, celebration: what I propose to conceptualize as an *aesthetics of inequality.* In the end, conservatism is the only political philosophy that offers us an authentic celebration of inequality. Thus, it offers us a solid basis for understanding the corporate regime, and what is so often problematic about it. Second, we need to be able to understand the key movement that characterizes contemporary conservatism, namely the shift from a conservatism of values to a conservatism of commerce, which embarks on the celebration of economic activity as the new locus of aristocratic politics.

Understanding the conservative nature of the corporation—its practices, tactics, institutions, discourses, and imaginaries—seems to be a crucial task for proponents of relational egalitarianism. Yet, despite Elizabeth Anderson's 1999 call to think about the "point" of equality as fighting unjust hierarchies and building equal social relations, relational egalitarians have largely failed to take seriously the fact that many are driven by the opposite, the maintenance and celebration of hierarchies.[61] The proponents of hierarchical orders (fair or unfair? How pretentious!) are well alive, and they are conservative.

---

[61] Elizabeth Anderson, "What Is the Point of Equality?," *Ethics* 109, no. 2 (1999): 287–337.

5

Self-Employment and Independence

Iñigo González Ricoy

Self-employment is as ubiquitous as it is philosophically neglected. Nearly half of the workforce in developing countries, and two-thirds in regions like South Asia, are self-employed.[1] And although the employment share of the self-employed negatively correlates with countries' GDP per capita, such that it accounts on average for just one in seven workers in affluent countries, in recent decades (nonagricultural) self-employment has ceased to decline and is now on the rise in such countries.[2]

Despite its prevalence, however, recent philosophizing about work has largely neglected self-employment.[3] This neglect is particularly puzzling when it comes to republican analyses of labor relations, at the core of which is the value of independence. For independence from a boss is precisely what self-employment promises to deliver. Indeed, much classic theorizing about work championed self-employment as a means to escape the "servile dependency upon their superiors" that, according to Adam Smith, wage labor comprised.[4] And independence from a boss is also the chief reason that the self-employed today cite for preferring self-employment to employee work.[5]

In this chapter I inspect the argument from independence, as I will refer to it, for protecting and promoting self-employment, which comes in roughly

[1] International Labour Organization, *Small Matters: Global Evidence on the Contribution to Employment by the Self-Employed, Micro-enterprises and SMEs* (Geneva: ILO, 2019), 12.

[2] Patrice Muller et al., *Annual Report on European SMEs 2016/2017: Focus on Self-Employment* (Luxembourg: European Commission, 2017), 46–82; Mark Baker et al., "To What Extent Do Policies Contribute to Self-Employment?," OECD Economics Department Working Papers, No. 1512 (2018), 1–31.

[3] Exceptions include Elizabeth Anderson, "Equality and Freedom in the Workplace: Recovering Republican Insights," *Social Philosophy and Policy* 31, no. 2 (2015): 48–69; Jahel Queralt, "Protecting the Entrepreneurial Poor: A Human Rights Approach," *Politics, Philosophy and Economics* 18, no. 4 (2019): 336–357; and Daniel Halliday, "On the (Mis)classification of Paid Labor: When Should Gig Workers Have Employee Status?," *Politics, Philosophy and Economics* 20, no. 3 (2020): 229–250.

[4] Adam Smith, *An Inquiry into the Nature and Causes of the Wealth of Nations* (Oxford: Oxford University Press, 1976), III.4.4.

[5] Christopher Dawson et al., "Why Do Individuals Choose Self-Employment?," IZA Discussion Paper, No. 3974 (2009), 34.

Iñigo González Ricoy, *Self-Employment and Independence* In: *Working as Equals.* Edited by: Julian David Jonker and Grant J. Rozeboom, Oxford University Press. © Oxford University Press 2023.
DOI: 10.1093/oso/9780197634295.003.0005

74 WORKING AS EQUALS

two versions. According to the "brute power" version of the argument, self-employment is valuable because being subject to the power of a boss is objectionable as such, no matter how suitably checked this power may be. On the "arbitrary power" variant of the argument, by contrast, self-employment is valuable because it confers independence not from the power of a boss as such, but from the risk of this power being deployed in a way that fails to track workers' interests—a risk that, given the open-endedness of employment contracts, may not be possible to entirely root out.

Both versions of the argument from independence rest on egalitarian premises, of two kinds. First, they stem from a complaint, whose specific content each version outlines differently, about the power inequality that the employer-employee relationship involves. Accordingly, they challenge the view, common among contemporary republicans and relational egalitarians, that, depending on the terms under which they occur, employment relations can be entirely unobjectionable. Second, both versions of the argument favor making self-employment accessible not just for some, as classic republicans often championed, but for all, demanding that barriers to becoming and remaining self-employed be universally removed as a result.

Some such barriers involve outright intrusions from governments, like bans on self-employment or bribe extraction from public officials. Other barriers are regulatory, like the legal hurdles that governments often create and uphold. For example, registering a business takes ninety-seven days and 179.7 percent of the per capita income in Haiti, but just one day and 2.1 percent of the per capita income in Georgia.[6] Yet other barriers, albeit not governmental in origin, like the financial constraints and poor skills that some would-be self-employed workers endure, governments can nonetheless mitigate them by actively promoting self-employment—for example, through capital injections, tax breaks, and training programs.

But how compelling is the argument from independence? I will argue that not as much as is often believed—or not enough, in any event, to conclude that self-employment merits not only protection from governmental intrusion and regulatory hurdles, but also promotion, given the forgone opportunities to promote employee work that promoting self-employment often entails. I proceed as follows. After introducing the notions of self-employment and independence in section 5.1, I inspect the "brute power" version of the

---

[6] "Starting a Business," Doing Business: Measuring Business Regulations, https://www.doingbusin ess.org/en/data/exploretopics/starting-a-business, accessed August 30, 2021.

argument in section 5.2, and argue that it yields false positives. If dependence on the power of a superior is objectionable as such in the workplace, I argue, then it is likewise objectionable—implausibly so—in other realms, such as in the state. Now, although the brute power concern may not be valid, some workers may have a preference for independence as such all the same. But, as I argue, attempts to justify that this preference should be satisfied, whether on the basis of the value of occupational freedom or on the basis of fair play duties stemming from the positive externalities that self-employment may generate, yield reasons to protect, but not to promote, self-employment.

The "arbitrary power" variant of the argument, which I examine in sections 5.3 and 5.4, does prompt compelling reasons to promote, and not just to protect, self-employment. But it only does so, I argue, when managers' power is not suitably checked. When managerial power is deployed under terms that suitably track workers' interests, such reasons are less stringent. And they are more easily outweighed by competing reasons, like those stemming from the further forms of dependence that self-employment may prompt—on suppliers and purchasers, in the case of the self-employed, and on self-employed bosses, in the case of the employees of small businesses.

Republicans and relational egalitarians are right to believe, I conclude, that employment relations need not be inegalitarian or objectionable. Much depends on the specific terms under which such relations take place. None of this necessarily entails, however, that self-employment merits no promotion, all things considered. Independent considerations, which section 5.5 briefly discusses in closing, may perhaps generate more compelling reasons to promote, and not just to protect, self-employment.

5.1. Which Self-Employment? Whose Independence?

Before turning to the two versions of the argument from independence, it pays to clarify the notions of self-employment and independence, and how this argument links them. Let us start with self-employment, which philosophers and social scientists have often conceived of as a kind of anachronism—as a category fated to vanish due to market competition with large firms. "The factory [now] rules, and the days of handicraft, of independent production, are numbered," socialist theorist Karl Kautsky stated

76 WORKING AS EQUALS

at the end of the nineteenth century.[7] But the rumors of the death of self-employment have been greatly exaggerated. For the decline of the employment share of the self-employed has not simply halted in recent decades. In many wealthy economies, it has reversed.[8]

The nature of self-employment and the composition of the self-employed workforce have also shifted of late. Social theorists in the past typically equated the self-employed with the petty bourgeoisie, and contrasted them with both capitalists and wage workers. George Steinmetz and Erik Olin Wright, for example, argued that the petits bourgeois, unlike capitalists, earn their income at least partly through their work. And, unlike wage workers, they do so without selling their labor to an employer in exchange for a salary.[9] But self-employment today offers a more complex picture. Traditional petit bourgeois self-employment (e.g., artisans, restaurateurs) is now in decline. And self-employment is growing in professional-managerial occupations (e.g., communications, consulting) and in unskilled occupations (e.g., construction, manual services) in which it was rare in the past.[10] Moreover, defining the self-employed as those who earn an income through their work without selling their labor for a salary, as Steinmetz and Wright do, is insufficiently discriminating. It fails to clearly distinguish those who really work for themselves from those engaged in new forms of "dependent" or "bogus" self-employment, which firms nowadays increasingly resort to as a means to bypass employer liabilities, like collective agreements and social security taxes.[11]

No wonder, then, that self-employment is increasingly defined as independence from an employer, which courts and labor organizations often test using three conditions: autonomy over how to run one's business, authority to hire and dismiss staff, and having more than one client. On this view, one in three self-employed workers in the European Union, failing to satisfy one or more of these conditions, counts as a dependent self-employed worker.[12] There is an ongoing debate about whether these workers should be classified

---

[7] Karl Kautsky, *The Class Struggle* (Chicago: Charles H. Kerr & Co., 1910), 12.

[8] Muller et al., *Annual Report on European SMEs*, 46–82.

[9] George Steinmetz and Erik O. Wright, "The Fall and Rise of the Petty Bourgeoisie: Changing Patterns of Self-Employment in the Postwar United States," *American Journal of Sociology* 94, no. 5 (1989): 973–1018, at 979.

[10] Richard Arum and Walter Müller, eds., *The Reemergence of Self-Employment* (Princeton, NJ: Princeton University Press, 2004), ch. 1.

[11] Colin Williams and Frédéric Lapeyre, "Dependent Self-Employment: Trends, Challenges and Policy Responses in the EU," ILO Employment Working Paper, No. 228 (2017): 1–64.

[12] Williams and Lapeyre, "Dependent Self-Employment," 16.

SELF-EMPLOYMENT AND INDEPENDENCE   77

as independent contractors, as employees, or as a separate category.[13] In what follows, however, I set such workers aside and focus on those who, meeting the three conditions just mentioned, are truly independent.

But why, if at all, is independence from a boss valuable? The value of independence is central to, and has been submitted to careful inspection by, republican thought. On this view, whose chief value is political freedom, "Liberty consists in an independency upon the will of another," as Algernon Sidney's classic formula has it.[14] How free people are hinges, then, on how dependent they are on the *arbitrary* power of another person—that is, on a power that is not forced to track, or to be justified in terms of, their interests.[15] Yet, as we will see in section 5.2, an alternative view proposes that, what undermines freedom is dependence on the power of others *as such*, no matter how suitably such power may be forced to track the interests of those on the receiving end of the power relation.[16] But, on the republican view, which I will discuss in sections 5.3 and 5.4, what undermines freedom is dependence not on the power of others as such, but on their arbitrary or uncontrolled power.[17]

On this last view, employee work potentially undermines workers' freedom not only, and not chiefly, because employees depend on those who own, rather than toil on, the means of production in order to make ends meet. Independent contractors, like restaurateurs and attorneys, may also depend on their suppliers and purchasers for their subsistence, as I will discuss in section 5.3. But, although they may be subject to their suppliers' and customers' power, independent contractors are not directed by them as to how, when, and with whom to do their job. In entering an employment contract, workers submit to a particular—and particularly worrisome, from a republican standpoint—kind of power: the power that their employers, and the managers acting on the employers' behalf, wield to direct them during

[13] Within philosophy, see Halliday, "On the (Mis)classification of Paid Labor."

[14] Algernon Sidney, *Discourses Concerning Government* (Indianapolis, IN: Liberty Classics, 1990), 17.

[15] Philip Pettit, *Republicanism: A Theory of Freedom and Government* (Oxford: Oxford University Press, 1997), and *On the People's Terms: A Republican Theory and Model of Democracy* (Cambridge: Cambridge University Press, 2012).

[16] Christian List and Laura Valentini, "Freedom as Independence," *Ethics* 126, no. 4 (2016): 1043–1074, at 1058ff.

[17] In both views, what undermines freedom is dependence on the *power* of others, whether or not such power may be actualized. A slave who is subject to the power of a master and a woman who is subject, under coverture, to the power of a noninterfering husband are unfree all the same, whether the powerful party may happen to interfere with their choices or not. See Pettit, *Republicanism*, 63–64; List and Valentini, "Freedom as Independence," 1051–1058.

78 WORKING AS EQUALS

their working hours. They submit, in brief, to their authority—understood, as I here will understand it, in its empirical or de facto, rather than its moral, sense, as the ability to issue commands whose content is generally conformed to.

Employers' authority is particularly worrisome, from a republican standpoint, because it is not limited to ensuring that the employee complies with the terms of the employment contract, which both parties have agreed upon at the outset of the relationship. Employers also wield residual authority over those aspects of the relationship that remain unspecified in the contract. And, given that employment contracts are particularly open-ended—as seeking to contractually specify the terms of the relationship for every contingency would be prohibitively costly, inefficient, and difficult for courts to enforce (see section 5.3)—employees are liable to a kind of power whose purview is far beyond their control, and which is particularly easy to abuse.[18]

It is unsurprising, then, that classic republicans typically conceived of employee work as a form of servitude. Aristotle, for example, equated it with "a sort of limited slavery."[19] Cicero defined the salary of wage laborers as "a pledge of their slavery."[20] And Immanuel Kant distinguished those who "earn a living . . . only by selling that which is his" from those who allow "others to make use of him," and argued that only the former should be granted the franchise.[21] It is likewise unsurprising that some classic republicans saw self-employment as a superior alternative to wage work. Amid the rise of cities and commerce in the seventeenth century, which prompted the emergence of yeoman farmers, artisans, shopkeepers, and other self-employed "masterless men," commercial republicans like John Locke and Adam Smith regarded self-employment as a way to escape dependence on the authority of a superior, which wage work and other forms of subordinated labor implied.[22]

Contemporary republicans, by contrast, have given little thought to self-employment. Many of them are as concerned with employee work as classic

---

[18] Nien-hê Hsieh, "Rawlsian Justice and Workplace Republicanism," *Social Theory and Practice* 31, no. 1 (2005): 115–142; Anderson, "Equality and Freedom," 60–61; Iñigo González-Ricoy, "Little Republics: Authority and the Political Nature of the Firm," *Philosophy and Public Affairs* 50, no. 1 (2022): 90–120.

[19] Aristotle, *Politics*, trans. Horace Rackham (Cambridge, MA: Harvard University Press, 1932), 1260b.

[20] Marcus Tullius Cicero, *De Officiis*, trans. Walter Miller (Cambridge, MA: Harvard University Press, 1913), XLII.

[21] Immanuel Kant, *Kant's Political Writings*, ed. Hans Rice, trans. H. B. Nisbet (Cambridge: Cambridge University Press, 1970), 7.

[22] Anderson, "Equality and Freedom," 53–54.

SELF-EMPLOYMENT AND INDEPENDENCE   79

republicans were. But they have instead focused on alternative ways to keep arbitrary management at bay, such as strengthening employees' rights to quit abusive jobs, to go on strike, and to have a say over firm decisions.[23] And those who, like Anderson, see self-employment as a means to skirt dependence on an employer have often discarded its universalization as an option that is largely out of step with modern economies.

Perhaps contemporary republicans are right to neglect self-employment as an alternative to employee work, given the competing reasons we may have to disfavor it, including those of economic efficiency, as I will discuss in the closing section. But this leaves unanswered the more fundamental question of whether the value of independence from a boss, which policymakers and workers themselves often cherish, yields reasons, as defeasible as these may be, to promote or at least to protect self-employment. In what follows, I address this question by exploring the "brute power" and the "arbitrary power" variants of the argument from independence, starting with the former.

5.2. The Brute Power Concern

Why, if at all, is self-employment valuable? The self-employed make less money, work longer hours, bear greater mental hazards, and more often become jobless than those who draw a paycheck from an employer.[24] Yet, unlike wage workers, they are independent from a boss. According to the "arbitrary power" version of the argument from independence, which sections 5.3 and 5.4 will address, independence is valuable because it eradicates the risk of arbitrary management. According to the "brute power" variant, by contrast, what is valuable is independence from bosses' power *in itself*, no matter how suitably checked such power may be. On this view, independence is valuable because it implies not having to submit to an employer's power to command,

---

[23] See, respectively, Robert S. Taylor, *Exit Left: Markets and Mobility in Republican Thought* (Oxford: Oxford University Press, 2017), ch. 3; Alex Gourevitch, "Quitting Work but Not the Job: Liberty and the Right to Strike," *Perspectives on Politics* 14, no. 2 (2017): 307–323; Keith Breen, "Freedom, Republicanism, and Workplace Democracy," *Critical Review of International Social and Political Philosophy* 18, no. 4 (2015): 470–485.

[24] David G. Blanchflower, "Self-Employment: More May Not Be Better," NBER Working Paper, No. 10286 (2004); Ari Hyytinen and Olli-Pekka Ruuskanen, "Time Use of the Self-Employed," *Kyklos* 60, no. 1 (2007): 105–122; Reto Odermatt, Nattavudh Powdthavee, and Alois Stutzer, "Are Newly Self-Employed Overly Optimistic about Their Future Well-Being?," *Journal of Behavioral and Experimental Economics* 95 (2021): 101779; C. Mirjam Van Praag and Peter H. Versloot, "What Is the Value of Entrepreneurship? A Review of Recent Research," *Small Business Economics* 29, no. 4 (2007): 351–382.

80   WORKING AS EQUALS

supervise, and sanction. It implies, in brief, not having to submit to the power of someone who can tell you when and how to do your job, who can snoop on your work email, and who can demote you if you lose a customer.

Although I will argue that this view is uncompelling, it is far from implausible, as anyone who has endured an inquisitive boss, however considerate and checked by labor law and union oversight, can probably attest. Indeed, this view may explain why a marked preference for self-employment exists even in countries whose labor law reasonably safeguards employees from managerial abuse—such that 64.5 percent of the Swiss, 63.3 percent of Italians, and 64.2 percent of New Zealanders claim to prefer it to employee work, if given the choice—and why independence from a boss is the chief reason that the self-employed cite for this preference.[25] It is less obvious, however, what exactly grounds the complaint that dependence on a boss as such prompts. It cannot be that the authority of employers, even when suitably regulated, always makes room for potential abuse, given the open-endedness of employment contracts. For if this prompts a legitimate complaint, it is a complaint whose source is not subjection to the authority of an employer as such, but rather subjection to their abusive authority.

Maybe, however, what renders dependence on a boss morally objectionable as such—thus yielding reasons to favor self-employment over employee work—is that it undermines workers' agency, and not just in the sense that bosses routinely issue directives whose content preempts, on pain of demotion or dismissal, competing reasons for action that workers may have. The complaint persists, albeit perhaps in a tempered form, when no such conflict arises. For, in general, employees act as they do because their bosses say so, backed by the threat of penalty, even when they would have acted similarly had they received no direction to act in that particular way. It is the alien source of the directive, not its content, or not just its content anyway, that arguably prompts the complaint, which self-employment addresses by removing managerial authority altogether.

The trouble with this view is that it is not discriminating enough. It yields false positives, for if dependence on others' authority is objectionable as such, in terms of undermining the freedom of the dependent party, then such dependence is also *ex hypothesi* objectionable in the state, in college, or in the family. It would entail, for example, that living under a state, however

---

[25] Blanchflower, "Self-Employment," 33; Dawson et al., "Why Do Individuals Choose Self-Employment," 34.

SELF-EMPLOYMENT AND INDEPENDENCE   81

democratic, is morally objectionable—and that there is no difference, in terms of how free its subjects are, between an autocratic state and a faultlessly democratic one. Given that this implication is implausible—although perhaps not if you are a philosophical anarchist—working under a boss as such cannot be objectionable either. After all, we all live embedded in an intricate, but not necessarily objectionable, network of dependencies. We routinely depend on the will of our doctors and teachers, parents and descendants, tax collectors and police officers, among countless others, without this dependence being necessarily objectionable. "I may be dependent on others for access to some of the things necessary for a decent quality of life," Philip Pettit contends, "without necessarily being dominated by them."[26] So perhaps what prompts a valid complaint is dependence not on an authority simpliciter, but rather on an arbitrary authority, as I will discuss in the next section. And this drastically weakens, and perhaps entirely disposes of, the reasons for self-employment that independence from a boss as such may prompt.

There are, of course, discontinuities between the forms of dependence we see in the workplace and those we see in other realms. Take the state. One difference is that it would be morally impermissible for public officials to issue directives that are as exacting, and whose compliance is as exactingly monitored, as those that bosses permissibly issue. Another is that it would be impermissible for public officials to assign ends to citizens—given that legitimate states are typically meant to merely enable citizens to pursue their own ends—in the way that employers permissibly do, within limits, when they tell their employees which financial products to sell, how to treat farmed animals, or what to put into baby food.[27] But are these differences enough to render managerial authority intrinsically more objectionable than state authority, in a way that would yield reasons to favor independence in the workplace that are lacking in the state? I think not. For, even if such differences were relevant enough—which some question[28]—they may be offset by other differences that make state authority, at a minimum, no less intrinsically worrisome than managerial authority. One such additional difference is that state officials can permissibly inflict physical force in order to elicit compliance, while employers cannot. Another is that state authority can only be

[26] Pettit, *Republicanism*, 159.
[27] John Rawls, *Political Liberalism* (New York: Columbia University Press, 1996), 41–42; Niko Kolodny, "Is There an Objection to Workplace Hierarchy," 10, https://philpapers.org/archive/KOL ITA-3.pdf (accessed November 15, 2022).
[28] Jeffrey Moriarty, "On the Relevance of Political Philosophy to Business Ethics," *Business Ethics Quarterly* 15, no. 3 (2005): 453–471, at 458–459.

82 WORKING AS EQUALS

avoided at great cost, if at all, while employees can avoid the authority of their employers by quitting, which is much less costly.[29]

There is nothing objectionable, in brief, in being subject to the power of a boss as such. Yet some workers may prefer not to have a boss, no matter how suitably checked her power may be, all the same. A separate question, then, is whether there are independent reasons to socialize (some of) the costs that satisfying a preference for independence as such involves—a question that may be usefully addressed in two ways.

One such way is in terms of occupational freedom, which we may conceive of in roughly two senses. According to one view, which is grounded in the value of self-ownership, freedom of occupational choice is wholly negative. It exclusively demands that regulatory barriers to becoming and remaining self-employed—like bulky registration procedures or steep fees—be removed, as they trespass on workers' right to their occupational decisions not being interfered with. According to a second view, which is grounded in the value of autonomy, occupational freedom is both negative and positive. It demands not only that barriers to self-employment be removed, but also that occupational options be made available. Now, the second view probably entails that those with a marked preference for occupations that the labor market cannot meet—because jobs as a restaurateur, plumber, or attorney are scant—should be able to become self-employed at a bearable cost. In fact, the second most popular reason that the self-employed give for their decision is the nature of their occupation.[30] But, even accepting this view, it is much less clear whether occupational freedom likewise demands that those wishing to enter self-employment due to a strong preference for independence, rather than in order to fulfill an occupational preference that the market cannot meet, be supported (for example, through legal assistance, start-up funding, or tax breaks) when jobs in their fancied industries abound. Freedom of occupational choice targets occupations, not the conditions under which occupations are pursued.

A second approach is in terms of the positive externalities that those with a marked preference for independence could produce if they were able to become self-employed. If, as a result of this preference being satisfied, the self-employed produce positive externalities—such as creating jobs, fostering innovation, or increasing aggregate productivity—that others willingly

---

[29] For a more detailed discussion of these differences, and their relevance for how to conceive of managerial authority, see Kolodny, "Is There an Objection;" González-Ricoy, "Little Republics."

[30] Dawson et al., "Why Do Individuals Choose Self-Employment," 11.

accept, then we may have reason to make the beneficiaries bear some of the costs of becoming and remaining self-employed. This argument is plausible because it meets two conditions that are needed for positive externalities to generate fair play duties to share some of the costs of producing them— namely, that the producers of the relevant externalities incur costs and that they produce them intentionally. I think that, on a plausible understanding of these conditions, like the one Serena Olsaretti has offered, we can safely argue that the positive externalities that the self-employed may produce would qualify.[31] For, although the self-employed may find joy in being their own boss, they also incur significant costs in becoming self-employed. And although creating jobs or fostering innovation may not be their primary aim, they do not produce such benefits unintentionally.

This argument is subject, however, to at least two difficulties. The first is that it is unclear whether self-employment yields, on balance, positive externalities. After reviewing the empirical evidence, Van Praag and Versloot conclude that, compared to large firms, the self-employed create and destroy jobs at similarly high rates, leading to more volatile employment creation. They fail to spend more on R&D and produce fewer patents, fewer new products, and fewer technologies. And they contribute less to the value of productivity levels.[32]

Second, even if we assume that the self-employed, or some of them anyway, produce net positive externalities as a result of their marked preference for being their own boss, many of these externalities may be "open benefits," in Simmons's classic terms: benefits that can only be avoided at great cost.[33] We cannot readily infer, then, that their putative beneficiaries willingly accept such externalities from the fact that, for example, they apply to jobs that self-employed businesses offer. Some of these workers may legitimately complain that the only reason they have to apply for those jobs is their desire to escape unemployment and destitution, and that, when it comes to deciding how to allocate scarce public funds, they would prefer job openings in large firms to job openings in mom-and-pop shops, whose pay and working conditions are on average not as good (more on this in section 5.4).

---

[31] Serena Olsaretti, "Children as Public Goods?," *Philosophy and Public Affairs* 41, no. 3 (2013): 226–258, at 242–247.

[32] Van Praag and Versloot, "What Is the Value," 376–379.

[33] A. John Simmons, *Moral Principles and Political Obligations* (Princeton, NJ: Princeton University Press, 1979), 138–139.

84 WORKING AS EQUALS

5.3. The Arbitrary Power Concern

According to the "arbitrary power" variant of the argument, to which we now turn, independence from a boss is valuable not in itself, but rather because it eradicates the risk of arbitrary management. This variant of the argument is much more congenial to republicanism, which opposes dependence not on others' power as such but rather on others' *arbitrary* power. To assess this variant, I introduce a distinction between vertical and horizontal forms of dependence, which correspond, respectively, to dependence on a superior's authority and to dependence on other contractors, such as suppliers and purchasers.[34]

Start with *vertical dependence* on a superior's directive power, which employers wield over staff, and which may be arbitrary on various levels, including direct command and supervision, decisions about the conditions under which employees work, including the conditions that shape the corporate culture of their company, and decisions that, although not directly about employees' tasks or their conditions, nevertheless significantly affect them, such as relocations.[35] On these three levels, employers may be able to abuse their open-ended authority by issuing directives that fail to track, or to be justified in terms of, their employees' interests. For workers surely have an interest in not being liable to the reckless allocation of perilous tasks, in eluding the capricious rescheduling of hours, in being able to comfortably speak out against bullies and sexual harassers, and in having a say over board-level decisions that significantly affect them.

Niko Kolodny has argued, however, that republicanism is not discriminating enough as to which managerial directives are objectionable.[36] If what renders managers' power over staff objectionable is that it fails to be justified in terms of the latter's interests, Kolodny argues, then managerial power is rarely ever unobjectionable, for managers tend to serve the interests of the client or the firm, rather than those of workers. "If the question is what is in the interests of the worker," Kolodny claims, "the answer, presumably, would be not to have to work at all."[37]

---

[34] I adapt this distinction from Nicholas Vrousalis, "Workplace Democracy Implies Economic Democracy," *Journal of Social Philosophy* 50, no. 3 (2019): 259–279, at 264.

[35] Hsieh, "Rawlsian Justice," 92.

[36] Kolodny, "Is There an Objection," 18–19.

[37] Kolodny, "Is There an Objection," 18.

SELF-EMPLOYMENT AND INDEPENDENCE   85

But this objection stems from an overly narrow understanding of what is in the interest of the worker, and of when managerial decisions may serve or neglect this interest. Given that work is especially well placed to serve the interest that people have in making a social contribution, as well as in social-ization, self-realization, and social recognition and esteem, it is questionable whether not having to work at all is what is in workers' interests.[38] Indeed, an interest in working that goes beyond its pecuniary dimension is some-thing that workers routinely avow when, financially able to get along without having to work at all, they choose to work all the same, even when the jobs available are not particularly stimulating.[39]

Moreover, although this is a point that republicans rarely acknowledge, workers have an interest not just in working, but also in the productive ef-ficiency of the companies they work for and, accordingly, in their managers efficiently serving the interests of the firm or client. For workers have an un-derlying interest in not having their working conditions undercut if their company does poorly and in not losing their jobs if it goes bust. Workers' interests in having a job, as well as in the efficiency of the companies they work for, need not outweigh the other legitimate interests they no doubt have when trade-offs arise. In other words, not every managerial decision to im-prove efficiency will be justified in terms of workers' overall interests, once we factor in these other interests. Yet many such decisions will be justified in terms of the interests that workers, and not just the firm or its customers, have. To be sure, there is the question of which means may suitably track workers' overall interests in order to minimize arbitrary management, as I will discuss below. But, for now, it suffices to note that, contrary to what Kolodny suggests, not every managerial decision will be objectionable on the republican view. Only those that fail to track, or fail to be justified in terms of, employees' overall interests, including their interest in the productive effi-ciency of the company they work for, will be so.

Self-employment is valuable, then, because it yields independence from the risk of having a boss who may fail to track the staff's overall interests,

---

[38] Anca Gheaus and Lisa Herzog, "The Goods of Work (Other than Money!)," *Journal of Social Philosophy* 47, no. 1 (2016): 70–89.

[39] See, among others, Reshmaan Hussam et al., "The Psychosocial Value of Employment," NBER Working Paper, No. 28924 (2021); Syon P. Bhanot, Jiyoung Han, and Chaning Jang, "Workfare, Wellbeing and Consumption: Evidence from a Field Experiment with Kenya's Urban Poor," *Journal of Economic Behavior and Organization* 149 (2018): 372–388; Axel Marx and Hans Peeters, "An Unconditional Basic Income and Labor Supply: Results from a Pilot Study of Lottery Winners," *Journal of Socio-economics* 37, no. 4 (2008): 1636–1659.

86 WORKING AS EQUALS

including their interests in not being underpaid relative to their marginal productivity or sexually harassed, but also in their companies being smoothly run. A plausible objection, however, is that if becoming self-employed is valuable just as a means of avoiding arbitrary management, then alternative means may also do the trick. Recent debates on how to keep arbitrary management at bay, such that bosses are forced to track workers' interests, pursue precisely this. Whether it is through strengthened rights to change jobs or to strike or through more exacting workplace regulation or board-level employee representation, means other than self-employment could perhaps make bosses suitably accountable to workers' interests, rendering the reasons for self-employment that stem from the value of independence less stringent and easier to defeat.

Consider two rejoinders, however. One is that means such as an improved right to strike or to quit abusive jobs, however successful in keeping bosses in line, fail to eradicate managerial domination. Workers' ability to quit the work but not the job—as Alex Gourevitch has referred to the right to strike—or to quit the job altogether if at risk of being abused—as Robert Taylor advocates—may, depending on the circumstances, induce bosses to track workers' interests in deploying their powers.[40] But they may also yield a situation of mutual domination, rather that one of nondomination.[41] For even if management and staff were to wield roughly equal power over each other, there would be no assurance that they would not deploy it arbitrarily.

A regulatory approach to arbitrary management—whereby bosses' authority is checked by labor law, collective agreements, and professional and craft standards—may be more modally robust. This approach may do better at providing all parties with certainty about how the others may act under both actual and nonactual circumstances. But it is liable to a second rejoinder—namely, that arbitrary management cannot be entirely rooted out because employment contracts are particularly incomplete. Moreover, they are desirably so for efficiency reasons. To cut a long story short, given that, on the influential view of the firm that Coase and others have developed, it is often more efficient to replace market exchanges between independent contractors with an administrative hierarchy—such that a person or group wields open-ended authority to direct workers as productive contingencies unfold—attempting to legally or contractually specify the terms of the

---

[40] Gourevitch, "Quitting Work"; Taylor, *Exit Left*, ch. 3.

[41] Andreas T. Schmidt, "Domination without Inequality? Mutual Domination, Republicanism, and Gun Control," *Philosophy and Public Affairs* 46, no. 2 (2018): 175–206.

SELF-EMPLOYMENT AND INDEPENDENCE   87

relationship for every possible state of the world would drastically undercut such authority, undermining the superior efficiency of firms relative to the market.[42] And given that, as argued above, the productive efficiency of the firm is in workers' interest, such attempts may not just harm firms but also unsuitably track employees' interests.

Now, although considerations of productive efficiency may discourage some means to check employers' authority, like those requesting that labor contracts be specific about everything that employees may be asked to do, they do *not* justify such authority's being unfettered or unaccountable to its subjects.[43] The reason is not only that workers have interests other than the productive efficiency of the companies they work for—interests that would surely prevail if their managers were to improve the firm's bottom line by cutting down on toilet breaks or by firing pregnant women. It is also that many of the regulations that safeguard employees from arbitrary management, such as protections against sexual harassment or taste-based discrimination and board-level employee representation, are likely to actually boost productive efficiency.[44] In brief, suitable regulatory means are available to force employers to track workers' overall interests, and to significantly reduce the risk of arbitrary management. When such means are in place, the reasons for self-employment that stem from the value of independence become much less stringent and easier to defeat.

When we factor in *horizontal forms of dependence*—that is, dependence on suppliers or purchasers, whose wills the self-employed are compelled to observe on pain of going under—things get even more complicated for the argument from independence. We should be careful, however, to avoid inferring personal dependence from dependence on the aggregate, lest we fall into an ecological fallacy. Although self-employed workers cannot depend on their bosses—for they have none—they no doubt depend on their customers and suppliers. Yet, in a competitive market, they do not depend on any single customer or supplier, whose particular wills they can easily skirt. "A tradesman or artificer," Adam Smith argued, "derives his subsistence from the employment, not of one, but of a hundred or a thousand different

---

[42] Ronald H. Coase, "The Nature of the Firm," *Economica* 4, no. 16 (1937): 386–405; Oliver Williamson, *Markets and Hierarchies* (New York: Free Press, 1975).

[43] For more detailed discussion, see Iñigo González-Ricoy, "Firm Authority and Workplace Democracy: A Reply to Jacob and Neuhäuser," *Ethical Theory and Moral Practice* 22 (2019): 679–684, at 682–683, and "Little Republics," 115–120.

[44] See, for example, Simon Jäger, Benjamin Schoefer, and Jörg Heining, "Labor in the Boardroom," *Quarterly Journal of Economics* 136, no. 2 (2021): 669–725.

88   WORKING AS EQUALS

customers. Though in some measure obliged to them all, therefore, he is not absolutely dependent upon any of them."[45] Pettit expresses a similar view: "I may not be dependent on any given individual or group—my dependence may be *anonymous*, as it were—and so may not be exposed to domination by any agent in particular."[46]

Horizontal forms of dependence, however, are not always innocuous. Take the easy case first: market concentration obtains. When the self-employed depend on a single supplier or purchaser, or on a handful of them, as when a single creditor has market power to set extortionate interest rates, dependence may no longer be anonymous, to use Pettit's term. Worse, contingent on how concentrated the market turns out to be, such dependence may no longer be solely horizontal either. It may become vertical, as when companies use their market power to direct self-employed suppliers as to when and how they should do their work.

Yet wholly horizontal and anonymous dependence in competitive markets may also be objectionable. Horizontal dependence on suppliers and purchasers is no doubt distinct from vertical dependence on an employer, who wields powers to command and supervise when and how one works. And anonymous dependence on manifold market actors is likewise distinct from interpersonal dependence on a single supplier or purchaser, who may end up wielding vertical power as well. Yet, depending on the circumstances, entirely horizontal and anonymous forms of dependence may also yield abuse, albeit not because market competition as such influences how the self-employed organize their work in order to remain competitive. Abuse may occur when market competition turns arbitrary power in the realm of employee work into arbitrary power over self-employed workers.

To unpack this idea, consider how market competition may affect the ways that the self-employed organize their schedule and pace of work. Ari Hyytinen and Olli-Pekka Ruuskanen, who have traced the timing of the tasks that Finnish self-employed workers perform in a typical working day, find that the self-employed follow routines almost identical to those that wage laborers follow.[47] In principle, self-employment confers independence in deciding when and how to work. In practice, however, market imperatives compel the self-employed to start their workday, allocate hours, and take breaks very much as those who work under the thumb of an employer do.

---

[45] Smith, *Wealth of Nations*, III.4.17.
[46] Pettit, *Republicanism*, 159; my italics.
[47] Hyytinen and Ruuskanen, "Time Use of the Self-Employed," 110–115.

SELF-EMPLOYMENT AND INDEPENDENCE 89

Now, the fact that market competition compels the self-employed to organize their work much as employees organize theirs does not, as such, prompt a valid complaint. This is the natural interdependence, as it were, that market competition yields—competition that, under suitable conditions, importantly improves overall economic outcomes, which stand to benefit everyone.[48] But suppose that employers deploy their staff in terms that grossly fail to track their interests. Suppose, for example, that employers, determined to improve their companies' bottom line, routinely allocate unpaid overtime, reschedule working hours on short notice, and assign tasks that seriously threaten their employees' health. When this occurs, market competition may compel the self-employed to follow suit, on pain of going broke, turning bosses' vertical arbitrary power over wage workers into horizontal arbitrary power over self-employed workers.

To sum up: the reasons for protecting and promoting self-employment, although stringent when workplace safeguards are absent or lax, are much weaker and easier to defeat when such safeguards are in place. Moreover, the self-employed rarely are wholly independent, for they are liable to horizontal forms of dependence. These are particularly worrisome when market concentration obtains, but are not necessarily innocuous when markets are competitive, as competition may turn arbitrary power within hierarchical firms into arbitrary power over self-employed workers.

5.4. What about Wage Workers?

Having inspected how self-employment bears on self-employed workers' vertical and horizontal independence, we now briefly turn to how it bears on wage laborers. I will first inspect wage workers in general, and next zoom in on a particular subset of them: those who are employed by self-employed owners of small businesses.

An important argument for making self-employment accessible at a bearable cost is that, when opportunities to become self-employed are abundant, employees can credibly threaten their bosses with resorting to them, if often only implicitly, to keep potential abuses at bay. This is particularly relevant

---

[48] Christopher McMahon, "Morality and the Invisible Hand," *Philosophy and Public Affairs* 10, no. 3 (1981): 247–277; Joseph Heath, *Morality, Competition, and the Firm: The Market Failures Approach to Business Ethics* (Oxford: Oxford University Press, 2014).

90 WORKING AS EQUALS

in developing economies, in which workplaces are often loosely regulated and employees' legal rights are poorly monitored and enforced. For example, studying industrial jobs in Ethiopia, Christopher Blattman and Stefan Dercon find that self-employment, despite being financially more volatile, offers conditions that workers often prefer, given how serious the safety risks of factory work are.[49] They find that two-thirds of sweatshop employees quit within the first months of starting their jobs, resorting to farming, street trade, and other forms of self-employment instead. And the case seems to generalize. Richard Arum and Walter Müller find that self-employment is more prevalent in countries with loose labor market regulation, and suggest that this link stems from the incentive that workers have to become self-employed when employee protection is inadequate.[50]

The point here is not merely that self-employment, as argued above, offers wage laborers an alternative when employee work involves dependence on arbitrary management. The point is rather that, when such an option is available under conditions that make it modally robust, bosses have a powerful incentive to track employees' interests. When most people can only become self-employed at an unbearable cost, workers can exit a particular job but cannot exit employee work altogether. By contrast, when employee work is not the only game in town, and workers can resort to self-employment with ease if at risk of being abused, bosses have an incentive to restrain themselves, on pain of losing firm-specific human capital and incurring recruitment and training costs if turnover increases. And although this reason for self-employment is weak when employee work is suitably checked, it is stringent when such checks are absent or lax.

The argument, however, cuts both ways. Opportunities for self-employment also make it easier for employers to resort to market contracting when workplace regulation is not to their taste, narrowing the range of viable workplace regulations as a result. When governments make it easier to become and remain self-employed—for example, by providing start-up funding, training, and tax breaks—they create an incentive not only for wage workers to switch to self-employment, but also for employers to outsource the supply of labor inputs to self-employed workers, instead of hiring them as employees. By adopting policies to foster self-employment, governments

---

[49] Christopher Blattman and Stefan Dercon, "The Impacts of Industrial and Entrepreneurial Work on Income and Health: Experimental Evidence from Ethiopia," *American Economic Journal: Applied Economics* 10, no. 3 (2018): 1–38.

[50] Arum and Müller, *Reemergence of Self-Employment*, 18–21.

SELF-EMPLOYMENT AND INDEPENDENCE 91

indirectly socialize part of the costs that employers would otherwise have to bear, such as social security contributions, on-the-job training, and paid holidays, as well as the risks that hiring employees with a fixed salary involves. Moreover, in so doing, they also make it harder for subsequent governments to enact further workplace safeguards.

Consider next a particular subset of employees: those whom the self-employed may hire. Although governments often portray the self-employed as Schumpeter-like entrepreneurs seeking to scale their companies up, most self-employed businesses—three in four among those with less than 20 employees—express no desire to grow big and never do so.[51] And the vast majority of the self-employed in poor countries, most of whom operate informally, do not hire others and never grow big.[52]

The fact that self-employed businesses that employ others rarely grow big is relevant for at least two reasons. One is that small firms are often exempted from the legal regulations, including employment protections, that medium and large companies have to conform to. Another is that small firms are more prone to using direct and personal supervision of their staff, instead of the bureaucratic and indirect rules that large firms usually employ. Employees of small firms are, then, not only more often dependent on bosses whose authority is less regulated, relative to employees in larger firms. They are also directed and supervised by more arbitrary means, even if some managers never happen to abuse them. Personal supervision in small firms, Randy Hodson has found, is closely linked to direct physical and verbal abuse, inappropriate firings, absence of job security, frequent layoffs, reductions in hours, and an absence of on-the-job training.[53] Self-employment, in brief, may yield some independence for the self-employed. But it seems to do so at the cost of yielding less independence for any employees they may hire.

5.5. Conclusion

Governments of various persuasions, and workers themselves, often argue that self-employment merits protection and promotion as a means

---

[51] Erik Hurst and Benjamin W. Pugsley, "What Do Small Businesses Do?," NBER Working Paper, No. 17041 (2011), 11–19.

[52] Abhijit Banerjee and Esther Duflo, *Poor Economics: A Radical Rethinking of the Way to Fight Global Poverty* (New York: Public Affairs, 2011), ch. 9.

[53] Randy Hodson, *Dignity at Work* (Cambridge: Cambridge University Press, 2004), 93–97.

92 WORKING AS EQUALS

to elude dependence on a boss. I have inspected two variants of this argument and found both wanting. There is nothing objectionable as such, I have first argued, in being subject to the power of a boss. And although becoming self-employed no doubt solves the risk of being abused by eradicating its cause, I have next argued, given that self-employment yields its own forms of dependence, it deserves promotion (and not just protection) only when managerial authority is unsuitably checked, as is often the case in poor economies. Republicans and relational egalitarians are right to believe, in brief, that employment relations need not be inegalitarian or objectionable. Much depends on the terms under which such relations take place.

Some may object, however, that independent considerations may recommend, on balance, that self-employment be promoted, and not just protected, when suitable workplace safeguards exist. I lack the space to discuss such considerations, including those of equality of opportunity, distributive justice, job creation, and efficiency—some of which I have inspected elsewhere.[54] But it seems doubtful. For, although philosophical reflection on self-employment is still in its infancy, employee work seems to outperform self-employment on various scores.[55] For example, the self-employed make less money, work longer hours, and bear greater mental hazards, on average, than wage workers. And self-employed businesses make a lower contribution to aggregate productivity, innovate less, and create more volatile jobs than larger companies do.

Acknowledgments

For valuable comments, I thank Daniel Halliday, Lisa Herzog, Julian Jonker, Jahel Queralt, Grant Rozeboom, and audiences at the Working as Equals workshop, the 2021 Society for Applied Philosophy conference, and the Queen's University Belfast political theory workshop. For discussion of

---

[54] Iñigo González-Ricoy and Jahel Queralt, "No Masters above: Testing Five Arguments for Self-Employment," in *The Politics and Ethics of Contemporary Work: Whither Work?*, ed. Keith Breen and Jean-Philippe Deranty (London: Routledge, 2021), 87–101.
[55] See Blanchflower, "Self-Employment"; Hyytinen and Ruuskanen, "Time Use of the Self-Employed"; Odermatt, Powdthavee, and Stutzer, "Newly Self-Employed"; Van Praag and Versloot, "What Is the Value."

some of this chapter's ideas, I also thank Adrián Herranz, Luke Newberry, and Chris Zhang. Research for this chapter was supported by an ICREA Academia award and project PGC2018-095917-A-I00, "Justice at Work: A Normative Analysis of Nonstandard Forms of Employment," funded by the Spanish Ministry of Science.

6

Hobby Lobby and the Moral Structure of the Employee-Employer Relationship

David Silver

6.1. Introduction

This chapter examines the "Hobby Lobby case" (*Burwell v. Hobby Lobby Stores, Inc.*, 573 US 682 [2014]) in order to explore the employee-employer relationship, and how it can be structured to be a relationship between equals. The case revolves around the Affordable Care Act of 2010 and its requirement that companies provide their employees with health insurance. When regulators determined that these insurance plans needed to cover a wide range of contraceptives, this raised a moral problem for Hobby Lobby Stores, Inc. Although the craft supply chain was large enough to fall within the law's mandate, it was closely held by a group of shareholders whose goal was to run the business in accordance with their socially conservative version of Christianity. This religious framework holds that human personhood begins at conception, and that forms of contraception that prevent the implantation of a fertilized human egg are as morally reprehensible as abortion.[1]

In order to avoid being morally implicated in the provision of such forms of contraception, the Hobby Lobby company sought an exemption from the contraceptive care mandate.[2] In *Burwell v. Hobby Lobby Stores, Inc.*, the US

---

[1] The company's objection was to forms of contraception that it believed prevented the implantation of a fertilized egg. The two main forms are contraception that they object to are the intrauterine device (IUD), and the Plan B and Ella emergency contraception pills ("the morning after" pill). While the evidence suggests that the Plan B and Ella emergency contraceptives do not prevent the implantation of a fertilized egg, it is not definitive (see Pam Bellick, "Science at Issue in Debate on Morning-After Pill," *New York Times*, June 5, 2012). Hobby Lobby could object to these morning after pills being part of the coverage plan on the *risk* that they do block implantation. The evidence indicates that when the copper IUD is used as emergency contraception, it *can* block implantation; however, when used as ongoing birth control, the evidence is again not definitive.

[2] Throughout the chapter, I speak of Hobby Lobby's beliefs and actions; however, I do not mean to take a controversial position here on the nature of corporate beliefs and agency. When I say that

---

David Silver, Hobby Lobby *and the Moral Structure of the Employee-Employer Relationship* In: *Working as Equals.*
Edited by: Julian David Jonker and Grant J. Rozeboom, Oxford University Press. © Oxford University Press 2023.
DOI: 10.1093/oso/9780197634295.003.0006

THE EMPLOYEE-EMPLOYER RELATIONSHIP   95

Supreme Court granted that exemption to Hobby Lobby and to other closely held firms whose principals had comparable religious objections to the law.

At one level this case concerns the kind of religious rights, if any, that *corporations* can have. In this chapter's *persons-based* analysis, whether a corporation has a particular moral right depends entirely on how the recognition or denial of that right affects the interests of human persons.[3] According to this understanding, the Hobby Lobby case concerns the moral structure of the employee-employer relationship and whether the religious views of Hobby Lobby's *shareholders*, in their guise as employers, merit accommodation within the liberal democratic order.[4]

I come to an understanding of this order by directly considering what individuals owe each other based on their equal status as self-governing agents, and focusing on the interest that each one of us has as a person *in charge of her own life*.[5] This interest in *self-sovereignty* cuts in two opposing directions. On the one hand, it makes moral sense of the shareholders' claim that they should not be forced to pay for a healthcare plan which might be used in ways that they find morally intolerable. On the other hand, it also makes moral sense of employees' claim that their contraceptive choices are not a matter of legitimate concern to the company or its shareholders.

In this chapter, I argue that the employees have the correct understanding of the matter, and that the Hobby Lobby company should not have been granted an accommodation from the contraceptive care mandate. According to this argument, the Affordable Care Act represents an equitable, democratic determination that employers must provide their employees with contraceptive care coverage, even if doing so forces them to contribute to actions that they find morally reprehensible. In passing the law, legislators thereby determined that employers like Hobby Lobby did not have a complicity-based

"Hobby Lobby is morally opposed to abortion," I mean something that can be explicated in terms of its stakeholders' beliefs, interests, and actions.

[3] Compare with Amy Sepinwall, "Denying Corporate Rights and Punishing Corporate Wrongs," *Business Ethics Quarterly* 25, no. 4 (2015): 517–534.

[4] For a discussion of the role of the philosopher in helping society develop a "common currency" for settling disagreements within that society, see Jean Hampton, "Should Political Philosophy Be Done without Metaphysics?," *Ethics* 99, no. 4 (1989): 791–814, at 809. One way that philosophers can contribute to the refinement of this common currency is by identifying the normative conception of the person which underlies the liberal, democratic constitutional order, and drawing out what this conception of the person dictates in particular cases.

[5] I am largely relying here on the version of contractualist moral theory presented in Thomas M. Scanlon, *What We Owe to Each Other* (Cambridge, MA: Harvard University Press, 1998). For the purposes of this chapter, though, I am describing the theoretical approach I am using in the more general Kantian terms of rational self-governance.

96   WORKING AS EQUALS

claim to an accommodation from the law. For employers to fail to see this point is a failure on their part to recognize and respect the status of their employees as equal self-sovereigns.

I proceed as follows: After reviewing the history behind the Hobby Lobby case, I examine Sepinwall's argument, which maintains that the company does indeed have a religious right to be exempted from the contraceptive care mandate. I show that this argument fails to provide a principled reason in favor of granting that religious accommodation and that, at best, it can show that the question of whether to grant the accommodation is a purely political matter to be decided through the democratic political process.

I argue, however, that this matter was democratically, and thus equitably, settled when Congress passed the Affordable Care Act. Because Congress chose to help secure every person in society affordable access to contraception through a mandate on employers, it made employers' claims of complicity in the contraceptive choices of their employees not worthy of a legal accommodation.

6.2. The History of the Hobby Lobby Case

The Supreme Court ruling in the Hobby Lobby case turns on an interpretation of the Religious Freedom Restoration Act (RFRA) of 1993. Congress passed the law with a huge, bipartisan majority in response to changes in how the Supreme Court tested whether the government was violating an individual's free exercise of religion. In earlier decades the Court had applied the Sherbert Test, which held that when a person has a sincere religious belief, and her ability to act on it is substantially burdened by a government policy, then the policy is legitimate only if

1) It furthers a "compelling state interest," and
2) The government has pursued that interest in the manner least burdensome to religion.

The Court jettisoned the Sherbert Test in the 1990 case *Employment Division vs. Smith*, in which it ruled against the claims of two men who had been denied unemployment insurance compensation after being fired for illegally using peyote within Native American religious rituals. The men

THE EMPLOYEE-EMPLOYER RELATIONSHIP   97

sought a restoration of their unemployment compensation benefits on the grounds that the law interfered with the free exercise of their religion.

Congress responded to the Court's ruling by passing the RFRA, which effectively reinstated the Sherbert Test as the legal standard for when religious beliefs and practices must be accommodated. In *Hobby Lobby*, the Court ruled that the contraceptive care mandate of the Affordable Care Act failed that test. This was because the law provided exemptions for certain religious nonprofit organizations by shifting the obligation to provide contraceptive coverage *to their insurers*. The existence of this workaround demonstrated that there was a less burdensome way to implement the desired policy objective, and the Court held that it should thus also be available to closely held for-profit companies.

This is not obviously the result that Congress intended when it passed the RFRA. The case which precipitated Congress's action concerned the religious freedom of *employees*, and the legislators did not necessarily foresee or intend that the test would apply to for-profit corporations in their role as employers. Nevertheless, the Court interpreted the act so as to recognize the right of closely held business corporations to be exempted from the contraceptive care mandate.

According to this interpretation, a corporation has a legal right to a religious accommodation from a law if it can be granted without undermining the state's legitimate policy objectives. Although the *Hobby Lobby* ruling does not dispute the legitimacy of the state's interests in passing the Affordable Care Act, it is worth rehearsing what these interests are from the perspective of the self-governance of individuals.

As the name of the Affordable Care Act suggests, the main policy goal of the law was to provide individuals across society with secure and affordable access to a decent standard of healthcare. Having this kind of access serves individuals' self-governance-based interests in health, financial security, and social recognition as meriting this decent standard of care. Either as part of this goal, or alongside it, the law specifically seeks to advance the ability of citizens to make their own choices about sex and reproduction without economic fear or pressure.

Practically speaking, individuals require affordable insurance coverage for contraceptives in order to ensure their reproductive autonomy. Many women who lack contraceptive coverage "will use no contraception or will use an imperfect form . . . inconsistently or improperly."[6] The IUD, for

---

[6] Brief amicus curiae of American College of Obstetricians and Gynecologists, Physicians for Reproductive Health, American Academy of Pediatrics, American Nurses Association, et al., *Burwell v. Hobby Lobby Stores, Inc.* (2014) 573 U.S. 682 (US Supreme Court), 16–17.

98   WORKING AS EQUALS

example, is particularly effective because it does not have daily compliance requirements; but it has large upfront costs that are difficult for many women to shoulder.

As a result of using no or less effective forms of contraception, women are more likely to have unintended pregnancies;[7] and, unintended pregnancy is a cause of poverty and diminished life prospects among women, which in turn impoverishes their children and perhaps their long-term health.[8] Both women and their children have self-governance interests in not having their life prospects so radically diminished, and it is this sort of interest that grounds a positive self-governance-based claim for affordable contraceptive coverage.

The *Hobby Lobby* decision, at least in theory, presents a policy outcome in which the company's employees retain access to the full standard package of benefits, including all those relating to contraception. At the same time, the policy lets the company extricate itself from *directly* funding activities that violate its shareholders' basic moral precepts.

6.3. Sepinwall's Argument in Favor of the *Hobby Lobby* Ruling

In her analysis of the Hobby Lobby case, Sepinwall argues that the company should have been granted an accommodation from the contraceptive care mandate because it attacks the personal integrity of the company's shareholders, and because their desired accommodation was neither based on hateful or discriminatory attitudes nor was overly burdensome for the company's employees. Let us consider these three elements in turn.[9]

First, Sepinwall's analysis focuses on the interests of the company's shareholders in not being complicit in behavior that they find morally intolerable. She notes that in their eyes, "mere facilitation of an act that has even a small potential to involve a wrong causes Hobby Lobby to be morally responsible for that wrong."[10] She argues that their resulting self-understanding

---

[7] American College of Obstetricians and Gynecologists et al, brief amicus curiae, 17.

[8] American College of Obstetricians and Gynecologists et al, brief amicus curiae, 12.

[9] For a functionally similar analysis of the case, see M. Paula Fitzgerald, Jeff Langenderfer, and Megan L. Fitzgerald, "Is It Ethical for For-Profit Firms to Practice a Religion? A Rawlsian Thought Experiment," *Journal of Business Ethics* 166 (2020): 159–174.

[10] Amy Sepinwall, "Conscience and Complicity: Assessing Pleas for Religious Exemptions in Hobby Lobby's Wake," *University of Chicago Law Review* 82, no. 4 (2015): 1897–1980, at 1935.

THE EMPLOYEE-EMPLOYER RELATIONSHIP   99

of their moral complicity in the contraceptive choices of the company's employees merits consideration within the liberal democratic order because it implicates their personal integrity.[11] As she argues, "Being made to contribute to conduct that one opposes is painful because it entails a dislocation from the self."[12]

In addition to these *integrity interests* of people who are forced to be complicit in an action that they oppose, Sepinwall identifies two other considerations that are relevant to determining whether someone merits a religious accommodation from a law. One consideration concerns how much of a burden it is fair to ask people to bear in order that others be able to live in accordance with their religious convictions. In general, she holds that the answer to this question has "no a priori, context-independent answer," and thus is a matter to be decided in the arena of democratic politics.[13] She argues, however, that *Hobby Lobby* presents a special case in which the company objectively merits accommodation. This is because, due to the workaround in which the company's insurer would provide its employees with contraceptive coverage, their desired accommodation would not impose "any significant costs on third parties."[14]

The final consideration in Sepinwall's analysis holds that a person's claim to a legal accommodation is undermined when it is based on discriminatory or hate-based views.[15] For example, a business would not have a legitimate claim to a legal accommodation from a law requiring it to serve all customers if it were based on its owners' thought they would be morally diminished by serving people from other racial or ethnic groups.

Each person has an interest not only in *being able to function* as a self-governor in charge of her own life, but also in *being socially recognized* as that kind of agent. The liberal conception of the person is an egalitarian one that denies that there is an inherent normative, social, or political ordering of persons. In light of this fact, all persons have a *recognition interest* in not being subject to any view which holds them to be inherently less worthy or less deserving than others, regardless of whether the holding of such attitudes negatively affects their capacities as self-governors. This is especially so in the

[11] Sepinwall, "Conscience and Complicity," 1909.
[12] Sepinwall, "Conscience and Complicity," 1958.
[13] Sepinwall, "Conscience and Complicity," 1975.
[14] Amy Sepinwall, "Corporate Piety and Impropriety: Hobby Lobby's Extension of RFRA Rights to the For-Profit Corporation," *Harvard Business Law Review* 5, no. 2 (2015): 173–204, at 201.
[15] Sepinwall, "Conscience and Complicity," 1973.

100 WORKING AS EQUALS

context of relationships, such as the employee-employer one, which involve either an imbalance of power or which have a history in which one party does not fully respect the moral status of the other.

While Sepinwall recognizes that an employer's objection to the contraceptive care mandate could be based on discriminatory views, she maintains that there are at least some people who object to the mandate "with entirely benign motives." With that in mind she presumes some of these objectors "really do care only for the state of their own souls," and examines whether they merit an accommodation from the contraceptive care mandate.[16]

One way that Sepinwall's analysis falls short is that it fails to recognize that our motives are not always fully transparent to us, and that lurking behind seemingly benign motives can be sources of subconscious bias. Employees might believe, for example, that the company's objection to paying for contraception was rooted in unacceptably patriarchal attitudes toward women's place in society.[17] The claim that Hobby Lobby's shareholders were "cognitively motivated" by such patriarchal attitudes would not involve accusing them of dishonesty or bad faith, but rather would maintain that they have been *nonrationally* motivated to adopt the belief that human personhood begins at conception *because* it supports views that make it more difficult for women to control their sexual and reproductive lives.[18]

This understanding of how people form their moral beliefs is consistent with a feminist rejection of theories that are based on a highly idealized understanding of the rationally autonomous person.[19] The particular suggestion is that a person can adopt moral beliefs *because* he holds unacceptably hierarchical views of human relationships, and that this in turn can be due

---

[16] Sepinwall, "Conscience and Complicity," 1926.

[17] There is direct evidence that the company and its shareholders hold such attitudes. According to David Corn and Molly Redden, "Hobby Lobby Funded Disgraced Fundamentalist Christian Leader Accused of Harassing Dozens of Women," *Mother Jones*, July 2, 2014, Hobby Lobby and its shareholders have jointly given millions of dollars to the Institute in Basic Life Principles. This ministry has published views which hold that there are "Biblical Authority Structures" in which God has "established a specific chain of command" in which a "wife is to submit to the leadership of her husband." Despite the ministry's insistence that this patriarchal "structure does not express superiority or inferiority," it patently fails to recognize the equal normative status of women and men. Institute in Basic Life Principles, "What Are God-Ordained Authority Structures?," April 4, 2013, http://iblp.org/questions/what-are-god-ordained-authority-structures.

[18] For a discussion on the idea that moral beliefs are not rationally motivated, see Jonathan Haidt, "The Emotional Dog and Its Rational Tail: A Social Intuitionist Approach to Moral Judgment," *Psychological Review* 108 (2001): 814–834.

[19] See Catriona Mackenzie and Natalie Stoljar, "Introduction: Autonomy Refigured," in *Relational Autonomy: Feminist Perspectives on Autonomy, Agency, and the Social Self*, ed. Catriona Mackenzie and Natalie Stoljar (Oxford: Oxford University Press, 2000), 3–31, at 6.

THE EMPLOYEE-EMPLOYER RELATIONSHIP   101

to the fact that he is part of a religious community that embraces these unacceptably hierarchical views.

Employees could also appeal to such an account of moral belief formation in order to maintain that Hobby Lobby's call for religious accommodation is based on an unacceptably hierarchical understanding of the employee-employer relationship. According to this understanding, an employee is expected to conform to the values of the employer with respect to any aspect of the employment relationship.[20] They may note that the company's concern for complicity arises within the context of an *employee benefit*, and that it is just as financially implicated in its proposed remedy, which moves the provision of the contraceptive coverage outside the employment relationship. (This is because the company will presumably end up paying higher insurance premiums to cover the insurer's increased costs in the workaround in which it assumes the obligation to provide contraceptive services to the company's employees.) Employees might thus feel stigmatized by seeing the state's recognition of the company's religious right to exempt itself from the contraceptive care mandate as a validation of the above unacceptably hierarchical view of the employee-employer relationship.

In raising the possibility that the objections of Hobby Lobby's shareholders toward the contraceptive care mandate are rooted in unacceptably hierarchical attitudes, I pose a challenge to Sepinwall's analysis. One way that she might respond is to agree that *if there is a compelling case* that Hobby Lobby's objections are cognitively motivated in this manner, then it would undermine the company's claim to a religious accommodation from the law. Alternatively, she might argue that this is a case where it is up to the democratic process to determine whether it is acceptable to place these potential burdens on the company's employees in order to serve the religious interests of the shareholders.

This latter response can be seen as fitting within a more general framework put forward by Seana Shiffrin. Her framework understands a number of moral issues in terms of how to balance the competing interests of persons in (a) not contributing to projects they find morally intolerable, and

---

[20] The Institute in Basic Life Principles document also puts forward a hierarchical understanding of the employee-employer relationship: "Employers are challenged to act with equity and care as they oversee employees, patterning their behavior after God Himself, Who is their authority. Employees are responsible to serve well, doing their work wholeheartedly as unto the Lord" ("What Are God-Ordained Authority Structures"). For a history of this hierarchical view of the employment relation, see Elizabeth Anderson, *Private Government: How Employers Rule Our Lives (and Why We Don't Talk about It)* (Princeton, NJ: Princeton University Press: 2017), 1ff.

102   WORKING AS EQUALS

(b) receiving some level of subsidization from others so that they may exercise a meaningful level of personal autonomy.[21] One can understand Sepinwall's approach to the Hobby Lobby case as concerning how much we can ask *of employees* in order to promote the religious interests of the company's shareholders, even if they reject the underlying religious beliefs. One could argue further that there is no a priori answer to how to settle this question, and thus it should be decided equitably via a democratic process.

6.4. Democracy, Equality, and the Demarcation of Self-Sovereignty

While I also accept Shiffrin's framework for understanding the Hobby Lobby case, my analysis reverses the roles of the employers and employees. I begin with the interest of all persons in society in being able to make their own decisions about contraception without financial pressure, and ask what burdens it is fair to impose on others in order to further this self-governance-based interest. My claim is not only that this is a matter to be decided democratically, but that this balance *was already democratically determined* when Congress passed the Affordable Care Act.[22] It decided that employers must positively contribute to the autonomy of their employees by providing comprehensive health coverage, and in so doing determined that *in this particular situation* the autonomy interests of the employees outclassed the interests of the employers in not being complicit in their contraceptive choices. In passing the law, then, Congress effectively demarcated the zones of self-sovereignty of both employers and employees; and, as we shall see in the next section, this has implications for how these two groups relate to each other as equals.

First, though, let me elaborate on the egalitarian nature of the democratic decision here. One important way that persons are equal is that each one of us is a self-governor in charge of her own life. As such, each one of us has interests both in receiving support from others in order to be able to exercise our self-governance, and in being free from contributing to things we find

---

[21] Seana Valentine Shiffrin, "Paternalism, Unconscionability Doctrine, and Accommodation," *Philosophy & Public Affairs* 29, no. 3 (2000): 205–250, at 245–246.

[22] I set aside concerns here that given the many nonrepresentative features of the US Congress, the Affordable Care Act was not the result of a genuine democratic process. In my view of things, this law was a case in which the democratic process worked, despite these unrepresentative features.

THE EMPLOYEE-EMPLOYER RELATIONSHIP   103

morally reprehensible. There will inevitably be disagreements about how to strike a balance between these two considerations, and the democratic process is the most egalitarian way to settle the disagreement. The question we will pursue in the next section concerns the kind of claims that people might have to a religiously based accommodation from a law passed through a democratic, egalitarian process.

6.5. Self-Sovereignty as a Relationship between Equals

In this section I appeal to the concept of self-sovereignty in order to explore the extent to which one might legitimately claim an accommodation from a democratic law on the grounds that it makes one complicit in actions that one finds morally intolerable. One way of articulating this concept is to look at the development of the idea of religious tolerance between political sovereigns. The acceptance of religious tolerance as a shared value in Western Europe arose after generations of warring between Catholic and Protestant princes. In the 1555 Peace of Augsburg, these princes agreed to let each one of them choose the religion for the territory that he ruled over. One way of understanding this doctrine of *Cuius regio, eius religio* was that both sides would have preferred to forcibly convert the other, but neither had the power to do so. On this understanding, the peace treaty came about only because peace was preferable to unending war.

Another way of understanding this arrangement was that it was—or developed into—more than a mere modus vivendi. Instead, it was a recognition of the equal status and authority *among the princely class*. Each prince was a sovereign power—which meant that he was entitled to choose a religion both for himself and for his territory without that choice undermining the possibility of a relationship on good terms with princes of the other confession.

This latter understanding of the Augsburg doctrine is essentially about the normative relationship between equal political sovereigns. It declares that they are entitled to a realm of conscience that they can exercise for their domains without their choices affecting the possibility of their having good relations with other sovereign powers.[23]

---

[23] Notably, this sovereign status did not extend to their subjects. According to the treaty, subjects within each territory must subserviently follow the beliefs of their lord. Those who did not wish

104   WORKING AS EQUALS

The liberal conception of the person as a *rational self-governor* extends this idea by viewing each person as an *equal* sovereign power in charge of her own life.[24] As such, we have an interest in self-sovereignty which guides both how we treat other persons and how they treat us. At a bare minimum, respect for the self-sovereignty of other people requires that we forswear the use of force to get them to organize their lives according to our own lights. If we want others to share our way of life, it must either be through rational persuasion or through the power of our lived example.

It is not enough, however, to forswear the use of force in order to demonstrate respect for the self-sovereignty of others. It is morally critical that we do not even consider forcing others to believe as we do because we reject the paternalistic idea that we are entitled to substitute our own judgment regarding how another person should run her life for her own judgment about that matter.[25] Moreover, respect for the equal status of others as self-sovereigns goes beyond a rejection of paternalism, so understood. One fails to demonstrate respect for another person as an equal self-sovereign simply by making how she chooses to organize her own life within her zone of self-sovereignty a matter of one's own concern. Each person's self-sovereign actions are *her own*, and thus do not morally implicate any other persons. It follows from the above that the liberal democratic order will not recognize a person's demand for a religious accommodation if it is based on that person's claims of complicity in the self-sovereign actions of other people.

For an example of a demand for religious accommodation that *does* merit recognition, consider the case of the men whose situation motivated passage of the RFRA. They presented a morally compelling claim that whatever interest the state has in denying unemployment benefits to those who are fired with cause, that interest could be served just as well by allowing exceptions for people who are fired due to their observance of religious rituals; and, importantly, their claim for religious accommodation in no way depended on a claim that they were complicit in how other people choose to govern their own lives.

One can make a comparably strong case for religious accommodation from legal requirements that one wear clothing or adopt a hairstyle that

to convert may have had the legal option to leave the prince's territory; but otherwise there was a dominating view of the relationship between lord and subject.

[24] Jeremy Waldron, *Dignity, Rank, and Rights* (Oxford: Oxford University Press: 2012), 34ff.

[25] See Shiffrin, "Paternalism," for a discussion of the concept of paternalism.

THE EMPLOYEE-EMPLOYER RELATIONSHIP   105

interferes with one's religious practices. When these calls *to dress oneself* or to wear *one's own hair* in a particular way are not based on avoiding complicity in how other people choose to organize their own lives, there is a compelling case for their accommodation for religious reasons, so long as that accommodation does not undermine the legitimate public purpose behind the law.

Such considerations provide the basis for recognizing that corporations have some religious rights.[26] These can serve both the interests of shareholders in not engaging in certain kinds of commerce, and the interests of religiously observant employees in not needing to seek special accommodations from their employer in order to practice their religion. In the case at hand, religiously observant employees at Hobby Lobby do not need a special arrangement to not work on Sundays, since this Christian business is closed for business on their Sabbath. For the sake of such integrity interests *the company* would plausibly have a moral right to be exempted from laws which required it to be open seven days a week.

The case for a religious exemption from a law is undermined, however, when part of the law's public rationale is to promote and protect individuals' interests in self-governance. Consider a law which requires employers to set aside time and space for their employees to engage in required daily prayers. An employer's call for an exemption from that law, on the grounds that the religious beliefs and practices of some of her employees are incompatible with her own, do not merit recognition within the liberal democratic order.

This is because democratic citizens collectively share the authority to determine how to structure the workplace in order to promote and protect the self-governance of everyone in society. It is up to these citizens, acting in an egalitarian manner through the democratic process, to determine what employers must do in order to accommodate the self-governance interests of their employees. The resulting laws that they pass effectively define the zone of employees' self-sovereignty in which they can act without that being a matter of concern to their employers. It follows that an employer's call to be exempted from the resulting laws does not merit recognition if it is based on the claim that she has been forced to accommodate her employees' ability to make choices that she is religiously opposed to.

---

[26] I thus disagree with Thomas Donaldson, who holds there that "many rights seem logically impossible to attribute to corporations: Can corporations have a right to worship as they please?" (*Corporations and Morality* [Englewood Cliffs, NJ: Prentice Hall, 1982], 23). It is worth reiterating at this point that I am not attributing religious rights to corporations because they are entities with moral or religious interests; rather, it is because the corporation is a legal entity through which human individuals associate and interact with each other.

106 WORKING AS EQUALS

This discussion highlights that it is within the authority of democratic citizens to require employers to use their property in certain ways in order to promote and protect the self-governance-based interests of their employees. Private property is morally valuable insofar as it furthers the self-governance-based interests of persons in pursuing their own projects, goals, and values with security; however, private property can just as readily be an instrument of oppression as one of empowerment, and this fact justifies placing legal requirements on how we use our property. It follows that when the democratic process requires that we use our property in certain ways in order to promote and protect individuals' interests in self-governance, we are not only morally obligated to comply—we are also obligated to not see ourselves as morally implicated in the resulting exercises of self-sovereignty.

The opposing view that one is morally implicated in *every* use of one's property is evocative of the libertarian conception of individual autonomy that animates feminist concerns about the concept as a whole. As Catriona MacKenzie and Natalie Stoljar maintain, it is not only important for "feminists to contest this particular conception of autonomy" but also necessary for them "to reclaim and reconceptualize the concept" in a way that is "more adequate from a feminist perspective."[27]

This chapter seeks to reclaim the concept of individual autonomy by incorporating a proper respect for the self-sovereignty of individuals. This reconceptualization denies that one is morally implicated in the actions of others when one is legally required to use one's property, or to allow it to be used, in order to promote and protect their self-sovereignty.

That being said, there are considerations which could make a valid case for a religiously based exemption from a law designed to promote and protect the self-sovereignty of individuals. Consider the case in *Masterpiece Cakeshop v. Colorado Civil Rights Commission* (2018), in which a baker sought an exemption from a public accommodation law that disallowed businesses from refusing to provide service on the basis of sexual orientation. The baker's religion did not recognize the validity of same-sex marriages, and on that basis he refused to make his specialized wedding cakes for same-sex weddings. Importantly, he was willing to comply with the public accommodation law with respect to any of his more generic baked goods.

One could understand this distinction regarding his willingness to comply with the public accommodation law on the grounds that creating a

---

[27] Mackenzie and Stoljar, "Introduction," 5.

specialized wedding cake is not just a commercial transaction, but also is an important form of participation in the wedding itself. One could thus understand his claim to be exempted from the public accommodation law as a demand to not be forced to *participate* in a kind of wedding that he does not recognize as valid.[28] As such, his call for a religiously based exemption is not based on his being complicit in the self-sovereign actions of other people, but rather is based on *his own forced participation in the wedding*.

This case raises an important distinction between a person's being forced to participate in religious practices that are not his own and his being forced to accommodate religious practices that he objects to. When one is legally forced to accommodate the self-governance of other people, including by being legally required to use one's property in a certain way, one may genuinely feel complicit in the actions of the people being accommodated; however, this kind of complicity does not provide grounds for a legal exemption.

One might note that the distinction between being forced to accommodate the religious practices of others and being forced to participate in their religious practices is not always clear. I would suggest, though, that there are factors that explain why a baker's being forced to provide generic baked goods to all customers is an example of the former whereas his being forced to create custom wedding cakes for all is an example of the latter. It is plausible, for example, that creating a customized wedding cake involves a degree of personal and interpersonal engagement that is not present in the creation and selling of more generic baked items. As we examine other claims for religiously based exemptions from laws designed to promote and protect individuals' interests in self-governance, then, we must be attuned to the plausibility of claims that they genuinely involve a forced *participation* in an activity that one opposes, rather than merely a forced accommodation of the self-governance interests of others.

This completes this chapter's framework for how to respect the self-sovereignty of persons within the liberal democratic order. Before applying it to the Hobby Lobby case, let me consider some objections. First, one might claim that people who hold religious views which do not fully demonstrate respect for the self-sovereignty of others may experience the failure of the

---

[28] I am arguing here that the law should view calls for religious accommodation in the way that it evaluates claims for conscientious objection. What matters in these claims is *one's personal participation* in an unjust system, rather than the fact that one participates in a system where there is an injustice. For a discussion of the law's view of conscientious objection, see Sepinwall, "Conscience and Complicity," 1938.

108 WORKING AS EQUALS

state to accommodate their views as stigmatizing. In response, I maintain this is an unfortunate, but unavoidable result in a society whose political order is structured around the equal value of persons as self-governors with a democratically determined zone of self-sovereignty.

This response reveals that this chapter's approach to political philosophy is not neutral between conceptions of the person or overarching views of the good.[29] In order to both affirm the correctness of its own conception of the person with interests in self-sovereignty, and to respect the interest that persons have in deciding on their own overarching view of the good, this chapter's approach to political philosophy holds that a liberal democratic society should tolerate *a person's holding of* illiberal ideas, but denies that such views generally merit legal accommodation.[30]

One might also present a feminist critique to this chapter's understanding of the role of self-sovereignty on the grounds that it presents a socially disconnected understanding of the human person.[31] To draw out this objection, one might think that according respect for the self-sovereignty of others requires only making sure that they have sufficient resources to organize their lives as they see fit, but otherwise that we should be *disinterested* in their lives.

In response, I argue that we can respect the self-sovereignty of other persons while having an interest in positively contributing to their lives. In the marketplace, we can offer goods and services to customers not simply because doing so serves our own interests, but specifically because *our customers have determined* that those products and services advance *their own.*

Putting these points together, I maintain that having a proper concern for the self-sovereignty of other people is compatible with coming to the market with an interest in advancing the well-being of other persons. In addition, we can also come to the market with other-regarding religious motivations, provided that the underlying religious views evince respect for the self-sovereignty of the people we seek to benefit. When they do incorporate this

---

[29] In the case at hand, it rejects the view of Hobby Lobby's shareholders that human personhood begins at conception because a newly fertilized human egg is not only not self-governing, but is not even conscious (cf. Scanlon, *What We Owe*, 185). This affects the structure of this chapter's analysis insofar as it considers the interests of zygotes only to the extent that they matter to the adult human beings involved.

[30] As Hampton notes, "There is a difference between tolerance of another's ideas and tolerance of another's holding of these ideas" ("Should Political Philosophy Be Done," 811).

[31] See Mackenzie and Stoljar, "Introduction," 8–10.

THE EMPLOYEE-EMPLOYER RELATIONSHIP   109

kind of respect, it is possible to enter the market without alienation from either one's own religious values, or from one's fellow human beings.[32]

6.6. Applying the Self-Sovereignty Framework to the Hobby Lobby Case

Drawing upon the above framework, I argue that Hobby Lobby and its shareholders have a positive duty to comply with a society-wide scheme for enabling all persons to have the kind of contraceptive coverage that allows them to have full control of their sexual and reproductive lives. The question of this chapter is whether they have a special integrity interest in not *directly* paying for contraceptive coverage which merits being recognized within the liberal democratic order.

According to the above framework, the call for accommodation by Hobby Lobby's shareholders does not merit this kind of recognition because it is based on their claims of complicity in the actions of the company's employees regarding how they organize their own lives within their democratically determined zone of self-sovereignty. The central claim of this chapter is that the liberal democratic order does not recognize the validity of such demands.

This result applies more generally. Consider the case of a closely held company owned by Jehovah's Witnesses who call for an exemption from covering blood transfusions in their employee healthcare plans, or the case of a company owned by Christian Scientists who claim a religious exemption from paying for *any* medical coverage for their employees.[33] Employees of these companies would not have the same basis as those of Hobby Lobby to understand these calls for religious exemptions as rooted in unacceptably patriarchal attitudes. Nevertheless, they could still reasonably object to their employer's call for religious exemptions on the grounds that their choices regarding their own healthcare are not a matter of legitimate concern to their employers.

One might respond to this analysis by arguing that we should not understand Hobby Lobby's call for religious accommodation as a call of its

---

[32] The view developed here thus stands in contrast to how many understand the French concept of *laïcité* to apply to the employment relationship. One can understand the concept to attempt to govern public relations in a way that respects the self-sovereignty of persons, but at the cost of the public expression of their religion.

[33] Sepinwall, "Corporate Piety and Impropriety," 174.

110 WORKING AS EQUALS

shareholders to be free from complicity in the self-sovereign actions of the company's employees, but rather as a call from them to not be forced to participate in actions which they find morally reprehensible. In response, I argue that in order to respect the principle of self-sovereignty, we must distinguish between a person's direct participation in an action and a person's compliance with a democratically enacted scheme to enable other persons to exercise their own self-governance.

Consider how this framework applies to the case where the government provides universal contraceptive coverage supported by general tax revenues. The owners of a company like Hobby Lobby could object to this scheme on the grounds that as taxpayers they were being forced to participate in something that they found morally intolerable. However, the liberal democratic order will not recognize this appeal because the company's shareholders are not being asked to participate in employees' contraceptive choices, but rather are being required to comply with a democratically approved scheme to enable their employees to make their own choices about sex and reproduction.

The moral calculus does not change when the government mandates that Hobby Lobby pay for an employee healthcare plan that covers forms of contraception that its shareholders object to. In this case the company is complying with a democratically approved scheme to advance the ability of their employees to exercise their own self-governance, rather than directly participating in the employees' contraceptive choices. Even though the line between being forced to participate in an action and being forced to accommodate the self-sovereign choices of others is not always clear, mere compliance with the law here could not reasonably be understood as a form of participation in the employees' contraceptive choices. To respect their employees' self-sovereignty, employers should thus not view themselves as complicit in how employees choose to exercise their options under the healthcare plan.

Hobby Lobby's call for an exemption from the contraceptive care mandate does not merit recognition within the liberal democratic order in virtue of the fact that it is based on the shareholders' claims of complicity in the self-sovereign actions of the company's employees; i.e., it represents a failure to recognize their *equal status* as self-sovereigns in charge of their own lives. The wrongness of recognizing that companies have a legal right to exempt themselves from the contraceptive care mandate, however, goes beyond a mere failure to respect the equality of the company's employees as self-sovereigns. Such a legal recognition provides a kind of validation for religious views which fail to respect the self-sovereignty of others *even when that failure of respect is rooted in unacceptably hierarchical understandings* of the human person. Indeed, the debate over whether to recognize the right of companies like Hobby Lobby to exempt themselves from the contraceptive care mandate can very much be seen as part of the larger culture war over whether such views merit this kind of legal and social validation. The argument of this chapter is that they do not.

Any stigma that Hobby Lobby's shareholders might experience through a denial of their right to a religious accommodation could be mitigated by adopting another scheme for providing citizens with affordable access to contraceptive services, such as paying for universal access out of general revenues. While it is important to consider ways to mitigate stigma when we design social policies, there may be good reasons for the democratic process not to settle on the least stigmatizing option. Consider that the Affordable Care Act was built upon an existing framework in which many people were satisfied with their employer-provided health insurance. It was both practical to build upon this existing framework, and a near political necessity to do so in order to advance the underlying policy objectives. The mere fact that there is a less stigmatizing option available for achieving the state's interest in providing secure and affordable access to contraceptive services to everyone in society, then, would not provide grounds for a religious accommodation from the contraceptive care mandate.

6.7. Conclusion

This chapter puts forward a general account of when claims for religious accommodation should be recognized within the liberal democratic order. This account is based on the egalitarian ideas that each person in society has equal status both as a self-sovereign and as a citizen who shares an equal role in defining the scope of self-sovereignty that all parties in the employment relationship enjoy.

It holds that someone has valid grounds for religious accommodation from a law when it is consistent with the achievement of its public purpose and when it is not based on claims of her being complicit in how other people organize their own lives within their democratically determined zone of self-sovereignty. It holds further though that this is compatible with recognizing that there can be grounds for accommodation so that one might not be forced to participate in a practice that one finds morally repugnant.

112 WORKING AS EQUALS

This discussion entails that while in principle corporations can have religious rights, there is a decisive reason for rejecting the existence of one in the Hobby Lobby case. Hobby Lobby and its shareholders do not have the religious right they claim because their call for accommodation from the contraceptive care mandate is based on their avoiding complicity in how their employees organize *their own lives* within a democratically defined zone of self-sovereignty. It is this interest, I am claiming, which does not merit being accommodated within a liberal democratic order that is based on an understanding of each person as an *equal* who both has a realm of self-sovereignty and a duty to support the self-governance of others. This suggests that the law should be revised so as to not recognize calls for religiously based legal exemptions which are based on a person's claim of complicity in the self-sovereign actions of other people. If the law were revised in this way, Hobby Lobby and other corporations would not have the legal right to exempt themselves from the contraceptive care mandate.

Let me end with one final point regarding the normative significance of the value of self-sovereignty within the liberal democratic order. This order provides normative guidance directly to citizens, legislators, and judges who have the power to make and interpret the law; however, there is an additional question of how corporations and their managers should make decisions when the law does not comport with the requirements of the liberal democratic order. It is beyond the scope of this chapter to fully address this question, other than to suggest that, out of respect for their employees' status as equal self-sovereigns, companies should not take advantage of their legally recognized right to exempt themselves from the contraceptive care mandate.

7

Justice in Human Capital

Michael Cholbi

Traditionally, the production of goods within the employment relationship has been envisioned along industrial lines, as an alchemy of employer-provided capital and employee-provided work. Employers provide physical capital, in the form of machinery or tools, while employees provide the sweat of their brow, in the form of physical or mental exertion. Production thus occurs when the latter is applied to the former. But this picture overlooks a factor of production that has become increasingly important over time. Most work in contemporary economies is no longer unskilled, for both employees and employers contribute to production by making use of their *human capital*, that body of skills, knowledge, or dispositions which enhances the value of their contributions to production. The human capital contributions to production often come from many different parties. Consider, for example, a seemingly straightforward production process such as a construction firm building a house. Such a process includes human capital contributions from carpenters and other building tradespersons, inasmuch as they draw upon their knowledge of building techniques; engineers, inasmuch as the house reflects their design; and professionals such as accountants, whose knowledge ensures that the house will be built within the firm's budget. Some of this human capital may be highly firm-specific (for example, the firm may have a patented design for a particular element of the house), while much of it will be more generic, including the various soft skills that allow for production to take place (for example, the ability to communicate in the language spoken by one's coworkers). "Management" itself may be seen as a human capital contribution to production as well.

Crucially, human capital *is* a form of capital, a resource that enables the production of goods for consumption or of additional capital goods. And for many individuals, human capital is the only form of capital readily accessible to them. The vast majority of individuals lack the physical (or financial) capital to produce goods on their own, and so earn their livelihoods

Michael Cholbi, *Justice in Human Capital* In: *Working as Equals.* Edited by: Julian David Jonker and Grant J. Rozeboom, Oxford University Press. © Oxford University Press 2023. DOI: 10.1093/oso/9780197634295.003.0007

114 WORKING AS EQUALS

exclusively by taking advantage of their human capital via employment. In an employment relationship, employers pay not for our human capital as such but for the work we perform, much of whose value nevertheless stems from the application of our human capital. The extent to which one's work is rewarded within competitive labor markets thus reflects, however imperfectly, the market value of one's human capital (or at least of what can produced thereby).

Moreover, although human capital can lose its value by becoming obsolete (being able to saddle a horse no longer has the labor market value it had a century ago), it is not *depleted* by use in the way that physical capital is. Physical capital can suffer from wear and tear, as can workers' bodies. But one's human capital and the value thereof is often enhanced rather than reduced through use. The practice of a skill, for instance, makes one more proficient at that skill and enables one to apply that skill in a wider array of circumstances. Human capital also tends to have some measure of portability. The market value of some parcels of human capital (an intimate knowledge of the different interpretations of Kant's Formula of Universal Law, for example) may be sufficiently idiosyncratic to be of market value only to a small number of prospective employees. But other parcels of human capital will be more multipurpose, able to contribute to the production processes implemented in many different firms or organizations. As such, human capital will often be critical to individuals' long-term economic well-being or security, since its portability increases the range of a person's employment prospects, the ability to obtain employment when unemployed, etc.

These considerations illustrate that for most people, human capital has a high degree of material value. Their human capital is a uniquely important asset in enabling them, over the course of their lifetimes, to be viable in labor markets whose mechanisms and prices reflect the value of said capital. Two developments in particular have amplified the importance of human capital. The first is the advent of the "knowledge economy." Gaps in wages and job security have grown in recent decades, gaps strongly correlated with educational levels and other rough indices of human capital.[1] A person's

---

[1] Though the positive relationship between educational attainment and wealth or job security is well established, that relationship may be diminishing over time, and the relationship between educational attainment and other employment-related goods (e.g., job satisfaction) appears more tenuous. See Lauren Schudde and Kaitlin Bernel, "Educational Attainment and Nonwage Labor Market Returns in the United States," *AERA Open* 5 (2019), https://doi.org/10.1177/2332858419874056; Hugh Lauder and Ken Mayhew, "Higher Education and the Labour Market: An Introduction," *Oxford Review of Education* 46, no. 1 (2020): 1–9, https://doi.org/10.1080/03054985.2019.1699714; Phillip Brown, Hugh Lauder, and Sin Yi Cheung, *The Death of Human Capital?* (Oxford: Oxford University

well-being, at least in economic terms, is increasingly contingent less on sheer exertion—the sweat of the brow—than on the application of human capital to the problems employers desire that employees analyze and solve. The second is the precarity that has increasingly come to dominate contemporary employment. Gone are the days in which workers could find security in the fact that they are likely to retire from the same firm that hired them. Workers are instead likely to have many employers in many industries over their lifetimes. Hence, to the degree that employment security is achievable today, workers now hope to achieve it by means of their human capital, i.e., the value and currency of the skill set by which they enhance the value of what they can produce.

The benefits of human capital are spread widely. Nevertheless, it is a good that economic actors can attempt to control or leverage to their own advantage. Such efforts are visible in policies and practices firms sometimes pursue. For instance, firms can attempt to privatize the value of human capital through the assertions of trade secrets and other claims of intellectual property. These are tools through which firms assert private control over intellectual assets. They are typically justified by appeal to the various interests that firms have in control over information or ideas they create.[2] Simultaneously however, any parcel of intellectual property also represents a parcel of valuable human capital, and so firms' assertions of intellectual property restrict employees' ability to exploit their own human capital and the ability of other firms to do likewise. Firms can also attempt to privatize the value of their employees' human capital through the use of noncompete agreements. Noncompete agreements limit employees' right to join or start a rival firm subsequent to their employment with their current firm.

Intellectual property assertions and noncompete agreements are instances where firms attempt to increase the human capital benefits that flow to them. But firms can also intervene in human capital distributions thorough efforts that target how the development of human capital is governed or supported. In recent years, for instance, industry actors have sought to ensure that publicly financed education is increasingly tailored to their own productive

---

Press, 2020); and Brittany C. Solomon, Boris N. Nikolaev, and Dean A. Shepherd, "Does Educational Attainment Promote Job Satisfaction? The Bittersweet Trade-offs between Job Resources, Demands, and Stress," *Journal of Applied Psychology* (2021), http://dx.doi.org/10.1037/apl0000904.

[2] Robert P. Merges, *Justifying Intellectual Property* (Cambridge, MA: Harvard University Press, 2011).

116   WORKING AS EQUALS

interests. Corporate philanthropy directed at educational institutions, for instance, flows increasingly to support initiatives (STEM education, technology research) that corporations view as serving their own human capital interests.[3] At the same time, corporate interests have succeeded in many nations in shifting the funding burden of human capital development onto individuals. The growth in university tuition since the 1990s corresponds to a period in which business and corporate taxation as a percentage of public revenue has shrunk, with the results that students and their parents now bear more of the costs of this form of human capital development. The United Kingdom government estimates that total student indebtedness will be around £560 billion by mid-century, about £8,000 for every resident of the United Kingdom,[4] and total educational indebtedness in the United States is currently $1.57 trillion, nearly $5,000 for every American and $28,000 per indebted student.[5]

It is not my purpose here to evaluate these particular firm practices. (Indeed, the conclusions I draw will illustrate the complexity of evaluating such practices.) They instead illustrate how human capital is a productive domain where various parties' interests can collide, and because human capital plays a large role in determining how our lives turn out and what sorts of opportunities are available to us, the development and distribution of human capital is subject to demands of *justice*.

The purpose of this chapter is to sketch an account of justice in human capital—what a morally defensible social arrangement would be with regard to our access to opportunities to create, acquire, and make use of human capital. In particular, I shall be concerned about what requirements our shared social life must meet with respect to human capital in order for it to instantiate whatever sort of *equality* is morally relevant in that domain. Societies and the individuals that comprise them are presumably better off when their overall store of human capital is greater rather than smaller, yet my concerns are entirely comparative and so do not engage with what justice requires with respect to the overall level of human capital. I also set aside questions arising from the intersection of egalitarian and nonegalitarian considerations. It

---

[3] Anand Giridharadas, *Winners Take All: The Elite Charade of Changing the World* (New York: Vintage Books, 2019).

[4] Paul Bolton, "Research Briefing: Student Loan Statistics," June 23, 2020, https://commonslibrary.parliament.uk/research-briefings/sn01079/.

[5] Ben Miller et al., "Addressing the $1.5 Trillion in Federal Student Loan Debt," Center for American Progress, June 12, 2019, https://www.americanprogress.org/issues/education-postsecondary/reports/2019/06/12/470893/addressing-1-5-trillion-federal-student-loan-debt/.

JUSTICE IN HUMAN CAPITAL   117

could well be that unjust inequalities could be rendered less objectionable by increasing overall levels of human capital (in the manner that Rawls proposes,[6] that inequalities in wealth might be unobjectionable if they work to the advantage of even the least advantaged). I mean only to address, with respect to human capital, what sorts of disparities are objectionable and why. Insufficient detail will be provided to deem what I offer here a *theory* of justice in human capital, yet I hope that my account will provoke further investigation of what has been a largely neglected topic in moral and political philosophy.

I begin by offering observations about the distinctiveness of human capital as a good. Human capital has a "metaphysics" that complicates efforts to normatively theorize about it. The appropriate unit of evaluation for thinking about justice in human capital is what I will call human capital *ledgers*. Section 7.2 puts forth and defend a principle to serve as a criterion for judging social arrangements with respect to how they produce human capital and allocate its benefits. That principle (roughly) says that a human capital allocation is just when and because it enables individuals to have equal probabilities of attaining their respective ends merely insofar as human capital is concerned. In sections 7.3 and 7.4, I attempt to elaborate the philosophical grounds for endorsing this principle. My elaboration will not contribute to settling recent disputes between distributive and relational egalitarians. Rather, it will strengthen each position by helping to answer challenges each theory faces. For distributive egalitarians, my account of human capital justice illuminates how distributions can be morally relevant independently of their significance for, or impact on, social relations. For relational egalitarians, my account will provide an example of how their ideal of equal relations can be distributively operationalized. In any case, that these two theories appear to converge on a common principle concerning human capital justice is an important practical result in its own right.

7.1. The Metaphysics of Human Capital

I earlier defined human capital as that body of skills, knowledge, or dispositions which enhances the value of our contributions to production. In theorizing about justice in human capital, we may be tempted to think of

---

[6] John Rawls, *A Theory of Justice* (Cambridge, MA: Harvard University Press, 1971).

118   WORKING AS EQUALS

human capital as analogous to other consumption goods (loaves of bread, say) or other capital goods (a computer or a tractor). From the standpoint of workers, human capital has a foot in both consumption and production. A worker's human capital is not typically consumed by working, but it has instrumental value in enabling her to acquire consumption goods by working in exchange for the wages that she in turn uses to purchase those goods. But at the same time, her human capital serves as a capital good, enabling the production of other goods.

This makes human capital metaphysically distinctive and ethically fraught. Its value is, on the one hand, strongly personal, linked closely to a person's ability to acquire what she needs or desires. But on the other hand, human capital has clear impersonal value, inasmuch as it enables production of goods with value to others besides the possessor of that capital. All benefit from the creation and exploitation of human capital. Questions of justice arise because it is obvious neither how individuals ought to contribute to its creation nor how they ought to benefit from it.

Further metaphysical challenges arise from how human capital is produced, made use of, and valued. Some human capital is innate, a reflection of employees' native endowments. But a good portion of human capital is instead *created*, and the number of contributors to its creation is typically large. Any given component of an individual worker's human capital is the product of contributions from schools and other community institutions, guild-like networks of other workers, a worker's family, employers, and workers themselves. Our human capital is a vital cog in economic production. Without it, the "cooperative venture for mutual advantage"[7] that we participate in when we work with others would flounder. But human capital is not only an input into that cooperative venture. It is also an output of that venture, one fed by many disparate streams operating in concert.

At any given time, a worker is likely to sit midstream in relation to human capital inputs and outputs. A worker will nearly always bring some measure of preexisting human capital to a given employment relationship, having been acculturated and educated so as to have the skills the employer desires. Indeed, it is hard to envision an employee whose skill set as an employment relationship begins is effectively a tabula rasa. And employment relationships at least sometimes contribute to individual human capital by fostering the refinement of existing skills or knowledge or by adding new skills or knowledge

---

[7] Rawls, *A Theory of Justice*, 4.

to the employees' human capital repertoire. In addition, the end of an employment relationship does not destroy an employee's human capital. It remains available for their benefit and for the benefit of prospective employers. With respect to human capital, then, almost any employment relationship has both a complex (pre)history and a future. And because human capital is cumulative, it can be difficult to see how to disaggregate the elements of one's human capital that accrete over time. A novice may become an expert with respect to some skill thanks to having been able to practice that skill in the course of doing a job. But the newly expert employee walks away from that job with a sheaf of interrelated skills, and it can be difficult, if not impossible, to disaggregate any one element of that sheaf from any other. She cannot plausibly enter into a subsequent employment relationship in which she uses *only* her novice skill set while setting aside her more expert capacities.

It is therefore daunting to disentangle the distinctive contributions that these various streams make to the development of human capital. Human capital emerges from the synergistic interplay of institutions and individuals. As such, it underscores how virtually all economic production is fundamentally cooperative. Any one institution's or individual's contribution to production depends for its success on others' contributions. Elizabeth Anderson invites us to contrast this reality of "joint production," wherein we "regard every product of the economy as jointly produced by everyone working together," with a "more familiar image that invites us to regard the economy as if it were a system of self-sufficient Robinson Crusoes, producing everything all by themselves until the point of trade." She observes that under this picture of "joint production," any attempt "to credit specific bits of output to specific bits of input by specific individuals represents an arbitrary cut in the causal web that in fact makes everyone's productive contribution dependent on what everyone else is doing."[8]

To ask, then, who is responsible for (say) a carpenter's ability to install windows correctly is tricky; the carpenter, yes, but also those individuals and institutions that educated and acculturated the carpenter, other carpenters whose work was emulated, the firms that offered opportunities to hone this ability, and so on. With respect to any given parcel of human capital, the correct answer to the question "Who produced or created that?" is "We (or they) did."

---

[8] Elizabeth Anderson, "What Is the Point of Equality?," *Ethics* 109, no. 2 (1999): 287–337, at 321.

120   WORKING AS EQUALS

Yet despite human capital being a collective product with collective value, it resides in, and is ultimately valuable to, individual human capitalists. This is not to deny that human capital can sometimes migrate outside of us in the form of technologies and artifacts created in order to substitute for human capital. Our human ability to create such substitutes is, ironically, an important feature of human capital. A barista who follows a set of instructions for pulling a shot of espresso is making use of others' human capital, as is the medical technician who performs a CT scan. Human capital's ability to devise technology that substitutes for human capital can enhance the value of human capital by making it more productive, yet at its limit, this same ability can automate the labor humans perform and render their human capital gratuitous.

These facts make human capital particularly ill-suited to any approach to justice that attempts to measure justice in terms of discrete historical events. In the manner of Robert Nozick's entitlement theory of justice, we might seek to articulate an account of justice in human capital that looks at the distribution of human capital and its benefits at a given point in time and considers how the discrete acts of the various contributors to, and beneficiaries of, brought about that distribution.[9] We might then apply one or more criteria (for example, that the acts were not performed under coercion, were Pareto-optimal, and so on) to the acts responsible for that distribution so as to ascertain whether the resulting distribution is just. Whatever the normative appeal of such an approach, it is simply infeasible with respect to a good like human capital. Portioning out the contribution that any specific individual or any of her specific acts made to the creation of her human capital or to the human capital residing in other individuals is well nigh impossible. So too are we unlikely to be able to identify the exact ways in which any individual benefits from the specific acts (either her own or others) that lead to the creation of human capital. On anything but the smallest economic scale, then, human capital is truly a collective achievement, rendering attempts to analyze justice in human capital in terms of relations between discrete acts and the creation or enjoyment of human capital difficult to envision.

The alternative is to compare different possible arrangements of human capital and ask, somewhat in the spirit of the Rawlsian original position, which such arrangements participants in a common human capital scheme would endorse. In doing so, we must take stock of both human capital

---

[9] *Anarchy, State, and Utopia* (New York: Basic Books, 1974).

benefits and *burdens*. Human capital benefits participants in such a scheme by enabling them to contribute labor to the production of goods where such contributions would be less valuable absent the role played by both their own human capital and that of others. The consequent benefits here are primarily material (wages and income), but may also include other goods whose value is more psychological or ethical in nature, such as the sense of pride at being able to contribute to the shared production of goods others value. But each beneficiary of human capital is also a contributor to its development, which is an equally large part of the equation in human capital justice. After all, human capital is the product of cooperative schemes from which individuals benefit but that cannot succeed without their help. Most prominent among the burdens of human capital creation will be the time devoted to education as well as its monetary costs. Note again that just as the human capital benefits one enjoys do not have their source exclusively in one's own human capital, so too do some of the burdens of human capital development lead to benefits for others (as when taxes support schooling for others).

With respect to any individual, then, an allocation of human capital benefits can run afoul of justice by providing her too little in the way of benefit, subjecting her to too much in the way of burdens, or both. To draw upon Amartya Sen's well-known example, we cannot here focus solely on who makes flutes, but also who would benefit from flutes and to what degree. (Indeed, to make the analogy more apt, we should think in terms of *designing* flutes).[10]

Crucially, we cannot address the benefits and burdens separately, since the facts about how burdened a person is with respect to human capital will often causally intersect with the facts about how advantaged she is with respect to human capital. Ideally, each of us should want to swap our own human capital burdens for others' human capital benefits. But as this discussion of the metaphysics of human capital indicates, benefits and burdens cannot be readily unbundled so as to facilitate such swaps. I may very much desire a specific human capital benefit that some other actor enjoys, but I cannot acquire that benefit without whatever burdens that actor (or other actors) had to bear in order to realize that benefit. Conversely, other actors may desire one of my benefits, but the causal interdependence of that benefit both on my own human capital burdens and the human capital burdens of others make it impossible for them to acquire that benefit without also subjecting themselves

[10] Amartya Sen, *The Idea of Justice* (Cambridge, MA: Harvard University Press, 2011), 12.

122 WORKING AS EQUALS

to the burdens. Thus, in assessing distributions of benefits and burdens, we should forswear efforts to evaluate alternative distributions in terms of the particular benefits and burdens that individuals have. We must instead evaluate alternative distributions holistically, in terms of what I call *ledgers* of human capital benefits and burdens. A ledger records transactions as assets or liabilities in relation to one another. Evaluating distributions of human capital benefits and burdens should not be envisioned in terms of interpersonal trade-offs of particular assets and liabilities residing within individuals' human capital ledgers. Rather, the relevant trade-offs are of ledgers themselves, i.e., whether rational individuals would be willing to trade their ledgers for those of others. This allows us to appraise possible trade-offs between burdens and benefits without supposing that the benefits and burdens can be disentangled from one other. Of course, all will prefer to maximize human capital benefits to themselves while minimizing their burdens. But preferences will vary with respect to the exchange rate between burdens and benefits, with some willing to tolerate higher benefits in exchange for slightly higher burdens, whereas some will be more burden sensitive, more eager to minimize burdens than to maximize benefit.

7.2. A Proposed Principle

Our goal is to identify a principle to serve as a criterion with which to assess whether some allocation of the benefits and burdens of human capital—again, as realized in individuals' human capital ledgers—is just, with a particular eye to a criterion that captures the respect in which the individuals are equals or are to stand in equal relations with one another.

One kind of criterion that we can reject is that every individual is to make an equal contribution to human capital development or to enjoy an equal set of benefits from human capital. One reason to reject this is that it would be inordinately difficult to ascertain what equal contributions or equal benefits consist in. As we observed in section 7.1, the metaphysics of human capital precludes simple judgments about what any one person has contributed to, or how much benefited from, the overall store of human capital. A second reason to reject this sort of criterion is that individuals will have different goals or tastes with respect to human capital. Some will be highly industrious and thus eager to contribute to human capital development, others less so. Some will be tenacious adherents to the Protestant work ethic, others beachcombers who place a high value on leisure or liberty. Some will have goals that require taking advantage of a great deal of human capital (either their own or that of others), whereas others' goals will be less reliant on human capital. It would, I take it, be onerous to insist that every actor (firms, individuals, etc.) make an equal contribution to human capital development and inefficient to insist that actors' shares of its benefits be equal. We require, therefore, a measure of justice in human capital that recognizes that although each person has an equal standing with respect to human capital, all people do not have equal interests with respect to human capital.

A criterion for justice in human capital should instead proceed in a contractualist spirit, by reference to actual individuals and the reasons they have to endorse or reject different possible ledgers of burdens and benefits. Individuals hypothetically considering how the benefits or burdens of human capital are to be distributed confront one another as fellow *agents*, i.e., as individuals who recognize that the production and use of human capital is in their interest inasmuch as it enhances the efficacy and reach of their own agency. Cooperation in the production and use of human capital makes it possible for these agents to pursue and attain ends that they could not pursue or attain by drawing only upon their native endowments. And yet their respective ends are diverse, as are the demands that these ends make on human capital. What principle(s), then, would individuals confronting one another as agents with a generic interest in pursuing their chosen ends believe it reasonable to endorse with respect to the benefits and burdens of human capital?

Such agents, I contend, would settle on the following principle for human capital justice:

> A distribution of burdens and benefits with respect to human capital development and allocation is just only if under that distribution, no individual prefers another's ledger of benefits and burdens to her own.[11]

Here is how such a test would unfold in action, so to speak: some individual S compares her current allotment of burdens and benefits of human capital (how much she contributes to its production alongside the value of the benefits she enjoys from that allotment) to the allotment enjoyed by some

---

[11] Savvy readers will recognize this as a variant of Ronald Dworkin's envy test (*Sovereign Virtue* [Cambridge, MA: Harvard University Press, 2004]). Because I do not have in mind that agents deploying my principle are motivated by envy, I refrain from giving my principle such a moniker.

124 WORKING AS EQUALS

individual T. S prefers T's allotment to her own, either because it requires lesser burdens, provides more benefits, or both. S would, in principle, be willing to trade her own human capital ledger for T's. S may perform the same procedure with respect to other ledgers, belonging to U, V, etc. So too may T perform this same procedure with respect to ledgers belonging to S, U, V, etc. If each individual within a society finds no one else's ledger preferable to her own, then the distribution of the burdens and benefits of human capital in that society meets a necessary condition for comparative justice, that is, that distribution is not unjust in that it treats individuals equally in the relevant sense.

Note that the principle refers to *individuals*. This allows for individuals to make use of firms, corporations, governments, etc. as instruments for the development and use of human capital. But these instruments do not themselves have preferences concerning human capital ledgers and are therefore excluded from the scope of the principle.

The principle requires an important qualification: as noted earlier, individuals vary in their goals, tastes, and aptitudes, and as such vary in their willingness to contribute to human capital development (either their own or others) and in their desire to exploit human capital (either their own or others). The principle therefore needs to incorporate such variations. This is accomplished by indexing the preferences for different ledgers of burdens and benefits to individuals and their respective goals, tastes, and aptitudes. So when S considers whether she prefers her existing ledger of benefits and burdens in connection with human capital to T's ledger, she does not ask whether T's ledger would be better for her in light of her goals, tastes, and aptitudes. Rather, S asks whether she would prefer T's ledger relative to T's goals, tastes, and aptitudes to her ledger relative to her (i.e., S's) goals, tastes, and aptitudes. In other words, S is not considering whether she would prefer to switch ledgers with T but whether she would prefer to switch *positions* with T, where their positions include both their ledgers and those idiosyncratic personal features that bear on human capital development and use. This allows S (or any other individual) to assess rival ledgers with respect to their instrumental effectiveness in relation to different ends that individuals may have. In effect, the principle is a probabilistic criterion, asking individuals whether others stand a better or worse chance of realizing their ends than those individuals themselves do—whether, in other words, we should prefer others' ledgers of human capital burdens and benefits relative to their ends. Note that the principle does not assume any particular level of the relevant probabilities within the status quo; S could prefer her ledger to T's despite its offering her a low probability of realizing her ends if, in S's estimation, T's ledger offers T a still lower probability. Again, we are concerned here with comparative justice instead of noncomparative justice, so questions about how much human capital a society produces writ large are not answered via the principle.[12]

My principle of human capital justice, like Rawls's original position, is not "moralized," by which I mean that individuals are evaluating the preferability of other human capital ledgers to their own in purely prudential terms rather than by appeal to any intuitions or antecedent principles regarding justice, fairness, or desert. They are, in Rawls' terms, rational and reasonable, cognizant of how cooperation in the domain of human capital could be beneficial to them and therefore willing to abide by principles applicable to that domain so as long as those principles answer to the reasons they have for such cooperation.

It is almost certainly true that no actual society has fully satisfied this principle. It therefore represents an ideal of justice with respect to human capital. All the same, the principle can be satisfied to varying degrees: within a given population, the number of persons unwilling to trade their ledgers for others' can vary. In addition, an individual can be more or less dissatisfied with her ledger relative to others'. Summed together, these two types of deviation comprise the total deviation from the ideal embodied in the principle, and it is in theory possible to compare two societies in how closely they approximate this ideal (or how closely a given society approximates it at different points in time). Furthermore, the principle could be deployed in a critical assessment of practices and policies bearing on human capital ledgers (such as intellectual property law, noncompete agreements, and taxation to support education). Sufficient knowledge of how these policies and practices move a society closer to, or further away from, the distribution of benefits and burdens described in the principle would be the grounds for such critical assessment.

---

[12] This in turn explains why the principle coincides with a necessary but not sufficient condition on human capital justice. A society with very low levels of human capital may satisfy the test but still underprovide human capital to a morally unacceptable degree.

126 WORKING AS EQUALS

7.3. Defending the Principle, Part I: Equal Distributions and Equal Respect

The previous section described a principle for human capital justice, but did not illuminate why the principle has moral force, and in particular, why social arrangements that fall short of the principle give rise to objections related to unequal treatment or consideration.

According to my principle, equality with respect to human capital does not mean having the same ledger of resources or obligations, nor does it mean that human capital confers equal benefits on all; rather, it means that (taking only considerations of human capital into account) individuals have an equal chance to attain their ends, whatever their ends may consist in. They will reject any social arrangement vis-à-vis human capital in which others are better positioned to attain their ends than they themselves thereby are. Deviations from such equal chances may well prove justifiable on noncomparative or nonegalitarian grounds. In the spirit of Rawls's maximin principle, we could, for instance, imagine some deviations from such equality being justified on the grounds that they increase instrumental chances for the worst off (moving from a distribution in which agents have only a 25 percent chance of achieving their ends in light of their human capital ledger to one in which some agents have a 50 percent chance could be justified if others also increase their chances to 35 percent, say). All the same, a cooperative scheme to which effectively all contribute—and the creation of human capital and the allocation of its benefits through employment is such a scheme—should enable individuals to enjoy their distributive fair shares of that scheme, and any deviation from equal chances seems to require a rationale that all can accept. At the very least, if some have human capital ledgers that better serve their ends than others' ledgers serve theirs, this discrepancy seems to require some moral defense.

It may appear mysterious, however, why the sort of equality incorporated into my principle—a kind of equality of chances—is morally relevant or a matter of justice at all. The principle implies that an allocation of human capital ledgers in which some thereby have a greater probability of attaining their ends than do others is, all other things being equal, unjust to the latter. I suggest that one dimension of the injustice in question rests on an ideal of equal respect for economic actors as rational agents. Individuals within societies confront one another as rational agents in Rawls's sense, as *agents* whose conceptions of the good include ends that they are seeking to advance but whose advancement requires productive cooperation with others. As we have seen, a central determinant of their success in this regard is how the human capital benefits and burdens that emerge within cooperative endeavors are allocated. If we are to be guided here by an expectation of equal respect, then we may not select allocations of human capital that favor some over others arbitrarily or by appeal to judgments about their conceptions of the good or the ends they include. Rather, equal respect for them as rational agents requires abstracting from the particulars of their aspirations so as to allocate human capital to them just insofar as and because they are rational agents. My principle does not assume that human capital is equally valuable to all (again, some will have projects or concerns that require more in the way of human capital, etc.). But it nevertheless reflects an ideal wherein cooperative production and exploitation—in this case, of human capital—should provide all agents with equal value relative to their respective ends. Patterns of human capital allocation conforming to my principle thus accord equal respect to individuals, and if Rawls is correct, the social institutions that contribute to such an allocation will also provide one of the social bases of self-respect as well.

Note that this justification of my principle ascribes moral significance to the distribution of human capital as such but does not take this significance as brute or unanalyzable. Allocations of human capital condemned by my principle are unjust because they implicate deeper moral inequalities in respect for individuals as rational agents. On this picture, the distributive significance of human capital allocation is nevertheless not interactional or relational. Obviously, unjust allocation results *from* interactions and relations among economic actors. However, insofar as human capital allocations represent unjust distributions, their injustice resides in the distributions instead of in inequalities in how those actors interact or relate to one another. In this regard, my principle assists distributive egalitarians in explaining how distributions themselves can embody injustice.

7.4. Defending the Principle, Part II: Equal Distributions and Equal Relations

In recent decades, however, relational egalitarians have argued that distributive facts are not normatively fundamental—that egalitarian justice consists in social relations free of domination and oppression that do not rest on

128 WORKING AS EQUALS

hierarchies or distinctions of status. If relational egalitarianism is to meaningfully contribute to our understanding of social justice writ large, including the material dimensions of social justice, its distributive implications should be spelled out. And it is clear the general direction that a relational egalitarian account of justice in distribution ought to go. Relational egalitarians should affirm that distributive facts can represent, instantiate, or contribute to unequal and morally objectionable social relations. On such a picture, distributive facts are "subsidiary to the broader value of relational equality" and "appropriately egalitarian distributes are determined *with reference to* that relational ideal, rather than via an appeal to an egalitarian distributive principle with any independent normative authority."[13]

A relational egalitarian interpretation of my principle for human capital justice along these is both feasible and attractive, in my estimation. Recall again that individuals choosing principles for producing and benefiting from human capital are confronting one another in a very specific context. They recognize the potential benefits to themselves of cooperation in the sphere of human capital, and in particular, how such cooperation might render their own agency more efficacious and more impactful, extending the range of ends they might pursue as well as increasing their capacity to attain these ends. All the more, these individuals confront one another as agents with equal standing. Suppose that a principle for comparative justice in human capital is proposed that leaves some with greater chances to pursue and realize their ends than others have. The ends of those for whom that principle entails a lesser chance of pursual and realization are thereby assigned lesser value. And unless nonarbitrary grounds are given for this entailment, the agency of those individuals has been assigned a lower status as well. Insofar as they are agents, they matter less to how human capital is created and utilized than do other agents. In contrast, my principle affirms their equal standing as agents, for the schemes of human capital cooperation my principle support do not regard the agency of some as more entitled to collective recognition or support than the agency of others. Schemes compliant with my principle do not organize individuals into agential castes or hierarchies.

My principle can thus be endorsed by relational egalitarians inasmuch as the principle incorporates a relational ideal in its standard of justification for different human capital schemes. But the principle also speaks in opposition

---

[13] Gideon Elford, "Survey Article: Relational Equality and Distribution," *Journal of Political Philosophy* 25, no. 4 (2017): e80–e99, at e81.

JUSTICE IN HUMAN CAPITAL   129

to social arrangements in which domination, oppression, or subordination of the kind relational egalitarians oppose is likely to arise. Suppose again that some principle of human capital justice is chosen other than my own, in which some are arbitrarily given greater agential efficacy and scope than others. A society organized in accordance with this principle gives wider berth for dominating, oppressive, or subordinating social relations to emerge. For those who have been arbitrarily assigned to a "higher" agential caste—those whose agential capacities have greater efficacy or scope—will be better equipped to establish such relations with those in lower agential castes. Such a society is likely to develop such that political or institutional power is hierarchical rather than democratic, so that those in higher agential castes exert greater influence over social relations. It is not inevitable that agential "elites" will establish such relationships, but they will probably be in a position to do so, and if their mindsets have been shaped by agential inequality over time, they may view themselves as entitled to do so. Whenever their ends are incompatible with the ends of those in lower agential castes, they may be both able and willing to use their greater agential efficacy to further limit the efficacy of others.

Injustice in human capital is therefore likely to be a nontrivial contributor to relational inequality inasmuch as it serves to structure options and opportunities in ways that afford some individuals greater ability to pursue their ends and others lesser ability to do so. Phenomena shaped by human capital, such as the workplace, will be a location in which such agential inequality plays itself out. Within workplaces and labor markets structured by such inequality, employers can come to enjoy greater benefits from human capital than employees and shift the burdens of human capital development onto employees. The interventions I described earlier—assertions of intellectual property, noncompete agreements, and divestment from public education—prove unjust if they reflect or enable unequal standing between employers and employees insofar as both are contributors to a cooperative human capital scheme. This does not mean that workers cannot achieve their ends in such a context. But it does mean they achieve their ends *despite* rather than because of how human capital is developed and distributed within their society. They may be successful despite being treated unjustly.

I thus follow Christian Schemmel in holding that, because relational egalitarians view "participation as equals in reciprocal cooperation as the foundational relationship of social justice, they have an intrinsic reason to

130   WORKING AS EQUALS

limit inequality in the goods produced by such cooperation."[14] A defeasible presumption of equality in goods generated via cooperation is thus a plausible starting point for relational egalitarian analyses of justice in human capital. And as I have argued, given that human capital is a cooperative endeavor whose value consists in its capacity to enhance the efficacy and range of human agency, the relevant metric of equality is equality of chances.

Relational egalitarians can thus embrace my principle of human capital justice inasmuch as it incorporates their concern for equal relations both in how a society that is just with respect to human capital is designed and in how such a society is likely to evolve over time. The principle accords individuals equal respect as agents and as cooperators. We of course relate to one another in other ways than as agents, and it is not my claim that justice with respect to human capital is the whole of justice. But a society that is just in this regard will go a long way in realizing two desiderata of justice that have been particularly influential in the Kantian and liberal traditions. First, such a society will have attained a union of wills with respect to a crucial dimension of social cooperation. Their cooperation in the development and use of human capital will rest on a harmony among agents wherein, by cooperating, their respective agential capacities are augmented to an equal degree. Second, such a society will have made progress in securing one of the social bases of self-respect. By ruling out unjust inegalitarian relationships in the domain of human capital, such a society promotes agents' understanding of themselves as "free and effective agents"[15] for whom others' agency does not stand as an objectionable obstacle to the exercise of their own.

7.5. Conclusion

Human capital proves to be a difficult matter to theorize about because of the complexity with which individuals create it and benefit from it. We must therefore assess different societal arrangements in terms of lifetime ledgers of human capital benefits and burdens, and my principle of human capital justice (a distribution of burdens and benefits is just only if no individual prefers another's ledger of benefits and burdens to her own) has defensible

---

[14] Christian Schemmel, "Why Relational Egalitarians Should Care about Distributions," *Social Theory and Practice* 37, no. 3 (2011): 365–390, at 370.

[15] Samuel Scheffler, "Choice, Circumstance, and the Value of Equality," *Politics, Philosophy and Economics* 4, no. 1 (2005): 5–28, at 24.

egalitarian credentials insofar as it captures what individuals who (a) confront one another as agents with equal standing, (b) are willing to reciprocally cooperate with one another in the production and use of human capital, and (c) aim thereby to extend the efficacy and scope of their rational agency, would embrace as a principle to govern human capital development and use. Both distributive and relational egalitarians can embrace this principle, thus showing that, whatever their differences at a theoretical level, these two species of egalitarian thought may well find common ground in practice.

8

Can Employers Discriminate without Treating Some Employees Worse Than Others?

Discrimination, the Comparative View, and Relational Equality

Kasper Lippert-Rasmussen

8.1. Introduction

There are many ways in which employers can treat employees badly. For most of these, whether employers treat some employees badly in this way has no implications for how they treat other employees. Suppose you accuse Andrea of taking advantage of Amina's delicate work permit situation to underpay her. Andrea dismisses your criticisms, retorting that all of her employees are in the same situation and are paid the same wage. I conjecture that your response would be that things are *even worse* than you thought initially: Andrea exploits not just Amina, but *all* of her employees.

Suppose instead that you accuse Andrea of discriminating against Amina, and Andrea replies that all her other employees are treated in the exact same way as Amina. Against *this* charge, Andrea's reply has some force. Arguably, this reflects that, as a conceptual matter, "discrimination is inherently comparative, and . . . what counts in the comparison is not how well or poorly a person (or group) is treated on some absolute scale, but rather how well she is treated relative to some other person."[1] Or as Justice Anthony Kennedy put

---

[1] Andrew Altman, "Discrimination," *Stanford Encyclopedia of Philosophy*, ed. Edward N. Zalta, Winter 2016 ed., accessed April 6, 2021, https://plato.stanford.edu/archives/win2016/entries/dis crimination/; see also Ben Eidelson, *Discrimination and Disrespect* (Oxford: Oxford University Press, 2015), 17; Kasper Lippert-Rasmussen, *Born Free and Equal? A Philosophical Inquiry into the Nature of Discrimination* (Oxford: Oxford University Press, 2014), 16; Sophia Moreau, *Faces of Inequality: A Theory of Wrongful Discrimination* (Oxford: Oxford University Press, 2020), 15, 17; Frej

TREATING SOME EMPLOYEES WORSE THAN OTHERS 133

it in the context of law: "One who alleges discrimination must show that she 'received differential treatment vis-à-vis members of a different group on the basis of a statutorily described characteristic.'"[2] Along these lines, one might embrace

> *The Simple Comparative View of Discrimination* (for short, the Simple View): X discriminates against Y only if
> (1) there is some relevant comparator, Z, different from Y such that X treats Y worse than Z; and
> (2) there is no good reason to treat Y worse than Z.[3]

I label this view the *Simple* View for reasons that will become apparent in section 8.2. For now, I draw the attention to three preliminary points. First, the Simple View—like most of the more complicated views that I discuss below—purports to state a necessary condition of discrimination. Hence, one could reject the Simple View and think that propositions (1) and (2) are jointly sufficient for discrimination.[4] Also, the Simple View pertains to what discrimination is, not to what makes discrimination wrong or what makes some forms of discrimination worse than others. Hence, it is no objection to the Simple View, e.g., that it does not provide any account of why some forms of discrimination are more morally objectionable than others. Third, it is a tricky question, determining whether there is no good reason to treat Y worse than Z. But nothing in the present discussion hangs on this, so readers are encouraged to read what follows with their own favorite account of when there is no good reason for differential treatment in mind.

Klem Thomsen, "Direct Discrimination," in *The Routledge Handbook of the Ethics of Discrimination*, ed. Kasper Lippert-Rasmussen (Abingdon: Routledge, 2018), 19–29, at 21.

[2] Olmstead v. L.C., 527 U.S. 581 (1999), at 611 (quoting Justice Thomas).
[3] For discussions of this view, see Deborah Hellman, "Two Concepts of Discrimination," *Virginia Law Review* 102, no. 4 (2016): 895–952, esp. 900–909; Denise Réaume, "Comparing Theories of Sex Discrimination: The Role of Comparison," *Oxford Journal of Legal Studies* 25, no. 3 (2005): 547–564; Timothy Macklem, *Beyond Comparison: Sex and Discrimination* (Cambridge: Cambridge University Press, 2003).
[4] Tarunabh Khaitan holds a view along these lines—see his *A Theory of Discrimination Law* (Oxford: Oxford University Press, 2015), 34–35, 71. However, his concern is what counts as discrimination from the point of view of law, whereas my main concern is with the folk concept of discrimination.

134 WORKING AS EQUALS

While the Simple View has some intuitive appeal, it is false.[5] In some cases, we are justified in thinking that a certain employee is discriminated against (e.g., a pregnant employee who is sacked on account of her pregnancy) even if we are uncertain about whether there is a comparator because we are uncertain who the better-treated comparator could be: a pregnant man? or a nonpregnant person?[6] Or "men otherwise similarly situated in their capacity or incapacity to work"?[7] This is not what one would expect if discrimination cannot take place in the absence of a relevant comparator being treated more favorably.

It matters whether the Simple View is correct. Practically, it makes a difference to the argumentative burden that complainants about discrimination have to bear at courts. Theoretically, the Simple View is closely connected with egalitarian accounts of what makes discrimination wrong. As Jonker nicely puts it: "By rejecting the comparative test we lose our grip on the intuitive thought that discrimination is centrally about unequal treatment."[8] Accordingly, if we reject the Simple View, perhaps we need to account for the wrongness of discrimination in terms of other values, e.g., freedom, welfare, (non-inequality-involving) disrespect, or desert.

The ideal of equality can be specified in many different ways. Here I focus on the ideal of equality as understood by relational egalitarians:

Justice requires that, for any X and any Y, X and Y relate as equals. X and Y relate as equals if and only if

(3) X and Y treat one another as equals;

(4) X and Y regard one another as equals.[9]

---

[5] Suzanne Goldberg, "Discrimination by Comparison," *Yale Law Journal* 120, no. 4 (2011): 728–812; Julian Jonker, "Beyond the Comparative Test for Discrimination," *Analysis* 79, no. 2 (2018): 206–214; Khaitan, *Theory of Discrimination Law*, 72–73.

[6] Geduldig v. Aiello, 417 U.S. 484 (1974), at 496 n. 20; Goldberg, "Discrimination by Comparison," 761–764.

[7] Neil S. Siegel and Reva B. Siegel, "Struck by Stereotype: Ruth Bader Ginsburg on Pregnancy Discrimination and Sex Discrimination," *Duke Law Journal* 59, no. 4 (2010): 771–798, at 773; Paul Lewis, "Pregnant Workers and Sex Discrimination: The Limits of Purposive Non-comparative Methodology," *International Journal of Comparative Labour Law and Industrial Relations* 16, no. 1 (2000): 55–69; J. G. Greenberg, "The Pregnancy Discrimination Act: Legitimating Discrimination against Pregnant Women in the Workforce," *Maine Law Review* 50, no. 2 (1998): 225–254; S. J. Kenney, "Pregnancy Discrimination: Toward Substantive Equality," *Wisconsin Women's Law Journal* 10, no. 1 (1995): 351–402.

[8] Jonker, "Beyond the Comparative Test," 213.

[9] Kasper Lippert-Rasmussen, *Relational Egalitarianism: Living as Equals* (Cambridge: Cambridge University Press, 2018), 71; see also Elizabeth Anderson, "The Fundamental Disagreement between Luck Egalitarians and Relational Egalitarians," *Canadian Journal of Philosophy*, supplementary vol. 36 (2010): 1–23; Elizabeth Anderson, "What Is the Point of Equality?," *Ethics* 109, no. 2 (1999): 287–337; Samuel Scheffler, "The Practice of Equality," in *Social Equality: On What It Means to Be Equals*,

As defined here, relational egalitarianism has both a behavioral, i.e., proposition (3), and an attitudinal component, i.e., proposition (4). One can treat someone as an equal even if one does not regard this person as such, e.g., for opportunistic reasons one treats them better than one thinks they deserve in view of their assumed lower moral status. And one can fail to treat someone as an equal, even if one regards them as such, e.g., because of peer pressure one refrains from treating certain people with the respect and concern one thinks they are entitled to qua persons.

The following argument—call it the Strong Connection Argument—indicates that there is a strong connection between discrimination, on the one hand, and violations of the requirements of relational egalitarian justice, on the other hand:

(5) If X discriminates against Y, then there is some Z such that X treats Y worse than Z for no good reason.
(6) If X treats Y worse than Z for no good reason, then X does not treat Y as an equal to Z.
(7) If X does not treat Y as an equal to Z, then X violates the ideal of relational equality.
(8) Thus, if X discriminates against Y, then X violates the ideal of relational equality.

Premise (5) follows from the Simple View, and premise (7) from the definition of relational egalitarian justice. Premise (6) seems plausible. It only states a sufficient condition of not treating as an equal. Moreover, treating unequally does not entail treating as unequals, e.g., if X benefits Y only, because the alternative is to benefit no one, this might not be a case of treating as unequals. Finally, in contexts involving discrimination, e.g., employment or promotion, typically treating members of a social salient group better than others for no good reason is regarded as not treating as an equal.

The conclusion of the Strong Connection Argument coheres nicely with a central selling point of relational egalitarianism, i.e., that there are social injustices, which cannot be adequately captured within the constraints of a

---

ed. Carina Fourie, Fabian Schuppert, and Ivo Wallimann-Helmer (Oxford: Oxford University Press, 2015), 21–44; Samuel Scheffler, "What Is Egalitarianism?," *Philosophy & Public Affairs* 31, no. 1 (2003): 5–39.

136 WORKING AS EQUALS

distributive approach to justice.[10] The injustice of discrimination is one of those. Of course, most forms of unjust discrimination do result in distributive inequalities, which are deemed unjust by plausible accounts of distributive justice. However, some intuitively unjust forms of discrimination, e.g., racial discrimination against members of a racial minority, whose members are unjustly privileged in terms of whatever is the distribuendum of distributive justice, might not. However, according to the Strong Connection Argument, they violate the ideal of relational equality.

Section 8.2 distinguishes between different comparative views and uses the Simple View as a springboard to propose a particularly plausible version, i.e., the complex, amended view. Section 8.3 assesses three objections to comparative views. Sections 8.4 considers how relational egalitarian accounts need to be reformulated in the light of wrongful discrimination, which does not involve any individual being treated worse than others. The chapter's main claims are that such discrimination—in the workplace as well as elsewhere— is indeed possible and that this implies that relational egalitarianism is not just about relating to other individuals as equals. However, discrimination is comparative in some, albeit more complicated, way than the Simple View suggests.

8.2. The Simple and Other Comparative Views

The Simple View implies that the relevant comparator has to be different, actual persons.[11] However, there is an amended version of this view, according to which the relevant comparator need not be a *different* actual person. Consider:

> *The Ageist Employer:* Imagine a world in which everyone dies at their seventieth birthday—the very same day they retire. Suppose that an employer uniformly treats employees forty-five years old and older better than younger employees due to stereotypes about younger people. Suppose all employees are hired at the age of twenty and work in the company until they retire. As the scenario is set out, no employee is treated worse than any other employee. Yet surely the employer engages in age discrimination.

[10] Anderson, "What Is the Point," 295–302, 317.
[11] Cf. Elizabeth Anderson, "Recent Thinking about Sexual Harassment: A Review Essay," *Philosophy & Public Affairs* 34 (2006): 284–311, at 306.

TREATING SOME EMPLOYEES WORSE THAN OTHERS 137

Per the Simple View, this employer discriminates based on age, even if all employees have been treated the same—promoted, paid well etc. during the time they were senior, and not promoted, paid well etc. during the time they were junior. Hence, the Simple View is false and, hence, discrimination is not about—or at least not all about—treating different individuals differently. (You might object that the Simple View implies that at no point in their lives must different individuals be treated differently. I turn to this matter below.)

To accommodate the Ageist Employer, we might suggest the following:

The Amended Comparative View: X discriminates against Y if
  (9) there is some relevant property F such that X treats Y worse when Y has F than when Y does not have F, and
  (10) there is no good reason to treat Y worse when Y has F than when Y has not.[12]

This view states a sufficient condition for discrimination. Accordingly, if it is true, then the Simple View is false. Differential treatment of one and the same person is often ignored due to the fact that, in many central discrimination cases, e.g., race and sex discrimination cases, the property in virtue of which people are discriminated against is such that if people have it at any particular time, they have it at all times.

Assuming these considerations are sound, we might propose:

The Actualist View: X discriminates against Y only if
  (11) there is some relevant Z such that X treats Y worse than Z, and
  (12) there is no good reason to treat Y worse than Z, *or*
  (13) there is some relevant property F such that X treats Y worse when Y has F than when Y does not have F, and
  (14) there is no good reason to treat Y worse when Y has F than when Y has not.

The Actualist View accommodates the case of the Ageist Employer, but it is false. Consider:

---

[12] During the time at which X does not have F, X discriminates *in favor of* Y.

138   WORKING AS EQUALS

The No-Female-Promotions Employer: Jack has a small company and only employs women (who are women at all times).[13] As a result of some statistical fluke, and that only, only women have ever applied for job openings in the company. Jack refuses to promote any of them. Had he had a different and male employee of the same caliber as his female employees, he would happily have promoted this person.[14]

The fact that Jack treats his female employees worse than he would treat his male employees, if he had any, suffices to show that he discriminates against female employees. Hence, the Actualist View is false.[15] A modified version of the No-Female-Promotions Employer supports the same claim:

Counterfactual Misogynism: Brenda, like her female colleagues, is not promoted. If she, or any of her fellow employees—all of whom are women—were to change sex, they would be promoted. Hence, it is true of each female employee that were she to become male instead, the employer would have treated her better. However, were the employer to hire additional otherwise relevantly similar employees who were men or had the employer hired male employees instead of some of the employer's present female employees, he would have treated these additional or alternative employees no differently than he treats his present female employees.

This case raises two questions. First, is it really possible and, second, assuming it is, does it involve discrimination? The correct answer to the first question is affirmative. Suppose that there is a Frankfurtian counterfactual intervener, i.e., a super-neuroscientist who has implanted a chip in the employer's brain that enables the neuroscientist to monitor the employer's brain and intervene should the employer be about to form an intention the neuroscientist does not like, present.[16] The counterfactual intervener would

---

[13] Like the other examples I use in this chapter, I do not intend to make or implicitly convey any view about the nature of gender, age, sexuality, race, etc. (though I realize that it is difficult not to). I use the examples solely to make conceptual points about the nature of discrimination. Readers who think my text conveys dubious views on these matters should (in addition to identifying and criticizing these) consider if these are inessential to my arguments regarding whether discrimination is comparative.

[14] "In one illustrative case, all of the relevant secretaries were female, which led the Second Circuit to reject a secretary's sex discrimination case because no comparator existed" (Goldberg, "Discrimination by Comparison," 760).

[15] EU directives on discrimination refer to counterfactual comparators (Council Directive 2000/43/EC, art. 2, 2000 O.J. (L 180) 22, 24; see also Goldberg, "Discrimination by Comparison," 805–806).

[16] Harry Frankfurt, *The Importance of What We Care About* (Cambridge: Cambridge University Press, 1988), 1–10.

TREATING SOME EMPLOYEES WORSE THAN OTHERS   139

have prevented the employer from treating different or additional employees any differently than how the employer treats his female employees. However, the counterfactual intervener has no power to prevent the employer from treating female employees who change their sex better than the employer presently treats them. In response to the second question, I contend that, clearly, this employer engages in sex discrimination. He refuses to promote Brenda, but would happily have done so had she been (or become) a man. Also, it is hard to see how counterfactual misogynism could be any different from No-Female-Promotions Employer discrimination-wise.[17]

If one accepts the reasoning so far, one might accept:

The Complex View: X discriminates against Y only if
(15) there is *or could be* some relevant Z (call "Z" the relevant comparator) such that X treats *or would treat* Y worse than Z, *and*
(16) there is no good reason to treat Y worse than Z, *or*
(17) there is some relevant property F such that X treats Y worse when Y has F than when Y does not have F *or such that X has F and X would have treated Y better if Y did not have F*, and
(18) there is no good reason to treat Y worse when Y has F than when Y has not.

This view accommodates all of the cases discussed so far. Propositions (15) and (16) enable it to accommodate No-Female-Promotions Employer and premises (17) and (18) to accommodate Counterfactual Misogynism. Unfortunately, we need to introduce one additional complexity. Consider:

Actual Sequence Misogynism: This case is identical to counterfactual misogynism except for the following two facts. First, the Frankfurtian counterfactual intervener would have prevented the employer from treating any employee who changed her gender to become male instead better. Second, the motivating reason behind the employer's treating his female employees badly is, or is rooted in, a negative, comparative attitude toward women, e.g., the belief that, unlike men, women ought not to occupy senior positions or a desire not to have to interact with women in senior positions.

---

[17] See also Jonker, "Beyond the Comparative Test," 207 on the counterfactual test.

140   WORKING AS EQUALS

What is special about this employer is that there is no actual employee who, during a time at which he is a male employee (which might be all the time), is treated better than the employer's present female employees. Nor is it the case—thanks to the now even more powerful Frankfurtian counterfactual intervener—that the employer would have treated employees who, at some period of time during their employment, are men better during that period of time. Yet, intuitively, this employer is sex-discriminating against his female employees on account of the motivational state from which he acts. He is what we might call an actual sequence discriminator. When individuals have discriminating attitudes toward members of certain groups, they will often discriminate against actual people belonging to this group, or it will often be true that, had they interacted with such people, they would have discriminated against them. Frankfurtian counterfactual interveners shows why this is not always the case. To support this view, compare actual sequence misogynism with an otherwise identical case in which the counterfactual intervener is absent. In my view, it is hard to see how this difference, which has nothing to do with how the putative discriminator treats the putative discriminatee or with the motivational state of the discriminator, can imply that only the former case is a case of discrimination. The actual sequence misogynist is not just someone who simply is prejudiced, even hostile to, women. He acts on those motivational states and refuses to promote any of his female employees.

If you accept my assessment of actual sequence misogynism, perhaps you should accept

The Amended Complex View: X discriminates against Y only if

(19) X discriminates against Y on the Complex View, *or*[18]

(20) X treats Y badly in some way because X holds a certain negative comparative attitude toward those with property F and Y has property F.[19]

---

[18] Proposition (19) is not redundant given proposition (20). It might be true both that X treats Y badly without having any particular, negative attitude toward Y and that X would treat a relevant comparator better if X interacted with such a comparator, e.g., because X would then form a positive attitude toward the comparator.

[19] Instead of accepting proposition (20), one might respond by proposing a more sophisticated counterfactual condition; e.g., instead of proposition (15) one might propose

(15*) there is *or could be* some relevant Z such that, in the absence of any counterfactual intervener, X treats *or would treat* Y worse than Z.

I suspect, however, that this condition might be vulnerable to counterexamples as well and that, in any case, acknowledging this possibility of such more sophisticated counterfactual conditions does not threaten my main argument below.

An attitude is a negative, comparative view directed against members of a certain group in the sense relevant to proposition (20) only if it involves some kind of negative comparison between members of that group and members of other groups. This negative comparison, which is internal to the content of an attitude, either the motivational state itself or some other state of the discriminator that the motivational state is rooted in, is what justifies regarding the Amended Complex View as a comparative view, broadly speaking.[20]

The Amended Complex View strikes me as defensible in the light of widely shared intuitions about when something is discriminatory.[21] This concludes the conceptual groundwork of this chapter.

8.3. Common Challenges to Comparative Views

In this section, I address four challenges to comparative views generally and specifically assess whether they defeat the Amended Complex View. First, sometimes we cannot apply a narrowly comparative view because there is no relevant comparator; e.g., it might be that there is no one whose treatment we can compare to that which pregnant women are subjected to in order to determine whether they have been discriminated against.[22] Hence, by default, a case which intuitively counts as discrimination does not count as such on narrowly comparative views. Call this the *lack of relevant comparator objection*.

While this objection might have force against the Actualist View, it has no force against the Amended Complex View. For all such putative problematic cases, we can either point to relevant counterfactual comparators or point

---

[20] Katherine M. Franke, "What's Wrong with Sexual Harassment?," *Stanford Law Review* 49, no. 4 (1997): 691–772, at 696.

[21] This is not to deny that proposition (20) needs to be specified further. First, "because" needs to be specified to avoid a problem of deviant, nondiscrimination involving causal chains. To borrow an illustration from Julian Jonker and Grant Rozeboom: Suppose an employer X has certain discriminatory views about Y, and decides to hire an antidiscrimination trainer. As a causal result of this costly hiring, X treats all employees, Y included, badly; e.g., X delays due pay increases. Presumably, we want to specify "because" in such a way that proposition (20) is not satisfied in this case, which, intuitively, does not seem to be a case of discrimination against Y. Second, I understand "treating badly" in a noncomparative way such that X can treat Y badly independently of any truth about how a relevant comparator would be treated better. One way to go here would be to offer a list of treatments that are bad in this way, e.g., refusing to promote an obviously qualified employee for a vacant position despite the absence of any other candidate.

[22] Narrowly comparative views imply that discrimination requires an actual or hypothetical comparator. Broadly comparative views such as the Amended Complex View do not have this implication.

142 WORKING AS EQUALS

to how the discriminator's adverse treatment of the putative discriminatee is rooted in negative comparative attitudes. This certainly is the case when it comes to pregnant women, e.g., plausibly such discrimination is rooted in the negative, comparative attitude that, unlike men, women ought not to continue working when expecting to have a child or the like.

The second problem is the *genus misidentification objection*, i.e., there are cases which do qualify as cases of discrimination, but which comparative views do not classify as such, or cases which are not cases of discrimination, but which the comparative view does classify as such.[23] Jonker illustrates this problem in its first version as follows:

> *Cheerleader.* B joins a cheerleading squad because it is a chance to show off her gymnastic ability and to support her favourite sport. But B discovers that she is required to do more than dance on field. Her dress, appearance, behaviour and social ties are all strictly controlled, on field and off field.[24]

Jonker notes—correctly in my opinion—that this case is difficult for the Actualist View. He then considers embracing a counterfactual version of the comparative view:

> Would a male cheerleader have been treated differently? The problem with this response is intimately linked to the nature of the discrimination complained of. The closest possible world in which our cheerleading squad hires men is one in which their attitudes to women are quite different. . . . We can perhaps conceive of a world in which the attitudes remain the same, but men find themselves—by accident or by external imposition—on the squad. In such circumstances, the comparative test would fail if these men were treated in the same way as the female cheerleaders.[25]

In the first counterfactual situation—the one with quite different, presumably nonsexist attitudes to women—plausibly a male member of a cheerleading squad would be treated better than B in Cheerleader. Hence, the relevant comparative views deliver the right results in this case. In the second counterfactual situation—the one with similar attitudes to women—the male

---

[23] See Goldberg, "Discrimination by Comparison," 773, on "merely benign variation in the workplace."

[24] Jonker, "Beyond the Comparative Test," 207–208.

[25] Jonker, "Beyond the Comparative Test," 208.

cheerleader would—so Jonker plausibly posits—be treated no better and, accordingly, the comparative views misclassify the case as one that does not involve discrimination. However, I do not see why this fact is a problem for counterfactual comparative views given that there are other relevant counterfactual situations which enable them to correctly classify the case as a case of discrimination. In any case, the Amended Complex View, which is not the comparative view which Jonker criticizes, is consistent with it being a case of discrimination. The treatment to which B is subjected is rooted in comparative, negative attitudes toward women and, thus, premise (20) of this view is satisfied.

This takes us to the third problem, which I shall call the *species misclassification objection*, i.e., the objection that there are cases of discrimination of a particular species which comparative views fail to identify as such. Jonker provides a clear objection of this kind, appealing to the following case: "*Mixed Marriage.* C, a white man married to a black woman, is fired from his job as a basketball coach because his white employer objects to his marriage."[26] This is a case of antiblack racial discrimination even if the (direct) discriminatee (or victim, at least) is white, and yet it is not clear what sort of comparison that one should apply on comparative views to classify it as such. Friends of comparative views might reformulate the relevant comparison in different ways. However:

> The problem with all of these reformulations is that they misidentify the real source of the mistreatment in each case. An employer who fires a white man for his marriage to a black woman does differentiate between white men in interracial relationships and white men in intraracial relationships. We can say that differential treatment of this sort amounts to discrimination; and if we had in mind a non-moralized conception of discrimination, we could add that discrimination on this basis is wrong. Yet having said all of this we will have missed an important feature of the discrimination: that it is a variety of racial discrimination, which we take to have special moral significance in our social context.[27]

Unlike the genus misclassification objection, the species misclassification objection does not assert that comparative views fail to classify cases of

---

[26] Jonker, "Beyond the Comparative Test," 209.
[27] Jonker, "Beyond the Comparative Test," 210.

144 WORKING AS EQUALS

discrimination as such. Rather, it claims that while comparative views might succeed in doing so, they fail to classify correctly what type of discrimination Mixed Marriage and similar cases involve, i.e., antiblack racial discrimination.

Mixed Marriage is a case of antiblack racial discrimination even if the direct victim is a white male. This is not problematic; e.g., indisputably in some cases male applicants whose names are mistaken for female names are the direct victims of an employer's sexist discriminatory hiring practices. However, it is unclear that Mixed Marriage shows that comparative views fail to do anything they should do. If all comparative views are supposed to do is to tell us *whether* a certain case constitutes a case of direct discrimination, then showing that they do not tell us *which form* of discrimination we are dealing with is not showing that they fail to do anything that they are meant to do and, thus, in a certain sense is no reason to reject the test. Similarly, comparative views as articulated here fail when understood as stating a necessary condition of indirect discrimination. However, that is not a criticism against comparative views, since they are intended as stating a view on the necessary conditions of *direct* discrimination.

In response, it might be said that what we are interested in is not just a view about *when* something counts as discrimination. We are also interested in developing a view about *what sort* of discrimination instances of discrimination are. If comparative views do not do that, this is not a reason to reject them as false, but it is a reason to criticize them for being seriously incomplete. But the obvious response then would be to supplement comparative views of *when* discrimination takes place with comparative views about *what sort* of discrimination takes place, e.g.:

The Amended Complex View of Discrimination Type: X discriminates racially against Y if

(21) there is or could be some relevant Z from a different racial category such that X treats or would treat Y worse than Z, and

(22) there is no good reason to treat Y worse than Z, *or*

(23) X treats Y worse when Y has the property of falling under a certain racial category than when Y does not or if Y were not to do so, and[28]

(24) there is no good reason to treat Y worse when Y has F than when Y has not, *or*

---

[28] Recall footnote 13.

(25) X treats Y badly in some way because X holds a certain negative comparative attitude toward people falling under the racial category under which Y falls or toward members of a certain racial groups with members of which Y associates.[29]

Due to premise (25), the Amended Complex View of discrimination type classifies Mixed Marriage as a case of antiblack racial discrimination, since it is because the discriminator in Mixed Marriage holds certain negative comparative attitudes toward black people that he fires the coach. No doubt, the view might nevertheless need refinement. But I see no reason to think that something similar would not be the case when it comes to noncomparative views on what type of discrimination is involved in associational discrimination.

Finally, some might note that the cases that motivate the introduction of the relevant complexities in the complex, amended view are far removed from real-life cases of morally objectionable discrimination of the sort that should concern us the most, given that we want to mitigate or eliminate wrongful discrimination. This might lead some to ask as follows: What do we gain by modifying the Simple View to allow us to claim that, say, cases involving Frankfurtian counterfactual interveners are cases of discrimination, even if no individual is being treated worse than any other individual? Some might go further and say that focusing on such rarefied cases of discrimination as those involved in my (farfetched) examples involves the risk of obscuring the more urgent moral issues raised by ordinary real-life cases of discrimination; e.g., nothing in the Amended Complex View speaks to the morally relevant differences between subordination-reproducing discrimination, on the one hand, and non-subordination-reproducing discrimination, on the other.[30]

In response to the first part of this challenge, I note, first, that section 8.2 uncovers what we mean by discrimination—the modifications of the Simple View that I propose are intended to fit the contours of our folk concept of discrimination. Admittedly, this aim does not prevent us from assessing possible revisions of our folk concept. However, one drawback of the specific motivation for revising it such that my hypothetical examples no longer

---

[29] Essentially the same argument can be made with regard to identity-policing-based discrimination.

[30] See, for instance, Charles W. Mills, "'Ideal Theory' as Ideology," Hypatia 20, no. 3 (2005): 166–172.

146   WORKING AS EQUALS

count as discrimination is that, on some accounts of the wrongness of discrimination, they involve the same wrong as ordinary, real-life cases of discrimination, e.g., disrespect of the discriminatee.[31] In response to the second part of the fourth challenge, it is a tricky, empirical question as to exactly what effects—good or bad—members of a specialized audience focusing on a theoretically important, but practically peripheral, issue have on the wider society. In order to be forceful, the present challenge must be backed up with a least some empirical evidence. Also, I want to preempt the worry about the potentially obscuring effects of my focus in this chapter by noting, first, that the amended, complex account expands the range of cases that can count as wrongful discrimination relative to the Simple View (see also next section) and, second, that these accounts are not accounts of what makes discrimination wrong. I conclude that none of the four challenges above is a good reason to reject the Amended Complex View.

8.4. Relational Equality

Let us now return to the Strong Connection Argument. On what I shall label the straightforward understanding of the ideal of relational equality, that ideal is about relating to different individuals as equals. On this understanding, the complex, amended view renders the Strong Connection Argument problematic. We can see this by noting that either the comparator is a different individual (actual or possible) or not. If the former, then premise (7) above looks unimpeachable. However, premise (5) is then false. Take the age discrimination scenario that I described above. Differential treatment that satisfies this view counts as discrimination. Yet such discrimination can take place even if there is no individual who is being treated worse than any other individual. True, at any given moment there are individuals who are being treated worse than other individuals. But whether or not that gives rise to a moral complaint—after all, there are other moments of time where these individuals are being treated better than those individuals who at the relevant moments of time are being treated less well—it does not seem to give rise to the complaint that some individuals are not being treated as equals given that, over the course of their lives, all individuals are being treated

---

[31] Larry Alexander, "What Makes Wrongful Discrimination Wrong? Biases, Preferences, Stereotypes, and Proxies," *University of Pennsylvania Law Review* 141 (1992): 149–219; Eidelson, *Discrimination*.

exactly the same way. Hence, on the assumption that the relevant comparator must be a different individual, the Strong Connection Argument fails. This implication is one that relational egalitarian should want to avoid in view of the fact that wrongful discrimination is one of those social injustices with which one expects the ideal of relational equality to clash. Hence, a natural move is to accept that the relevant comparator need not be a different person, but might be the same person with different properties.

If the relevant comparator can be both different individuals or the same individual with different properties, premise (5) looks more secure, though this premise needs to be tweaked to accommodate cases where the discriminator would in fact treat other individuals or the same individual with different properties no differently (recall Actual Sequence Misogynism). More interesting here is that on the present, liberal interpretation, premise (7) looks problematic. For if the relevant comparator is the same individual with different properties, it is unclear that the individual is not being treated as an equal. Admittedly, of any person, it is true that her older self is being treated worse than her younger self. However, these are both phases in one and the same person's life. This implication is particularly problematic in the light of the argument in the previous section, since discrimination in such cases does look as if relational egalitarianism is supposed to capture the sort of disrespect they involve.

In view of this dilemma, the best response might be to accept that one can discriminate against someone in a way which is disrespectful of that person even if there is no other person such that the discriminator would treat that person better and even if one would not treat that person better if she had different properties of the relevant kind. Since disrespectful discrimination is one core form of injustice that relational egalitarianism should accommodate, we must revise our understanding of what it is to relate as equals in such a way that the following otherwise appealing inference is invalid:

(28) If X and Y do not relate as equals, then they relate as superior individuals to inferior individuals.

(29) People do not relate as superior individuals to inferior individuals in cases where they relate to one another as if their standing is the same.

(30) Hence, people relate as equals in cases where they relate to one another as if their standing is the same.

148   WORKING AS EQUALS

To relate as equals, it is not enough to relate to one another as individuals with an equal standing; i.e., premise (28) is false. It is also required that one relate to one as another as if having certain properties, e.g., gender, race, or age, makes no difference to one's standing at the time at which one has these properties.[32] This aspect of relational egalitarianism has been undertheorized, and in the remaining part of this section, I explore some of its ramifications.

To support the undertheorization claim, consider Elizabeth Anderson's characterization of relational equality and its competing distributive egalitarian sibling, distributive equality:[33]

> The two camps disagree about how to conceive of equality: as an equal distribution of non-relational goods among individuals, or as a kind of social relation between persons—an equality of authority, status, or standing. . . . Relational egalitarians claim that inequality is unjust when it disadvantages people: when it reflects, embodies, or causes inequality of authority, status, or standing. This is the thought expressed in the general form of Rawls's difference principle, which requires that "social and economic inequalities are to be arranged so that they are . . . reasonably expected to be to everyone's advantage." This principle endorses many Pareto-improving deviations from equality.

Rawls famously thought that utilitarians ignore the significance of the separateness of persons and, as an aspect thereof, ascribe no significance to the unity of the lives of single persons. The point here is that core commitments of relational egalitarians contradict the thought which Anderson claims informs Rawls's difference principle. Consider a case where "inequality of authority, status, or standing," e.g., taking-turns ageism where everyone turns old and is then subjected to anti-old-people ageism, is "reasonably expected to be to everyone's advantage." This is highly unrealistic, but it is possible. Under such a situation, there would be no one who would have a complaint based on the thought, according to Anderson, informing Rawls's difference principle: "There can be no injustice without an injury to someone's interests."[34] Yet relational egalitarians find taking-turns ageism

---

[32] One important issue here is that if by "standing" we have something else in mind than the moral worth of persons, then, for some properties, many relational egalitarians would acknowledge that certain properties make a difference to one's standing.

[33] Anderson, "The Fundamental Disagreement," 1–2.

[34] Anderson, "The Fundamental Disagreement," 5; see also her remarks on Salieri in ibid., 8.

unjust.[35] Hence, on their view there can be injustice even if there is no injury to anyone's interests.

Could Anderson say that even though, in the scenario described, taking-turns ageism promotes everyone's interests overall, it harms specific interests of theirs, e.g., their interest in being related to as an equal when old? She could, but not without putting Rawls's justification of inequality of primary goods into question. For almost any incentive-based inequality there will be some (groups) who have a specific interest which the scheme harms, e.g., their interest in occupying the positions that more talented people will be attracted to occupy given inequality-producing incentives is set back, even if, all things considered, their interests are promoted by the inequality-producing incentive scheme.

Anderson mentions the "freedom" of gays and lesbians "to appear in public as who they are, without shame or fear of violence, the right to get married and enjoy benefits of marriage, to adopt and retain custody of children" as examples of ambitions reflecting relational egalitarian concerns.[36] A plausible form of relational egalitarianism must embrace these ambitions. Given how the world is, realizing them can be captured under the heading of creating a "community in which people stand in relations of equality to others."[37] However, in a world where it is not the case that some people are gays and lesbians and others are neither, but all of us are one at some point in our lives and the other at other times in our lives, the pertinent ambition is not adequately characterized as one in which individuals stand in relations of equality to one another. Rather, what relational egalitarians want is to create a community in which people stand in relations of equality to others *and* no one is related to as if their being gay or lesbian somehow gives them a lower standing during the times in their lives when they are so.

Why not simply say that relational egalitarians want to create a "community in which people at any given time stand in relations of equality to one another"? I do not think that will do either. Consider a society in which all old people are women and young people are men. Suppose this society is

---

[35] Or: at least they should if they object to ageism. See also Juliana Bidadanure, "Making Sense of Age-Group Justice: A Time for Relational Equality?," *Politics, Philosophy & Economics* 15, no. 3 (2016): 234-260.

[36] Anderson, "What Is the Point," 288.

[37] Anderson, "What Is the Point," 289. Many of the examples of the hierarchies "of human beings ranked according to intrinsic worth" that Anderson offers as illustrations of the "inegalitarian systems" are examples of inequalities where people do not change places at all, or only in very few cases, e.g., hierarchies of race, sex, nationality, caste, class, or genetic endowment; see "What Is the Point," 312-313.

150 WORKING AS EQUALS

sexist and anti-young-people ageist. There is a sense in which this might be a community in which people stand in relations of equality to others at any given moment.[38] Yet it is objectionable from the point of view of relational egalitarianism.

Turning now to another influential relational egalitarian's work—that of Samuel Scheffler—he notes that the "real motivation for egalitarianism . . . lies in a commitment to a certain ideal of society, a conviction that members of society should relate to one another on a footing of equality."[39] This ideal is a complex one, according to Scheffler, and "draws on values other than equality itself," e.g., mutual respect. It does, however, contain a distinctively egalitarian component, i.e., the egalitarian deliberative constraint:

> In a relationship that is conducted on a footing of equality, each person accepts that the other person's equally important interests . . . should play an equally significant role in influencing decisions made within the context of the relationship. Moreover, each person has a normally effective disposition to treat the other's interests accordingly. If you and I have an egalitarian relationship, then I have a standing disposition to treat your strong interests as playing just as significant a role as mine in constraining our decisions and influencing what we will do. And you have a reciprocal disposition with regard to my interests. In addition, both of us normally act on these dispositions. This means that each of our equally important interests constrains our joint decisions to the same extent.[40]

Scheffler notes that "the egalitarian deliberative constraint is best understood diachronically rather than synchronically. The point is not that each decision taken individually must give equal weight to the comparably important interests of each party. . . . The point is rather that each person's interests should play an equally significant role in determining the decisions they make over the course of the relationship."[41] This makes good sense. However, in the light of my example of a society of old women and young men discrimination, we can see that a plausible egalitarian deliberative constraint is not just about treating the interests of different individuals equally, whether

---

[38] There is also a sense of relating as equals in which this is not a society of equals. That sense is captured by premise (25) in section 8.3.

[39] Scheffler, "The Practice of Equality," 22.

[40] Scheffler, "The Practice of Equality," 25; for the societal version of this constraint, see ibid., 35–36.

[41] Scheffler, "The Practice of Equality," 26.

TREATING SOME EMPLOYEES WORSE THAN OTHERS   151

synchronically or diachronically. It is also about not discounting interests of certain kinds or on certain grounds, e.g., ageist and sexist grounds, whether or not that involves treating the interests of different individuals unequally.

I believe Scheffler would not want to resist this. However, one might say that what this shows is that discounting interests of certain kinds or on certain grounds—the sort of kinds and grounds that are at stake in the examples I have offered—is disrespectful and, thus, clashes with the ideal of mutual respect which Scheffler submits informs the relational egalitarian ideal.[42] Perhaps that is the right thing to say here, but if it is, then the egalitarian deliberative constraint is not a distinctively egalitarian component of that ideal that, unlike other components, does not draw on values other than equality—even that component can only be adequately specified in the light of such nonegalitarian values.

Alternatively, it might be pointed out that, according to Scheffler, the primary concerns of people who want to relate to one another as equals is "with their attitudes toward one another and with how seriously each takes the interests of the other in contexts of deliberation and decision."[43] Consider again the situation of a sexist, anti-young-people ageist society in which all women are old and all men young. In one sense, people in this society might take others' interests equally seriously; e.g., an old woman might think that the interests of a young man should constrain their collective decisions as much as her own, because even though they should be discounted because she is a woman, their significance is boosted to an equal degree because she is old. In another sense, however, it might be said that people do not take the "interests of others" equally seriously because doing that involves a certain modal robustness; e.g., the old woman should not think that, had she been a young man instead, "her" interests would have been more constraining of their collective decisions.

8.5. Conclusion

I have argued that the Simple View, i.e., that discrimination requires better treatment of a relevant comparator, is false. In its stead I have canvassed the

---

[42] Perhaps his fourth and fifth complication also speaks to this question (Scheffler, "The Practice of Equality," 28–30).
[43] Scheffler, "The Practice of Equality," 34.

Amended Complex View. This view still implies that discrimination is comparative, broadly speaking, though in a much more complex way than the Simple View entails. Specifically, it implies that discrimination does not rest on the postulation of a relevant comparator. The Amended Complex View also raises the question of whether there are unjust forms of discrimination that cannot be accommodated within standard accounts of the ideal of relational equality, because they do not involve some individuals being treated as being of lesser worth than others. In response to this problem, I have suggested that, actually, it is misleading to say that respect and relational egalitarianism are all about different individuals relating as equals. Undoubtedly, it is also about that. However, the ideal of relational egalitarianism must be reformulated to account for cases of inegalitarian treatment of individuals that do not involve treating some individuals worse than others. Bad treatment on the basis of comparative attitudes can be disrespectful and inegalitarian even if everyone is treated the same all the time.

9

A Cooperative Paradigm of Employment

Sabine Tsuruda

9.1. Introduction

The employment relation traditionally has a hierarchical authority structure at its "heart."[1] Employment contracts are often, and perhaps unavoidably, incomplete.[2] It can be hard to specify in advance what a given job will require, and workplaces may need to evolve in ways that are difficult to predict at the time an employment relationship is formed. Rather than vest authority over how an employment relationship develops in employees and employers alike, the law traditionally vests such authority in the employer. An employee, for instance, is normally under a legal duty to "obey" and comply with the employer's unilateral determination of matters such as how a job is to be performed and what the ultimate direction of the enterprise will be.[3]

---

[1] *Williston on Contracts*, vol. 19, 4th ed. (Minnesota: West Group, 2018), § 54:23.

[2] See Hugh Collins, *Employment Law* (Oxford: Clarendon Law Series, 2012), 9–12.

[3] See *Williston on Contracts*, § 54:23; Mair v. Southern Minn. Broadcasting Co., 32 N.W.2d 177, 178 (Min. 1948) ("The defendant, when contracting with plaintiff, did not abdicate his right to manage his own business; nor did he surrender his position as owner of the farm. . . . He still retained the right to control his own affairs in his own way, and any behavior of his servant in opposition or in violation of his reasonable orders and commands amounted to insubordination, which has always been held sufficient ground for the discharge of a servant."). This chapter uses the duty of obedience as its primary example of hierarchy in the employment relationship. This duty is not the only source of employer power over employees. When employment is at will, an employer can fire an employee for any lawful reason or for no reason. As many egalitarians have argued, at-will employment can give employers an objectionable degree of control over the lives of employees. See Elizabeth Anderson, *Private Government: How Employers Rule Our Lives (and Why We Don't Talk about It)* (Princeton, NJ: Princeton University Press, 2017), 55–57 (detailing the many ways in which employers can use their control over access to material resources to exercise power over the on- and off-duty lives of employees); Samuel R. Bagenstos, "Employment Law and Social Equality," *Michigan Law Review* 112, no. 2 (2013): 225–273, at 227 (arguing that "individual employment law should be understood as targeting the threat to social equality posed by a boss's ability to leverage her economic power over workers into a more general social hierarchy in and outside of the workplace"). But even when employment is not at will and employees can only be terminated for "cause," employees are still subject to the duty of obedience, and breach of that duty can paradigmatically supply cause for dismissal. This chapter thus targets the duty of obedience because it is an underappreciated source of hierarchy that is not necessarily affected by reforms to at-will employment.

Sabine Tsuruda, *A Cooperative Paradigm of Employment* In: *Working as Equals*. Edited by: Julian David Jonker and Grant J. Rozeboom, Oxford University Press. © Oxford University Press 2023.
DOI: 10.1093/oso/9780197634295.003.0009

154 WORKING AS EQUALS

This hierarchical core of the employment relation has survived liberal reform. Employment standards legislation and antidiscrimination law constrain employer authority in ways that still leave employers with largely unilateral authority over central aspects of work, such as workplace policies and practices and the ends of work. Even labor law, which gives employees an effective say over a variety of material working conditions, such as pay, preserves an employer's authority over the "ultimate direction of the firm"[4] and "managerial policies related to the mission" of the enterprise.[5]

The liberal neglect of hierarchical authority in employment is problematic. In this chapter, I argue that unilateral employer authority over even quotidian aspects of work—such as the ends our jobs further and the processes by which we pursue those ends—threatens to render occupational freedom illusory. Occupational freedom is a basic liberty.[6] What makes a liberty "basic" is that it is an essential social condition for securing our status as free and equal persons.[7] Employment is life shaping, enlisting our minds and bodies in the ongoing pursuit of particular ends in association with others, and structuring our projects and relationships outside of work. Occupational freedom is thus essential for being able to exercise meaningful agency over our lives under terms that treat us as equals. And exercising such freedom requires, at a minimum, being able to choose how we labor and for what ends.

The hierarchical authority structure in the employment relation places precisely such choices about the means and ends of our work under the unilateral authority of the employer. Even when that authority is constrained, employers can still unilaterally determine how we work and for what ends— for instance, whether we are supposed to design software for self-driving cars or for weapons systems. So even if the formation of an employment relation

---

[4] Good Samaritan Hosp., 265 NLRB 618, 626–627 (1982) (holding that federal labor law does not protect employee collective action to change a hospital's "the ultimate direction, philosophy, and managerial policies" because such matters are within the scope of an employer's managerial prerogatives).

[5] Marburn Acad., Inc. & Levi, NLRB, No. 09-CA-224092, 2019 WL 651473 (Feb. 14, 2019) (finding that a schoolteacher's complaints about pay scales and favoritism were protected by federal labor law in part because they did not seek to "attack[] . . . managerial policies related to the mission or operation of the school").

[6] See Samuel Freeman, *Liberalism and Distributive Justice* (New York: Oxford University Press, 2018), 17. John Rawls is at times ambivalent about whether occupational freedom is a basic liberty or merely a "constitutional essential." Compare John Rawls, *Political Liberalism* (New York: Columbia University Press, 2005), 228 (noting that occupational freedom as a "constitutional essential"), with John Rawls, *Justice as Fairness: A Restatement*, ed. Erin Kelly (Cambridge, MA: Harvard University Press, 2001), 169 (explaining that occupational freedom is, along with freedom of association and liberty of conscience, a "civil liberty" that is "necessary for the development and exercise" of our "capacity to form, to revise and rationally to pursue what one views as worthwhile in life").

[7] See Rawls, *Justice as Fairness*, 169.

A COOPERATIVE PARADIGM OF EMPLOYMENT   155

is ostensibly free, the relationship is nevertheless subordinating, placing "central range[s]" of occupational freedom's "application" under the unilateral legal authority of the employer and thus giving the employer an intolerable degree of authority over our bodies and our ends.[8]

Employer authority is therefore not only problematic when it is arbitrary or insufficiently circumscribed;[9] its hierarchical nature precludes employment from being a cooperative enterprise among free and equal persons. Appropriately responding to workplace subordination accordingly requires radically rethinking the basic hierarchical paradigm of employment.

To that end, this chapter advances a cooperative paradigm of employment according to which the workplace must be governed by forms of joint and collective authority. First, authority over the requirements and purposes of a particular job should generally be vested jointly in the employee and the employer. This means that the employee and the employer alike must look to common ground to resolve disagreements and ambiguities in their relationship. Such common ground includes the parties' shared understanding of the purposes of the employee's work and how those purposes are to be pursued. By requiring the parties to exhibit fidelity to such a shared understanding, the law can help make it the case that the parties' relationship develops under terms that reflect ongoing and meaningfully voluntary cooperation.[10]

Second, securing occupational freedom also requires placing broader workplace policies, along with decisions about management, ownership, and the broader direction of the workplace, under the collective authority of affected employees and the employer. Unilateral changes with respect to such matters compromise the freedom of the employee's choice to undertake employment. For instance, had a university employee known in advance that their work would need to further the ideological aims of donors rather than raise general funds for student scholarships, they might not have accepted the job. Such a change in the direction of an enterprise would thus be a material change to the employee's working conditions, and so should not be unilaterally imposed on the employee. But for the same reason, a single

---

[8] Rawls, *Justice as Fairness*, 297 (explaining that basic liberties have a "central range of application" and that the "institutional protection of this range . . . is a condition for the adequate development and full exercise of the two moral powers of citizens as free and equal persons").

[9] See Anderson, *Private Government*, 52–54; Bagenstos, "Employment Law," 227.

[10] This chapter thus develops a conception of promissory fidelity in employment that resembles aspects of, but is not identical to, the US duty of good faith in contractual performance. See section 9.3.3; Sabine Tsuruda, "Good Faith in Employment," *Theoretical Inquiries in Law* 24, no. 1 (2023): 206–228.

156   WORKING AS EQUALS

employee and their employer together lack the authority to make this kind of decision for the workplace because of the decision's like implications for other employees.

Implementing a cooperative paradigm of employment thus requires replacing the duty of obedience with a mutually binding duty of promissory fidelity, and adopting mechanisms and protections for facilitating joint and collective forms of workplace decision-making. A cooperative paradigm of employment in turn points to a liberal conception of meaningful work, according to which our work is an expression of our individual agency and of our social, interdependent nature. Implementing a cooperative paradigm of employment can accordingly vindicate the Rawlsian and Marxian conviction that the solution to workplace subordination is not to stop working for one another, but to "produc[e] as human beings"[11] by engaging in "willing and meaningful work in a just union of social unions in which all can freely participate as they so incline."[12]

This chapter begins by arguing that the hierarchical core of the employment relation is incompatible with occupational freedom. It then advances an alternative cooperative paradigm of employment according to which the workplace must be governed by joint and collective forms of decision-making authority. This chapter closes by considering how a cooperative paradigm of employment yields a liberal conception of meaningful work.

9.2. Occupational Freedom

Deciding whether to accept employment is one of the most morally significant kinds of choices a person can make. Our jobs implicate our financial and physical well-being and shape how we exercise basic liberties. For example, when and where we work structure our opportunities for participating in a variety of community and civic associations, as well as for spending time developing interpersonal relationships, such as familial relationships and friendships. Our fundamental freedom to set our own ends is also implicated in our work. For the more privileged among us, our jobs can engage us in projects that coincide with our own views of the good. But no matter how

---

[11] Karl Marx, "Excerpts from James Mill's *Elements of Political Economy*" (1887), in *Early Writings*, trans. Rodney Livingstone and Gregor Benton (London: Penguin Books, 1992), 259–278, 277.

[12] John Rawls, *A Theory of Justice* (Cambridge, MA: Belknap Press of Harvard University Press, 1971), 529.

privileged or disadvantaged we are, our jobs engage our minds and bodies in the pursuit of particular ends—such as healthcare, building cars, making money for wealthy capitalists, and the like. As a result, our opportunities to set and pursue our own ends are in significant part shaped by the institution of employment.

Because employment implicates practically every core agential interest a person has, it is largely uncontroversial within liberal egalitarianism that occupational freedom is itself a basic liberty.[13] What makes a liberty basic is that it is an essential social condition for exercising meaningful agency over our lives, and for developing and acting on our capacity to treat others fairly and view others as having lives that are equally valuable to our own.[14] A basic premise of liberal egalitarianism is that we are each fundamentally and equally entitled to develop and exercise such agential capacities. So given the influence of employment on some of the social and material preconditions for exercising such capacities, it is imperative that how we labor—with whom, by what means, for what ends—be, in some meaningful sense, up to us as individuals.

9.2.1. Authority

The traditional hierarchical authority structure at the heart of the employment relation is incompatible with securing conditions of meaningful occupational freedom.[15] To see why, first notice that employment agreements are typically incomplete.[16] Not only do parties often fail to fully specify what a given job requires, it is also just generally difficult to fully specify each task and activity that a given job will require. Furthering the purposes for which one was hired can require the exercise of independent judgment and depend on a variety of dynamic and evolving circumstances that are difficult to foresee and beyond the control of the parties to an employment contract. Gaps between the express terms and underlying purposes of employment contracts are thus endemic.

Rather than place the resolution of such ambiguities under the joint authority of the parties to an employment contract—as is standardly the case

[13] See note 6.
[14] Rawls, *Political Liberalism*, 309.
[15] *Williston on Contracts*, § 54:23.
[16] Collins, *Employment Law*, 9–12.

158 WORKING AS EQUALS

under the general common law of contract[17]—the common law of employ-ment vests such interpretive authority primarily in the employer. An em-ployee is subject to an implied contractual duty to obey all their employer's reasonable, lawful orders.[18] What makes an order reasonable is tradition-ally a matter of the employer's own understanding of the purposes of the relationship—of how the relationship will serve the employer's public image, aspirations of economic domination, and the like.

The duty of obedience thus empowers employers—indeed, gives employers the legal right—to develop and give content to the employment relationship in ways that are unmoored to employees' reasonable expecta-tions about their jobs. So, for instance, a casino could unilaterally change its dress code to require bartenders to wear revealing clothing, and those bartenders are legally obligated to comply unless their contract or the law specifically provides otherwise. Likewise, an artificial intelligence company can unilaterally decide that its engineers are now going to design software for weapons systems, rather than self-driving cars as originally planned, unless their contracts specifically give those engineers some control over that type of decision.

The duty of obedience thus has the potential to render occupational freedom illusory. The conditions for exercising meaningful occupational freedom are in part epistemic. To make a meaningful choice about whether to accept a job, you must know how the job will fit in your life. What ends will your labor further and how? With whom and through what kinds of relationships will you be working? (And so forth.) Notwithstanding the in-completeness of employment contracts, we typically seek out and accept our jobs based on readily available answers to such questions. The recruitment process, marketing materials, and our prior knowledge of an employer often supply such information. So even if the moment of formation is ostensibly free—the employee had reasonably good alternatives to accepting the job, the employee had access to a good deal of information about the nature of the work—unilateral employer authority within the employment relationship can compromise the epistemic conditions for occupational freedom. How can you meaningfully assess how a job will shape your life if your employer is not bound to the understanding that reasonably informed that assessment?

---

[17] See section 9.3.3.
[18] *Willison on Contracts*, § 54:23; *Restatement of the Law of Agency*, 3rd ed. (American Law Institute, 2006), §§ 1.01, 8.09.

A COOPERATIVE PARADIGM OF EMPLOYMENT   159

It is, of course, possible to accept a job in full knowledge that the nature of that job may change in numerous material ways. But this points to a further problem. The purpose of occupational freedom is not just to ensure that our labor is consensual. What makes occupational freedom a basic liberty is that it enables us to exercise other basic liberties and, perhaps even more fundamentally, to set our own ends and exercise moral authority over how we use our bodies and minds.[19] The duty of obedience, because it grants the employer largely exclusive authority over how to fill gaps in the employment contract—and, hence, over what the employment contract requires—gives the employer unilateral authority over what ends we are to pursue and how we are to use our bodies and minds in pursuit of those ends. Such an authority relationship is thus subordinating, enabling employers to effectively purchase our rights to engage in core exercises of fundamental freedoms and to exploit our capacities for exercising such freedoms. So although extant hierarchical employment relationships are of course less objectionable than relationships of indentured servitude, they are similar in kind.

9.2.2. Exit

An employee could, of course, quit instead of acceding to their employer. And, in a more just world, quitting could (and probably should) be far less costly. We could, for instance, have high-paying unemployment insurance, available even for voluntary quits. As a result, since an employee need not necessarily obey their employer, one might accordingly question whether the duty of obedience compromises occupational freedom.

In response, first, this skepticism misunderstands the nature of the objection to hierarchical employment raised thus far. The problem is not simply one of forced labor. Rather, it is that largely exclusive employer authority over how to fill gaps in employment agreements and over the ends of our work compromises the warrant we need to make an informed choice about whether to accept a job, and that contracting for such employment involves the alienation of core exercises of occupational freedom.

Second, we should be cautious in our use of idealizations to guide reform of social circumstances mired in various forms of oppression and inequality,

[19] See Rawls, *Justice as Fairness*, 169.

160   WORKING AS EQUALS

such as employment.[20] In our social reality, it is often extremely costly to quit. Under extant conditions, an employer's unilateral authority over material aspects of the employment relationship is oppressive, allowing the employer to economically coerce employees into performing labor in ways and for ends they never agreed to. This should suffice to condemn unilateral employer authority over the meaning and requirements of employment contracts. The many workers who currently lack the economic means to easily quit their jobs should not have to wait for a more just distribution of income and wealth before they are free from what are effectively conditions of coerced labor.[21]

Third, money, in any case, does not exhaust our interests in employment. A variety of personal, social, and moral goods are often and predictably attached to our jobs—our sense of community belonging, valuable interpersonal relationships with colleagues, our pursuit of meaningful life projects through our work, and so on. And this is not necessarily a bad thing. If we stripped paid work of its moral content, our opportunities for association and our pursuit of value would be limited to our off duty lives. This would not only yield a dreary existence but would be incompatible with the core liberal principle that economic life should support our flourishing as moral agents. Detaching paid work from its personal, social, and moral value would subordinate our agential interests to production, rendering work even more alienating than it already often is. It is therefore a fiction that exit from a job could ever be truly costless, even within a just liberal democracy.

9.2.3. Cooperation

Finally, if exit were an employee's only alternative to obeying their employer, the legal institution of employment would likely fail to facilitate ongoing cooperation. Because employment contracts are often incomplete, they contain the conditions for disagreement. So, predictably, employees will sometimes disagree with their boss's understanding of what the job requires. A legal institution of employment that sought to facilitate employee freedom primarily,

---

[20] See Alex Gourevitch, "The Right to Strike: A Radical View," *American Political Science Review* 112, no. 4 (2018): 905–917, at 910 (arguing that we should be cautious in our use of idealizations when we theorize workers' rights, for we risk "obscuring the oppression of [the] social reality").

[21] For a similar set of arguments in favor of an expansive right to strike, see generally Gourevitch, "The Right to Strike."

A COOPERATIVE PARADIGM OF EMPLOYMENT   161

if not exclusively, through the power to exit would therefore be unstable as an institution for facilitating ongoing cooperation. There needs to be another way to resolve disagreement.

And employment should facilitate ongoing cooperation. Liberal democracy is an ideal of cooperative interdependence. As John Rawls explained, "It is a feature of human sociability that we are by ourselves but parts of what we might be. We must look to others to attain the excellences that we must leave aside, or lack altogether."[22] By working together and for one another's ends, the members of a liberal democracy can maintain and enjoy social conditions of freedom and equality.[23] We can administer healthcare, grow food, and stably provide for other necessary means for living, leaving ample space in our lives and culture to attend to matters beyond survival.[24] We can create art, give life to our political and religious commitments, develop and share knowledge, and make possible myriad other human goods. And we can legislate, litigate, and adjudicate to facilitate such mass collaboration and to ensure that the production and enjoyment of such social conditions is compatible with the equal and fundamental value of each of our lives.

As a result, although exit rights are crucial to securing meaningful occupational freedom, exit rights cannot be the primary solution to workplace subordination in a liberal society. An employee must have a secure and reasonable alternative to quitting in the face of disagreement in the employment relationship.

9.3. Joint Authority

Rather than give employers largely exclusive authority over the meaning and, hence, the requirements of an employment contract, the parties to an employment contract should be bound by their shared understanding of their relationship and should accordingly exercise joint authority over the requirements and purposes of the contract.

---

[22] Rawls, *A Theory of Justice*, 529.
[23] Rawls, *A Theory of Justice*, 523–529.
[24] See Joseph Raz, *The Morality of Freedom* (Oxford: Clarendon Press, 1986), 374.

162 WORKING AS EQUALS

9.3.1. Interpretation

Governed by such a joint authority structure, the parties to employment relationship have reason to cooperate in the face of disagreement and uncertainty. Because it is the parties' *shared* understanding that determines what the relationship requires, the parties to an employment relationship have reason to seek out one another's views about what the job requires and to thereby uncover common ground.

For example, if the express terms of an employment agreement leave it ambiguous whether a particular employee's shift can be changed from the day shift to the night shift, the employer cannot resolve this ambiguity on their own. And that is a good thing. The time of day can make a material difference to a person's ability to fulfill parental obligations, on a person's opportunities to form and maintain a variety of intimate and voluntary associations, and other like agential interests. An employer's unilateral resolution of this ambiguity can accordingly conflict with the understanding that informed the employee's choice to form the relationship and compromise the employee's freedom over their labor.

In contrast, in a legal regime where the parties' shared understanding of an employment relationship determines the relationship's scope and content, the employee is equally an epistemic authority with respect to interpretation. The employer therefore has reason to consult the employee, to give equal weight to the employee's own views on the matter, and to resolve the matter with the employee based on their shared understanding. Vesting joint authority over interpretation in the employer and employee thus helps to ensure that the employment relationship develops under terms that give effect to the employee's exercise of occupational freedom in deciding to form the employment relationship.

The employer's agential interests are also served by the parties having joint interpretive authority over their agreement. Although employers are not identically situated to employees—an employer does not normally labor for its employees[25]—employers (or the persons represented by them) also have agential interests in deciding whether to entrust their ends to another person and in having a say over how those ends are to be pursued. Those interests can accordingly be compromised if the employee can unilaterally

---

[25] In worker-owned and worker-managed firms, though, employees could count as laboring for one another, rather than for an employer.

A COOPERATIVE PARADIGM OF EMPLOYMENT 163

change material aspects of the employment relationship or unilaterally resolve ambiguities in the relationship.

In turn, by cooperating to resolve ambiguities and fill gaps in employment agreements, the parties can engage in forms of communication that further their productive enterprise. Suppose, for instance, that an employment agreement does not expressly settle how a warehouse worker is supposed to receive cargo. The employer tells an employee to engage in one type of receiving process. In response, the employee reasonably believes that such a process would be inefficient (or unsafe, bad for business, or would otherwise implicate an employer interest or obligation under the agreement). Treating the employee as a joint authority over the interpretation of the employment contract would require insulating the employee from dismissal for raising this objection in good faith to their employer, and an employer, seeking to implement such an authority structure, would have legal reason to listen.[26]

Treating the employee and the employer as joint legal authorities over the interpretation of their employment contract could therefore facilitate communication that enables the parties to better fulfill contractual obligations and achieve their productive ends. Exercising joint authority is thus an alternative to exit that gives effect to the parties' respective choices to form the employment relationship and facilitates ongoing cooperation.

9.3.2. Modification

Legally binding the parties to an employment relationship to their shared understanding of their relationship would also give the parties joint authority over material changes to that relationship.

First, if the parties are bound by their shared understanding, an employer should not make unilateral changes to that relationship that would defeat the employee's legitimate expectations under that understanding. For example, an employer cannot require that an employee relocate from San Francisco to Vancouver if the shared understanding at the time of formation was that the employee would be based in San Francisco. Such a change would compromise the meaningfulness of the employee's agreement to take the job in light

---

[26] For an elaboration of how joint contractual authority, implemented through the legal duty of good faith in performance, ought to protect employee speech, see Tsuruda, "Good Faith in Employment."

164 WORKING AS EQUALS

of the significance of location to maintaining a variety of intimate and other associations, as well as the significance that location may have to other important aspects of a person's life.

Instead, when a party to an employment relationship seeks to make such a material change, they should do it in ways that treat the other party as an equal authority over whether the change should be made. The employer should therefore not seek to obtain the employee's agreement by threatening to fire the employee or to withhold a benefit that the employee legitimately expected under their employment relationship.[27] Instead, the employer should seek to persuade the employee by appealing to shared reasons or purposes, or other sources of common interest.[28] The employer might, for instance, try to convince the employee that moving to Vancouver will be attached to new and interesting professional opportunities, or that the move will further their mutual interests in, say, providing legal support for migrant workers or in developing cutting-edge artificial intelligence technology.

By appealing to such sources of common interest, an employer appeals to the kinds of considerations the parties would be able to rely on in deciding to form an employment relationship under conditions of meaningful freedom in production. Engaging in such persuasion is thus a way of treating the employee as a free and equal person.

9.3.3. Good Faith

Implementing a joint authority structure in the employment relation would therefore require replacing the duty of obedience with a duty to perform in good faith. The parties should fill gaps and resolve ambiguities in that agreement in ways that evince a "good faith effort to redeem" that understanding.[29] And when one party believes that circumstances call for a material change in the relationship, the parties should negotiate such changes in

---

[27] See section 9.2.2.

[28] Such persuasive efforts should of course be honest; otherwise, they risk circumventing the employee's rational agency and thereby failing to treat the employee as having moral authority over their labor.

[29] Seana Valentine Shiffrin, "Common and Constitutional Law: A Democratic Perspective," *Tanner Lectures on Human Values* 37 (2018): 145–222, at 182; see also *Restatement (Second) of the Law of Contracts* (American Law Institute, 1981), § 205 cmt. a. For a critical discussion of the incomplete implementation of the duty of good faith in the law of employment contracts, see generally Tsuruda, "Good Faith in Employment."

A COOPERATIVE PARADIGM OF EMPLOYMENT   165

good faith—in ways that treat one another as equally moral authorities over their labor and ends.

Thus described, this duty of good faith in employment resembles the common-law duty of good faith in performance in US contract law. In the United States, the parties to a contract are generally subject to a nonwaivable duty of good faith in performance.[30] The duty requires that the parties exhibit "faithfulness to an agreed common purpose and consistency with the justified expectations of the other party."[31] By requiring such fidelity, the duty of good faith is standardly thought to bar parties from using vulnerability within the contractual relationship to secure unbargained-for benefits.[32] In turn, by holding the parties to their shared understanding of their contractual relationship and its purposes, the duty of good faith is thought to help ensure that the contractual relationship develops in ways that reflect a joint and voluntary undertaking over time.[33]

There are, however, important differences between the duty of good faith advanced here and the duty in the United States. The US duty of good faith is typically interpreted as a "thin" duty—a duty that just gives effect to the parties' shared understanding of their relationship, neither adding to nor constraining that understanding.[34] So to the extent that the duty of obedience is a part of the parties' shared understanding of their contract, the duty of good faith will require that the parties give effect to that duty and its underlying purposes.[35]

In contrast, I have argued that the duty of obedience should be unenforceable because the duty is incompatible with treating occupational freedom as a basic liberty.[36] The duty of good faith advanced here thus requires giving

---

[30] See Restatement (Second) of Contracts § 205; Uniform Commercial Code [UCC] (American Law Institute, 2012), § 1-203.

[31] Restatement (Second) of Contracts § 205 cmt. a; UCC §§ 1-201, 2-103.

[32] See, e.g., Peter Benson, Justice in Transactions: A Theory of Contract Law (Cambridge, MA: Belknap Press of Harvard University Press, 2019), 155–164; Daniel Markovits, "Good Faith as Contract's Core Value," in Philosophical Foundations of Contract Law, ed. Gregory Klass et al. (Oxford: Oxford University Press, 2014), 272–293.

[33] As Markovits explains, "Good faith in performance is the attitude that [parties] must adopt towards their plans in order for the plans to be joint plans at all. It is, quite literally, the matrix in which a shared perspective is possible." Markovits, "Good Faith," 293.

[34] See Benson, Justice in Transactions, 155–164; Markovits, "Good Faith," 278–280.

[35] Even at-will employment, which enables an employer to avoid liability for the vast majority of representations and promises about the nature of the job, is thought to be compatible with the duty of good faith. See Restatement of Employment Law (American Law Institute, 2015), § 2.07; Murphy v. Am. Home Prod. Corp., 448 N.E.2d 86, 91 (1983) (holding that an employer did not breach its duty of good faith by firing an at-will employee, an accountant, for internally reporting accounting improprieties even though he was led to believe that reporting such improprieties was part of his job).

[36] See section 9.2.2.

166　WORKING AS EQUALS

effect to the parties' shared understanding of their relationship, but because and only to the extent that giving effect to such an understanding treats the parties as equally moral authorities over how they labor and for what ends. In comparison to the duty of good faith under current US law, the duty of good faith developed here is therefore radically egalitarian, requiring that the parties to an employment relationship exercise joint authority over many material aspects of their relationship.[37]

9.4. Collective Authority

An employer and an employee's joint authority over their employment relationship is not unlimited. Securing social conditions for occupational freedom also requires placing a variety of workplace policies and practices, along with decisions concerning the direction of the enterprise, management, and company ownership, under the collective authority of affected employees and the employer.

9.4.1. Shared and Collective Interests

Some aspects of an employment relationship should not be settled just between an employee and an employer because those aspects implicate material aspects of other employment relationships in the workplace. For example, a single employee and an employer lack the joint authority to determine a new dress code or pay scale for the workplace if doing so would impose new material working conditions on the other employees.

An employee and employer similarly lack the joint moral authority to change the ends of the workplace. A single Facebook employee and Facebook should not be able to decide that all of Facebook's employees will further the creation of a "metaverse." A single employee and their employer, an artificial intelligence company founded for ostensibly peaceful purposes, should not be able to decide on their own that the company's engineers will now build AI software for weapons manufacturers. Both cases would involve imposing

---

[37] For an argument that the duty of good faith in employment can and should be developed in ways to protect employee speech and refusals to work in ways commonly associated with labor law, see generally Tsuruda, "Good Faith in Employment."

A COOPERATIVE PARADIGM OF EMPLOYMENT   167

changes in the working conditions of other employees that would have been material to their decision to form employment relationships.

Changes in management can similarly compromise occupational freedom. For example, the personalities and dispositions of our bosses can determine the moral character and tenor of our employment relationships. Managers are the employer representatives that coordinate how employees labor. How a manager speaks to and communicates with an employee,[38] interprets the ends of the employer, and coordinates quotidian matters across the workplace, such as shift scheduling, shape an employee's life in important ways. The identity of the people we work for may therefore reasonably matter to us.[39]

Changes in ownership can also compromise occupational freedom. For example, it may reasonably matter to someone employed by a small, independent bookstore that the store is about to be acquired by Amazon. The fact that the employer was an independent bookstore, rather than a large corporate entity, could have been one of the primary reasons for the employee's choice to work at the bookstore. The employee might also find Amazon's business and employment tactics morally objectionable. A change in ownership would thus be a material change to the employee's working conditions because it implicates the employee's ability to harmonize her work with her broader values. Such a change should therefore not be unilaterally imposed on the employee (or other employees) by the employer. But for the same reason, the employee and the employer lack joint authority to make this decision on their own, given its implications for the occupational freedom of other employees in the workplace.

9.4.2. Workplace Democracy

Ensuring that employees' occupational freedom is not undermined by changes in the ends of work, management, ownership, and other matters touching on multiple employees' working conditions thus requires giving employees a collective say over such matters. How, exactly, such collective

[38] See Sabine Tsuruda, "Working as Equal Moral Agents," *Legal Theory* 26, no. 4 (2020): 305–337, at 313–318.

[39] See Seana Valentine Shiffrin, "Hidden Delegations: Rights, Duties, and the Assignment of Debt" (unpublished manuscript), 24–25 ("An employee has many reasons to be concerned about who has the right to her performance where the identity of the right holder may affect how those duties are discharged.").

168   WORKING AS EQUALS

authority should be implemented cannot be fully addressed here. But briefly considering a few familiar candidates can offer guidance for later theorizing the appropriate institutional response.

First, implementing collective authority in the workplace is likely incompatible with a scheme of unanimous consent. Such a scheme would give each member of the collective a veto right. This would be inappropriate since a veto right could empower an employee (or the employer) to unilaterally determine the character of the workplace.[40]

Second, standard models of collective bargaining would need to be reformed to implement the requisite collective authority. Labor law typically empowers employees to come together to negotiate only a narrow band of terms with their employer. In the United States, such subjects of bargaining typically include pay scales, health insurance, vacation time, and other basic working conditions—all, of course, important matters for employees to have a say in. But employers are not obligated to bargain with employees on subjects such as high-level hiring and managerial decisions, including the ends that the employees' labor is supposed to further and the basic types of processes by which those ends are to be furthered.[41] In order for labor law to implement collective authority over working conditions, such managerial and high-level policies would have to be included in the mandatory subjects of bargaining.

Third, it may also be that collective bargaining is not the appropriate mechanism for implementing collective authority in the workplace. Collective bargaining is a limited form of representative democracy. It is a form of representative democracy because a union representative, elected by the members of the bargaining unit, negotiates on behalf of the members of the bargaining unit.[42] And it is a limited form of representative democracy because the outcome of the bargaining process is not determined democratically, such as by a vote, but rather through a negotiation process where, as

[40] Overriding an individual employee's objection would not necessarily pose the same kind of moral problem as an employer's unilateral imposition of a new working condition on that employee. This is because the employee never had the authority to either unilaterally or jointly determine the matters that are under the collective authority of the workplace to begin with. The dissenting employee may, of course, still have a moral objection to the group's decision. The decision might, for instance, be discriminatory, it might unduly burden employees' off-duty lives, or it might improperly control the employee's expression. As in politics, majoritarian rule in the workplace is insufficient for treating people in accordance with the equal and fundamental value of their lives.

[41] See note 4.

[42] See Benjamin I. Sachs, "Enabling Employee Choice: A Structural Approach to the Rules of Union Organizing," *Harvard Law Review* 123 (2010): 655–727, at 664–667.

in other transactional settings, the relative bargaining power of the parties shapes the resulting terms.

As a result, determining how to implement collective authority in the workplace would require further examination of the values at stake in representative versus direct workplace democracy, in addition to consideration of how and whether bargaining power dynamics should influence how workplace policies, practices, and ends evolve over time. Determining how to implement collective authority in the workplace would also require considering the extent to which procedural democracy can be removed from a decision-making process about working conditions and yet still facilitate voluntary collaboration between and among equals. These are issues that warrant their own sustained inquiries.

9.5. Meaningful Work

So far, I have been arguing that the law must implement a cooperative paradigm of employment to ensure that, in one of the most socially significant areas of social life, we treat one another as free and equal persons. This cooperative paradigm requires that the workplace be governed by forms of joint and collective authority, and that members of the workplace negotiate disagreement and effectuate change by looking to sources of common ground. Before closing, I want to briefly consider how a cooperative paradigm of employment yields a liberal egalitarian conception of meaningful work.

Employment, reimagined as a cooperative relationship, is a site for working under terms that express our nature as interdependent moral agents. A cooperative paradigm of employment makes work an ongoing exercise of occupational freedom, regularly calling on us to judge whether the ends of our work are worth taking up and require revision. And making such judgments cannot be entirely inward looking or self-serving. Instead, we must look to common ground to work out disagreements, seeking to develop a mutual understanding to guide the direction of our work. Cooperative employment relationships thus also express our social and moral nature.

So whether we are manufacturing computer chips or teaching philosophy, under a cooperative paradigm of employment, our jobs will regularly engage our moral and rational capacities. By exercising joint and collective authority over employment under terms that treat us as free and equal, we can,

170 WORKING AS EQUALS

as Karl Marx contemplated, "produc[e] as human beings."[43] Implementing a cooperative paradigm of employment can accordingly vindicate the egalitarian conviction that the solution to workplace subordination is not to stop working for one another, but to engage in "willing and meaningful work in a just union of social unions in which all can freely participate as they so incline."[44]

Thus, although this conception of meaningful work is not a perfectionist conception of meaningful work—it does not, for example, hold that work expresses our nature because it is creative or develops our talents[45]—this conception can nevertheless offer a shared, public basis for objecting to working conditions that are "deadening to human thought and sensibility."[46]

Making work meaningful by rendering it cooperative may, of course, yield lower productive gains than decision-making under the hierarchical status quo.[47] Some liberals might accordingly worry that, for the sake of equality and freedom in one limited sphere—the workplace—we risk compromising our ability to produce the social and material goods needed for meaningful freedom in our broader lives. Consequently, adopting a cooperative paradigm of employment might leave us with a less extensive liberty than we would otherwise have under a hierarchical, albeit constrained and regulated, paradigm of employment.

In response, first, I agree that our economic system should support the broader exercise of a variety of basic liberties. But liberal egalitarianism is not a liberty-maximizing view. As Rawls explained, the point of recognizing certain liberties as basic and thus giving them priority in the design of our society is "to guarantee equally for all citizens the social conditions essential for the adequate development and the full and informed exercise" of our moral agential capacities to set our own ends and relate to one another

---

[43] Marx, "Excerpts from James Mill," 277–278 ("Let us suppose we had produced as human beings. In that event, . . . in my individual activity I would have directly *confirmed* and *realized* my authentic nature, my *human, communal* nature.").

[44] Rawls, *A Theory of Justice*, 529.

[45] Meaningful work is often characterized as work that involves creativity or the development of talents. See, e.g., Richard J. Arneson, "Meaningful Work and Market Socialism," *Ethics* 97, no. 3 (1987): 517–545; Joseph Chan, "Legitimacy, Unanimity, and Perfectionism," *Philosophy & Public Affairs* 29, no. 1 (2000): 5–42; Adina Schwartz, "Meaningful Work," *Ethics* 92, no. 4 (1984): 634–646.

[46] Rawls, *A Theory of Justice*, 529.

[47] See R. H. Coase, "The Nature of the Firm," *Economica* 4, no. 16 (1937): 386–405; Michael C. Jensen and William H. Meckling, "Theory of the Firm: Managerial Behavior, Agency Costs and Ownership Structure," *Journal of Financial Economics* 3, no. 4 (1976): 305–360.

A COOPERATIVE PARADIGM OF EMPLOYMENT   171

as equals.[48] And a cooperative paradigm of employment is, as I have been arguing, among such social conditions. So even if implementing a cooperative paradigm of employment would yield lower productive gains than the status quo, the productive gains associated with the status quo cannot supply a productive benchmark—those gains are the product of an unjust scheme of labor and employment that subordinates workers to employers. As Rawls explained, "Deviations from market perfection are not especially worrisome. It is more important that a competitive scheme gives scope for the principle of free association and individual choice of occupation."[49]

Second, we should be careful not to exaggerate the productive costs of a more collaborative employment relationship. Employment relationships, precisely because they may be underspecified, often depend for their smooth operation on mutual trust and mutual respect. Cooperating in the face of uncertainty and disagreement can lay a foundation for such trust and respect, supplying employees and employers alike with the warrant to believe that their legitimate interests in the employment relationship will be adequately considered and protected. Such a foundation of trust and respect might in turn reduce agency costs and improve employee retention, thereby lowering costs associated with recruitment and training.[50] It therefore seems to be a nonobvious empirical matter whether a cooperative employment relationship would have any seriously deleterious effects on production.

Indeed, as has been noted, contracts for the sale of goods and other types of contracts governed by the general common law of contracts already have a similar collaborative structure.[51] Extant employment relationships are, by contrast, exceptionally uncooperative, and the cooperative character of many other contractual relationships in core commercial zones of life has certainly not brought about a productive collapse. Nor do unionization, German codetermination, and other forms of workplace democracy seem to have hindered many enterprises from thriving.

---

[48] Rawls, *Political Liberalism*, 332; see also Freeman, *Liberalism and Distributive Justice*, 17–18; Rawls, *A Theory of Justice*, 290.

[49] Rawls, *A Theory of Justice*, 310.

[50] This may in part explain why, in jurisdictions outside of the United States, such as England, good faith has long been a "cornerstone of the legal construction of the contract of employment." Collins, *Employment Law*, 106; see also 105–110.

[51] See section 9.3.3.

9.6. Conclusion

Objectionable hierarchy in the employment relation has survived liberal reform. The hierarchical authority structure at the heart of the employment relation authorizes employers to take unilateral action to change employees' working conditions in ways that are incompatible with occupational freedom. Hierarchical authority in the employment relation is thus not merely problematic when an employer's authority is arbitrary or insufficiently circumscribed; its very nature cannot be reconciled with our free and equal status. It is therefore not enough to constrain employer authority and to increase workers' contractual bargaining power. Authority within the employment relationship must itself be radically rethought to give employees an effective voice in how they work. Workplace democracy must be part of the solution to workplace subordination.

In focusing primarily on how to redistribute authority in the workplace, I have not meant to suggest that the distribution of authority is the only morally salient aspect of employment. As in politics, procedural democracy does not guarantee substantively egalitarian outcomes. Employer authority—whether collective, joint, or unilateral—must be subject to substantive constraints. To work as equal moral agents, we must work under nondiscriminatory conditions that treat us as equally entitled to exercising basic liberties of speech, association, and the like.[52] So in addition to redistributing authority over the ends and means of production in the workplace, a cooperative paradigm of employment will also require implementing antidiscrimination norms, occupational safety law to protect the basic liberty of the person, job protection to ensure that employment does not subordinate worker political agency to production, and other like substantive antihierarchy principles.

Moreover, sharing authority in the workplace does not guarantee that, as a society, we will fairly share the burdens of production. Under extant social conditions, many, but not all, people must work in order to live, and such people provide asymmetrical support for other people who are wealthy

---

[52] For a defense and discussion of the implications of this principle for workers' speech rights, see generally Tsuruda, "Working as Equal Moral Agents."

A COOPERATIVE PARADIGM OF EMPLOYMENT   173

enough to simply profit from their ownership of the means of production.[53] Such circumstances are a gross failure of reciprocity. So in order for the members of society to work as free and equal persons, it may well be that ownership of the means of production also needs to be democratized.[54]

---

[53] See Lucas Stanczyk, "Marginal Liberalism," in *Work, Ethics, and Democracy*, ed. Keith Breen and Jean-Phillipe Deranty (forthcoming) (arguing that the "asymmetrical subordination of working-class adults to the members of the business-owning class" should be concerning for liberals as "one of the most pervasive forms of hierarchy in modern social life").

[54] See generally Stanczyk, "Marginal Liberalism"; Freeman, *Liberalism and Distributive Justice*, 17–50; Rawls, *Justice as Fairness*, 44 (explaining that "[a] free market system must be set within a framework of political and legal institutions that adjust the long-run trend of economic forces so as to prevent excessive concentration of property and wealth").

10

The Workplace as a Cooperative Institution

Julian David Jonker

Individuals have their own commitments and projects, and these may conflict with the commitments and projects of others. A liberal society permits such conflicts, and provides a framework in which we may live together despite the disharmony. We find the workplace within such a society, and not apart from it.[1] Even those for whom work is among their most important projects bring other commitments to the workplace, and these may conflict with the commitments of other workplace participants. So the question arises where to draw the line between the demands of work and the permissiveness of a liberal society. How shall we fit the demands of working together with the demands of living together?[2]

One apparent difference between the workplace and social life is that we enter the workplace through bilateral agreement. Philosophical discussion of the workplace often questions the quality of the agreement between employer and employee.[3] But I am more interested in questioning

---

[1] By "*the* workplace" I have in mind that social arena roughly indicated by paradigmatic examples of workplaces, from the factory to the hastily cleared work-from-home desk to the ride-share vehicle. These spaces share a social significance despite their diversity. It is their shared social significance that I have in mind when I abuse syntax and talk of "the workplace" as if there were one such thing. In talking in this way, I am helping myself to the claim that the workplace *is* a relatively unified institution. Against this assumption, one might object, like Thatcher, that there is no such thing as the workplace, only individuals working in particular places. To that, my response is this chapter's argument that there is, at the abstract level of institutions, a distinctive perspective which makes sense of the demands of work.

[2] This is one aspect of the challenge to integrate political philosophy and business ethics issued by Joseph Heath, Jeffrey Moriarty, and Wayne Norman, "Business Ethics and (or as) Political Philosophy," *Business Ethics Quarterly* 20, no. 3 (2010): 427–452. That is, understanding the normative dimensions of the labor market, and markets more generally, involves understanding the interface between the demands of political justice and those of interpersonal morality.

[3] At the extreme, the near necessity of work for those without capital ensures that employment relations are more a product of coercion than voluntary agreement. See the interpretation of Marx presented in Richard Arneson, "What's Wrong with Exploitation?," *Ethics* 91, no. 2 (1981): 202–227. A less extreme version is that the reserve labor pool (as may be maintained by anti-inflationary monetary policy) ensures unequal bargaining power; see Joan Robinson, *An Essay on Marxian Economics*, 2nd ed. (London: Macmillan, 1966), 31–33. Complementing this less extreme view is an argument that the possibility of exit does not save the voluntariness of employment relations, given what is at

---

Julian David Jonker, *The Workplace as a Cooperative Institution* In: *Working as Equals*. Edited by: Julian David Jonker and Grant J. Rozeboom, Oxford University Press. © Oxford University Press 2023. DOI: 10.1093/oso/9780197634295.003.0010

THE WORKPLACE AS A COOPERATIVE INSTITUTION   175

the bilateral nature of workplace relations. A most conspicuous departure is that workplace practices determine social outcomes beyond the workplace: for example, working hours and parental leave policies may generate unequal burdens of domestic labor,[4] and racialized differences in employment opportunities may generate segregation beyond the workplace.[5] The social externalities of the workplace are not purely negative. The fact that most have little choice whether to work, or where to work, means that employees are thrown together more arbitrarily than in the rest of their lives, and so workplaces are often more socially integrated than families and entirely voluntary associations. Employees, so thrown together, must work in relative peace and stability in order to achieve shared goals, and so the workplace may (at its best) serve as a model for wider social cooperation.[6] These observations suggest ways in which the employment relation impacts those outside the workplace.

Yet the bilateral analysis of the work relation is insufficient even within the workplace. The counterexample I focus on is the exercise of workplace authority in the face of disagreement. The exercise of such authority is particularly prone to being understood in terms of a bilateral relation between employer and employee.[7] Against this, I claim that any exercise of workplace authority is subject to a *workplace justification constraint*: workplace directives must be justifiable to all reasonable participants in the workplace. This criterion is a way of accommodating disagreement to the degree we expect of other liberal institutions. It provides a basis for using workplace authority to achieve the goals of work while respecting the fact that individuals may reasonably diverge in their conceptions of the good. The criterion has an egalitarian justification, but one that aims not at equalizing some dimension of the bilateral relation between employer and employee, but rather at providing an institutional perspective which gives each workplace participant equal standing.

---

stake. See Elizabeth Anderson, *Private Government: How Employers Rule Our Lives (and Why We Don't Talk about It)* (Princeton, NJ: Princeton University Press, 2017).

[4] Gina Schouten, *Liberalism, Neutrality, and the Gendered Division of Labor* (Oxford: Oxford University Press, 2019).

[5] Elizabeth Anderson, *The Imperative of Integration* (Princeton, NJ: Princeton University Press, 2013), 23*ff.*

[6] Cynthia Estlund, *Working Together* (Oxford: Oxford University Press, 2003).

[7] I abstract from the difficult question of who exactly counts as an employee. However, I suspect my arguments apply more widely than narrow legal definitions of employment.

176   WORKING AS EQUALS

10.1. The Problem of Disagreement

Liberalism places great importance on accommodating (as opposed to set-tling) disagreements about the good. A liberal society therefore grants polit-ical and civil liberties that allow and even encourage individuals to develop distinctive conceptions of the good, and requires that the exercise of polit-ical authority be justifiable in light of this reasonable disagreement about the good. Famously, this requirement leads *political* liberals to argue that the ex-ercise of political authority is justifiable in a liberal society only if it meets a *public justification constraint*: i.e., that the exercise of authority is justifiable in terms of reasons that could be accepted by all reasonable members of the political community.[8] Can we reconcile the liberal accommodation of disa-greement with the need to reach consensus in order to work together?

There are various kinds of disagreement that can arise in the workplace. One broad kind of disagreement concerns production (what is to be produced and how), and this sort of disagreement can be an obstacle to productive ef-ficiency and the motivation of workplace participants. Another broad kind of disagreement concerns how the benefits of production are to be shared among workplace participants, and this can affect participants' sense of fair-ness and, as a result, their motivation. Both kinds of disagreement might arise simply because workplace participants occupy different roles, and not because of any disagreement they carry beyond the workplace. For example, two workers, A and B, may have the exact same preferences over methods M and N for manufacturing a widget, but disagree about which method to use because M has A doing her least preferred job (say, painting the widget) while N has B doing her least preferred job (also painting the widget). This kind of workplace disagreement need not be grounded in reasonable disa-greement about the good, and so it does not raise a distinctive problem from the perspective of political liberalism that such disagreements are settled by the exercise of an employer's unilateral authority.

However, other kinds of workplace disagreement are the product of deeper dissent about the good of the type that political liberals seek to accommodate as reasonable. For example, a restaurant dress code may be contentious be-cause its gender-specific style is endorsed by some and rejected by others on

---

[8] John Rawls, *Political Liberalism* (New York: Columbia University Press, 1993); Jonathan Quong, *Liberalism without Perfection* (Oxford: Oxford University Press, 2010); Gerald Gaus, *The Order of Public Reason: A Theory of Freedom and Morality in a Diverse and Bounded World* (Cambridge: Cambridge University Press, 2011).

THE WORKPLACE AS A COOPERATIVE INSTITUTION   177

the basis of different normative conceptions of gender identity. Arguments about production and its benefits may also be grounded in this deeper kind of disagreement. For example, the decision whether to pursue a contract to supply the military (supposing the decision is left open by the requirements of justice) may activate a dispute between different workplace participants about the value of the military and their willingness to participate in this kind of production. Is it permissible to settle these kinds of disagreement by the use of employer authority, or must the disagreement be accommodated in some other way?

I focus on this problem of political disagreement in the workplace not because it is an obstacle to production (though it surely can be), but because it is a challenge to the compatibility of a liberal society and our current way of organizing production. While liberalism advertises its ability to accommodate political disagreement, we would be overselling its achievements if it turned out that workplace relations fail to do so, since workplace relations are a pervasive way of structuring interpersonal interactions in contemporary liberal societies.

A second concern about the effects of capitalist production on liberalism's promise has to do with the stability of justice in a society in which workplace relations pervasively structure our lives and everyday experiences. Consider Rawls's optimism that a just society's institutions will foster the sense of justice that is required for maintaining those institutions.[9] Perhaps that is true of the political institutions of a well-ordered liberal society, but if much of our lives are spent in the workplace, then we also need to be assured that workplace relations will foster the sense of justice. Without this assurance, it is reasonable to worry that if workplaces do not accommodate political disagreement as liberal political institutions do, then the common experience of being silenced by unilateral employer authority will undermine the sentiments and virtues required for maintaining liberal political institutions.[10]

The concern I hope to have highlighted is not strictly the same concern about hierarchy that has dominated republican and democratic discussions of the workplace.[11] The motivating ideal is not intrinsically one of equal

---

[9] John Rawls, *A Theory of Justice*, rev. ed. (Cambridge, MA: Harvard University Press, 1999), ch. 8.

[10] See Debra Satz's chapter in this volume for an elaboration of this concern.

[11] Of course they overlap: "A paradigmatic way we can fail to treat each other as equals is by legally authorizing a person or entity to act as a moral authority over the lives and choices of other adults. The employment relationship often treats employees as laboring precisely under such authority relations in the workplace." Sabine Tsuruda, "Working as Equal Moral Agents," *Legal Theory* 26, no. 4 (2020): 305–337, at 307.

178 WORKING AS EQUALS

authority, but rather of equal standing to hold and live according to one's own conception of the good. I assume that political liberals are motivated by this sort of concern, and that it is fundamentally a concern about the equality of persons.[12] Asking whether workplace authority can accommodate disagreement is therefore a way of asking about the compatibility of capitalist work relations and a commitment to the basic moral equality of persons.

I focus on the problem of disagreement as a distinctive egalitarian concern because it acknowledges the role that equality has in shaping justification. Consider that institutions involving unequal relations of authority could conceivably be justified by the fact that they contribute to efficiency or other impersonal values. Such a justification need not involve weighing equality against other values, but it would treat equality as one consideration among others. In contrast, the problem of reasonable disagreement steers our attention toward the equal standing of each individual's conception of the good, which requires that a relation of unequal authority be justifiable to each member of the relation, and not simply justifiable in impersonal terms.[13] Equality is not simply one consideration among others within acceptable justification, but is a formal constraint on it.

10.2. The Nature of Workplace Authority

Although I am concerned with disagreement, rather than hierarchy, the problem of disagreement arises most sharply when employers are able to settle controversies and exclude opposing perspectives by the unilateral exercise of their authority. A prefatory question, then, is how seriously we should take the commands of workplace authority.

---

[12] Many political liberals identify respect as their grounding value; e.g., Charles Larmore, "The Moral Basis of Political Liberalism," *Journal of Philosophy* 96, no. 12 (1999): 599–625; Quong, *Liberalism without Perfection*; Schouten, *Liberalism, Neutrality*; for a contrary view, see Han van Wietmarschen, "Political Liberalism and Respect," *Journal of Political Philosophy* 29, no. 3 (2021): 353–374. I assume that the appeal to respect is itself motivated by a relational ideal of equality. Consider that Rawls's basic commitment is to persons as free and equal, and that while disagreement arises because people are free (in the sense that they have the moral powers to develop and act from a sense of justice and a conception of good), political liberalism is a response to the reasonableness of their views, and therefore their equality (in the sense that their moral powers allow for cooperation as a society); Rawls, *Political Liberalism*, especially Lecture III.

[13] This notion of justifiability is shared by contractualists like Rawls, Scanlon, and Scheffler, and gives contractualism its relational character. See Julian Jonker, "Contractualist Justification and the Direction of a Duty," *Legal Theory* 25, no. 3 (2019): 200–224.

THE WORKPLACE AS A COOPERATIVE INSTITUTION   179

There are really two questions concerning the normative status of employment authority:

(1) What, if anything, justifies employers' right to address workplace directives to their employees?
(2) What, if anything, grounds employees' obligation to obey their employer's directives?[14]

The first question has independent moral importance because even if an employee has no obligation, a directive may give her strong prudential reason to obey, and we want to know whether and why an employer may exercise such power over the employee. The second question has independent moral significance because even if an employer lacks the aforementioned power (perhaps because he cannot monitor the employee's compliance), we want to know whether the employee nonetheless has a moral reason to obey. These questions are much like, first, the traditional question about the state's right to rule; and, second, the traditional question about the duty of citizens to obey the state. So I will treat the state and employer as parallel cases to the extent that I treat them as raising parallel questions about the interplay of power and moral reason.

A tempting approach to both questions begins with the claim that employees agree to employment authority. This suggests that an employer has the right to direct the employee because the employee has consented to his doing so, and an employee has a duty to obey the employer's directive because she has promised to do so. Philosophers sometimes worry about whether employment agreements are truly voluntary, given that in our form of society, most find it necessary for survival to work for another.[15] But that may be true without impugning the voluntariness of agreements with particular employers. In any case, the idea that voluntary agreement justifies both aspects of employment authority is a useful stalking horse, since it appears to limit the scope and force of authority only by the content of the agreement— call this the "strong voluntarist conception" of employment authority.

---

[14] I do not believe these are Hohfeldian correlatives, as in the case of the right of a promisor and the duty of a promisee. The first question concerns the employer's right to address something as a directive to employees, which is not the same as commanding them; in addition, the right to direct is not the same as whatever right is granted by a successful directive.

[15] E.g., Serena Olsaretti, "Freedom, Force, and Choice," *Journal of Political Philosophy* 6, no. 1 (1998): 53–78.

180 WORKING AS EQUALS

With strong voluntarism in mind, note that employment authority is typically temporally extended (it is the basis of ongoing interactions rather than a single interaction) and open-ended (it not only allows an employer some choice as to how to direct an employee, as from a menu, but allows the employer to direct the employee in novel and unpredictable ways as the circumstances of production change). These features of employment authority play an important role in production. Economic theories of the firm teach us that the firm exists in order to overcome transaction costs and information asymmetries that make it difficult for production to proceed through market arrangements.[16] Open-ended and temporally extended authority is a natural part of such arrangements because it allows firm production to be flexible as well as committed in the face of changing market conditions.

The strong voluntarist conception is certainly compatible with authority's extended and open-ended nature, treating it as a product of the incompleteness of the employment agreement. Yet these features of employment authority also create morally problematic opportunities for abuse. The extended nature of employment authority can create dependence on the part of the employee that makes it difficult for the employee to speak her mind or negotiate extensions of the agreement on a fair footing, or enables the employer to issue many directives that are each unobjectionable but that cumulatively create an objectionable situation. The open-ended nature of authority leaves unforeseeable the ways in which the authority will be exercised, and this leaves room for directives that would not have been agreed to if their possibility had been considered during bargaining. One important mitigating factor is the employee's right to exit, which is part of what distinguishes employment from servitude. But exercising the right may be unappealing in light of the employee's other options, and the fact that this is very frequently the case leads some to say that employees do not have a real choice whether to exit. That is an exaggeration, but a useful way to emphasize the true claim that exit is often enough an inadequate way to curb abuses of employer authority.

Aside from the possibility of abuse, there is also the chance that an employer will direct an employee to do something other than what she has most moral reason to do, all things considered. In some cases, morality will require such an employee to disobey the directive in order to avoid doing something

---

[16] R. H. Coase, "The Nature of the Firm," *Economica* 4 (1937): 386–405, and Oliver Williamson, "Markets and Hierarchies: Some Elementary Considerations," *American Economic Review* 63, no. 2 (1973): 316–325.

THE WORKPLACE AS A COOPERATIVE INSTITUTION 181

morally wrong. But in many such cases, the employee will not have been directed to do anything wrong, but simply to do something that is not her morally best option. An employee who follows such a directive does not do what she is morally required to do, yet we do say that she does what her employer requires of her, and that in a sense (related to the sense in which she is required) she would be criticizable for not doing it. These sorts of cases suggest that employment authority is not a variety of moral authority, as we may suppose promissory authority is, but that it is nonetheless authority in a sense.

These are reasons to think that we *do not* treat employment authority as a kind of moral authority. There is also reason to think that we *should not* (when deciding whether to revise our concepts) treat employment authority as a kind of moral authority. One such reason is that the precarity of the employee's power to exit together with the thought that employment authority is moral authority would result in apparently moral obligations that have been entered into on grounds of their optionality, but that are in fact inescapable. In this way, the apparently moral aspect of employment authority would add significantly to the way in which open-ended and extended authority creates vulnerability on the part of the employee.

Similar concerns can be raised about legal authority, and positivist legal philosophy suggests an answer: legal authority is perspectival, in the sense that its participants adopt an internal perspective from which exercises of authority have the force of moral obligations, or set standards of criticism for noncompliance.[17] Similarly, I want to suggest, we should treat workplace authority as perspectival: having force from within a workplace perspective, though it is morally optional whether workplace participants adopt the perspective (setting aside facts about reliance and other contingent considerations). Those who adopt the workplace perspective thereby view certain patterns of behavior as standards of criticism, and one such pattern is that employees generally follow the directives of the employer and its agents. Therefore employees who adopt such a perspective will generally think they have good reason to comply with the employer's directives, and that they are subject to criticism and justified sanctions if they do not.

Workplace positivism of the sort I am assuming here treats employer authority as optional in a way that moral authority is not. An employee may

---

[17] H. L. A. Hart, *The Concept of Law*, 3rd ed. (Oxford: Oxford University Press, 2012), and Scott J. Shapiro, *Legality* (Cambridge, MA: Harvard University Press, 2011).

182 WORKING AS EQUALS

take up the perspective which accords her employer authority but is not required to do so, depending on whether she thinks she has reason to, and is likely to do so on the basis of not just habituation but her belief that she has reason to take up the perspective. What is more, she may come to abandon the perspective even while employed, and there is no reason intrinsic to the employment relation (rather than contingent upon reliance interests and so on) why she may not. So I do not assume that an employee has a moral obligation to treat her employer as an authority, even if she adopts the workplace perspective, and therefore believes she has an obligation to comply with her employer's directives. From anecdote and experience, I believe employees are somewhat likely to adopt the workplace perspective at times, and so to believe their employers' directives have the force of genuine obligations. But adopting the perspective, even on the basis of what one believes is good reason to adopt it, does not in itself provide one with reason to adopt the perspective, and does not make employer directives obligatory in fact.

10.3. The Cooperative Conception of the Workplace

The question remains whether an employee has good reason to take up the workplace perspective, even if doing so falls short of a moral requirement. Some employees will not because they are alienated in the sense of Holmes's "bad man," who does not adopt the internal perspective toward the law but cares only about the empirical prediction that noncompliance will have negative consequences for him.[18] Similarly, the "bad employee" will follow an employer's directives only because prudence counsels that noncompliance will bring sanction or some other negative outcome. What makes her a bad employee is not that she takes herself to have merely prudential reason rather than moral reason to comply with her employer's directives, but that she takes herself to have reason only to avoid the negative outcome rather than to treat her employer's directives as emanating from a legitimate authority. This is bad from the workplace perspective, since it is a form of misalignment between the employee's motivation and the workplace's values and plans.

An employee who does adopt the workplace perspective will comply with employer directives and sometimes feel compelled to go beyond them.

---

[18] Oliver Wendell Holmes Jr., "The Path of the Law," *Harvard Law Review* 10 (1897): 991–1009, at 993.

THE WORKPLACE AS A COOPERATIVE INSTITUTION 183

She does so not because she fears that she will otherwise be fired, or not promoted, or subjected to awkward interactions. She instead thinks that she should generally comply because otherwise she will be slacking off, or not doing her part, or not living up to her role, and so on. These sorts of statements could be understood as claims about what morality requires, but they make more sense as statements from within the workplace perspective. That is because the same employee who believes such things may over time, without any change in her moral views or moral character, become more like the bad employee—say, because she no longer thinks that her work serves an important purpose, or because her career comes to occupy a different place in her life priorities. The reasons presented by the workplace perspective will become correspondingly less gripping as her commitment to the perspective fades in relative importance.

These last points suggest reasons why an employee might adopt the workplace perspective. She might think that the work she does serves an important social role. She might be neutral about the social benefit of her organization's work, but think that her role is important to the organization. She might be neutral about the importance of her role and her work, but think she owes it to her colleagues to adopt the workplace perspective, since she cares about them and they place importance on their work. She might simply have a traditional and unreflective attitude to working for others as something one ought to do.[19] That is, an employee could have any of a number of reasons for adopting the workplace perspective, reasons that are as various as the commitments and motivations of individuals.

A reasonable hypothesis is that many employees will be more likely to adopt the workplace perspective and see their employer's authority as legitimate and binding if they also consider their workplace a fair scheme of cooperation aiming at mutual benefit—that is, if they adopt a *cooperative conception* of the workplace.[20] It is also reasonable to hypothesize that employees who adopt the workplace perspective will have higher morale and therefore be more productive. Furthermore, it is reasonable to think that an employee who adopts the cooperative conception of the workplace is more likely to think it reasonable to adopt the workplace perspective, and to think it reasonable for her colleagues to do so. The result is that she is able to see

---

[19] Cf. Hart, *The Concept of Law*, 203.

[20] This is parallel to Rawls's animating conception of society as a fair system of cooperation (*Political Liberalism*, 15–22).

184   WORKING AS EQUALS

herself as standing under a reasonably shared normative order, rather than participating in a kind of modus vivendi in which cooperation is merely a by-product of each acting according to prudence and self-interest.

There is some value in the experience of standing with others under a shared normative order, an experience that is often the basis of solidarity.[21] The value of that experience gives us reason to seek it out where it is readily available, and so employees who work at a cooperative workplace have reason to adopt the workplace perspective. This reason, unlike the other reasons to adopt the workplace perspective that I have so far mentioned, is not tied to employees' idiosyncratic motivations. What is more, workplace participants who adopt the workplace perspective are likely to act in ways that maintain the workplace as a fair scheme of cooperation, which is a valuable outcome. This provides an additional reason of stability to adopt the workplace perspective, one that is dependent upon the behavior of the workplace participants but not upon their idiosyncratic motivations. So the cooperative conception provides a surer basis, in the form of at least two kinds of further reason, for workplace participants to adopt the workplace perspective.

The cooperative conception of the workplace might also be important for the stability of a just society more generally. Recall that the idea of stability—of a just society rather than of cooperative workplace—is that members of a just society will, through being subjects of just institutions, develop a sense of justice that motivates and enables them to maintain such just institutions. Since much of life is presently spent in the workplace, it is especially important for the stability of a just society that workplaces be arranged in a way that encourages the cultivation of the sense of justice. I conjecture that, in our present form of society, the cooperative conception of the workplace, which makes fairness and reciprocity the basis for submitting to workplace authority, is an important mechanism for developing the sense of justice, given that for many the workplace provides the primary experience of cooperation and authority, and so in the best circumstances is a model for the reciprocity that liberalism demands of our political institutions (and in the worst circumstances, for its failure).

Finally, the cooperative conception suggests one solution to our first question about authority, i.e., whether an employer has a right to direct employees. I have been claiming, in response to the second question about an

---

[21] Samuel Scheffler, "The Good of Toleration," in *Equality and Tradition: Questions of Value in Moral and Political Theory* (New York: Oxford University Press, 2010), 312–336.

employee's obligation to obey, that employer authority is perspectival, such that an employee may for good reason come to see herself as having such an obligation, though this is not the same as her in fact having such an obligation. But this availability of a workplace perspective does not yet establish that the employer has a right to direct an employee who adopts the perspective, let alone one who does not.

I claim that an employer has the right to direct employees if the directives are consistent with the cooperative conception of the workplace. This conclusion is based upon two premises:

(1) An employer has the right to direct an employee in a certain way only if the directive does not count as an abuse of the employer's workplace authority.

(2) Directives that are consistent with the cooperative conception do not abuse the employer's authority. (This is not a necessary condition on being nonabusive, and so my conclusion is not a necessary condition on the right to direct employees.)

The first premise will seem tautological to the extent that we think of abuse of authority as whatever the holder of an authority does not have a right to command. But we can also get an intuitive grasp of the content of abuse of workplace authority by considering examples of the ways in which the open-ended and extended nature of the authority can be used to take advantage of an employee. There are at least three categories of such abuse. An *abuse of fairness* involves allocating more or less work to an employee than is fair, given the nature of the work, the needs of production, and the allocation of work to other employees. An *abuse of purpose* involves giving directives to employees that serve no legitimate purpose of the firm. Such an abuse goes further than unfairly allocating a task to an employee, but involves allocating work to the employee for no good reason at all. This may be the case where a manager gives an employee mere busy work, or issues directives that serve the manager's personal aims alone. An *abuse of professionalism* involves giving too much or too little attention to the fact that employees have private lives and personal circumstances that may appropriately be sealed off from managerial scrutiny while nonetheless requiring reasonable accommodation from workplace directives.

The point of this taxonomy is not to rigidly distinguish one type of abuse from another, but to gesture at the various ways in which employment

186 WORKING AS EQUALS

relations that are necessary for production inherently create the conditions for managerial actions that are not necessary for production, or even obstruct it. But the abuses gestured at here are not problematic simply because they are superfluous from the perspective of production. In some cases, an unfair workload or personal intrusion is compatible with the firm's productive aims, and can even further them. These practices are abusive but not because they fail to optimize productivity. The problem is that they fall short of the normative standard set by the cooperative conception of the workplace. That is the contrapositive of premise (1).

The argument for premise (2) (that conformity with the cooperative conception is sufficient for avoiding abuse) has a contractualist flavor. A workplace is cooperative to the extent that it is an arrangement in which the benefits and burdens of the productive process have been allocated in a reasonable way, that is, in a way which is justified by the aims and circumstances of production (including the need for flexible aims in the face of uncertainty and for the sake of innovation), and which treats the workplace participants fairly given these aims and circumstances. That is to say that the cooperative conception of a particular workplace is, though highly contingent, one that can be justified to all reasonable participants in that workplace. But then any directive that is consistent with this cooperative conception is one which could also be justified to all reasonable workplace participants. That in turn means that the directive could not be an abuse, since it affects the allocation of benefits and burden not simply so that one person might take advantage of another or ignore their vulnerabilities, but on the basis of reasons that can be accepted equally by those who are burdened and those who are benefited.

10.4. The Workplace Justification Constraint

The above contractualist characterization clarifies that the reasons of a cooperative workplace perspective are not the same as the reasons of production. That accords with our experience of actual deliberation within the workplace. While efficient production is a default aim of most workplaces, some firms allow a degree of exploration and flexibility that do not translate immediately into productive gains, while others will take up commitments that are tied to social goals, such as benefiting a local community or pursuing important technological projects. The cooperative conception allows for a wide range of values and commitments other than (but including) productive efficiency,

THE WORKPLACE AS A COOPERATIVE INSTITUTION   187

and that means that determining what is required by the perspective of a particular workplace can be difficult or indeterminate. But that is no different from the challenges for figuring out what the internal perspective of a legal system requires. In particular, it is not for us to say in the abstract whether the idea of the cooperative workplace gives relatively more or less priority to efficiency than to other values and commitments. What the perspective of a cooperative workplace recommends will depend on many contingent facts about that particular workplace.

Yet more can be said in the abstract about the perspective of a cooperative workplace. Just as the cooperative workplace can be justified to reasonable workplace participants, so too the directives of a cooperative workplace are justifiable to reasonable workplace participants. The idea of workplace justification appealed to here is both narrower and wider than that of agreement among all workplace participants. It is narrower because it sets aside any need to appease the preferences of those unreasonable workplace participants who are not concerned whether a directive is consistent with the fair allocation of benefits and burdens given the aims and circumstances of production. It is wider because it calls for considering the perspective of hypothetical reasonable workplace participants who are not currently represented in the workplace. That is, workplace justification requires going beyond the preferences of actual workplace participants in order to ask whether a directive could be justified to any reasonable member of society who aimed to participate in the workplace as a cooperative concern. This is a strong criterion, appropriately for a sufficiency condition, and can be characterized as the Workplace Justification Criterion (WJC): that the exercise of authority could be justified in terms of reasons (*workplace reasons*) that could be accepted by any reasonable member of society who took up the cooperative conception of that workplace and their role in it.

Workplaces vary in their agreeability. Larger organizations in liberal societies tend to contain great diversity of thought and identity, and therefore disagreement about the good. But some organizations have a large degree of consensus, particularly where the organization aims at goals that can be described in religious or political terms. What shall we say about a directive that is justifiable to all workplace participants on the basis of religious reasons that they each accept? One response to the most extreme version of this scenario is that the problem of disagreement that I am concerned with does not arise; nor, in practice, does any question about whether the employer has a right to use his authority to settle any disagreement.

188 WORKING AS EQUALS

Still, the WJC does present a challenge for an employer operating in circumstances of widespread agreement, since it requires that the exercise of authority be justifiable to any reasonable member of society who took up the workplace perspective. This means that the WJC has an outward orientation, requiring that the exercise of authority in even a very agreeable workplace be evaluated according to its ability to be justified to a wide range of the members of a liberal society who are not in fact active participants in the workplace. This does not mean that the WJC holds workplace authority to the standards imposed by political liberals upon political authority, since not every reasonable viewpoint in society could be consistently held together with the workplace perspective. But the WJC, insofar as it is taken up as a constraint by an employer, does apply pressure to ensure that directives are justifiable in terms of all liberal viewpoints that are also compatible with taking seriously the norms and values that make up the workplace perspective. This might seem demanding, given the liberal commitment to freedom of association, but it should be understood as an attempt to reconcile a commitment to social stability (thus its outward orientation to reasonable viewpoints outside the organization) and a robust commitment to free association (thus the restriction to viewpoints compatible with the workplace perspective). In practice, the WJC will permit justification in terms of religious and comprehensive reasons to the extent that these are given a place by the cooperative conception of the particular workplace, perhaps because the productive aims of the organization are to be characterized in similar terms.

I have been trying to show that the WJC is not overly permissive when applied in contexts of great agreement. But is it too quick to exclude the personal reasons of employees who reasonably have attachments and projects (such as religious identities or partisan political projects) that have little to do with work but nonetheless unavoidably accompany them into the workplace? Here it seems reasonable to conclude that the cooperative conception requires accommodation of the fact that human beings have personal projects and private lives that cannot be easily separated from work. Difficult questions arise as to what form and degree of reasonable accommodation of employees' personal reasons are required by workplace justification, and it is doubtful that we could settle these in the abstract. But in applying the WJC, these personal reasons find a place in justification indirectly, in the sense that the cooperative conception of the workplace recommends accommodating personal reasons to the extent required by the fair allocation of the benefits

THE WORKPLACE AS A COOPERATIVE INSTITUTION   189

and burdens of production. Since personal reasons appear in justification in this indirect way, they are placed within a framework for limiting the tensions that might arise between a firm's productive goals and an employee's private reasons, and between the different conceptions of the good held by different employees.

We should not expect too much of the WJC. My aim is not to provide a standard from which all other conditions of a just workplace can be derived. It is instead to show that there is a conception of the workplace which can reconcile the authority we currently need for satisfactory economic production with the diversity of thought that is permitted by the liberal commitment to the equal standing of each to devise their own conception of the good. The WJC achieves this reconciliation by requiring that the exercise of workplace authority be justifiable to all reasonable workplace participants. This entails that workplace authority cannot impose a partisan normative view upon one who does not accept it. Therefore accepting someone as a workplace authority does not require accepting that person as an authority in matters beyond the workplace. In this way, the WJC is a somewhat antihierarchical principle. But I do not think that the WJC is enough to check all of the hierarchical aspects of work about which egalitarians have worried.

I will briefly consider a case to illustrate the application of the WJC. Suppose an entertainment establishment introduces a dress and grooming code for its front-of-house employees, such as waiters and bar staff. The grooming requirements are designed to make staff easily recognizable as such and to maintain a neat appearance that will be appealing to customers. The dress code is not onerous, and some employees might welcome the sense of professionalism that accompanies it. But a female employee rejects the gendered nature of the requirements, accusing them of reinforcing stereotypes, and insists that she does not need to wear makeup as the code requires.[22] I pick this sort of case because it is not as obviously discriminatory as other instances in which expressions of gender identity are repressed in the workplace. I assume that where an employer engages in outright discrimination, his action is not an exercise of an authority he has, since it runs counter to moral (and legal) principles that already constrain the employment agreement. But the present case does not obviously fall outside of the employer's

[22] The case is reminiscent of Jespersen v. Harrah's Operating Company, Inc., 444 F.3d 1104 (9th Cir., 2006), which held that a similar dress code was permissible under employment discrimination law.

190   WORKING AS EQUALS

authority, since a dress code need not be applied in a discriminatory or objectionably stereotypical way.

Supposing the code is permissible, the employer still faces two questions: whether it is generally reasonable, given the cooperative conception of the workplace; and if it is, whether it nevertheless must allow exceptions in order to accommodate the personal convictions of particular employees. The WJC constrains the answers that may be given to these questions by excluding private reasons that the employer may have for adopting the code, such as a strong aesthetic preference for women who wear makeup, or a religious conviction that certain forms of appearance are gender appropriate. However, it permits such workplace reasons as that the dress code is appealing to customers, or that it motivates employees to meet higher standards of professionalism—to the degree that these reasons are in fact compatible with a fair allocation of the benefits and burdens of production.

The WJC does not only exclude certain reasons. By imposing the requirement that a directive must be justifiable to reasonable workplace participants, it also focuses attention on employees' reasonable expectations of accommodation. A liberal society admits a diversity of ways of identifying, and these identities may be based on the rejection of social norms of gender appropriate appearance. Moreover, identities are often based on or accompanied by strong convictions, such as the belief that social norms of appearance normalize and reinforce gender injustices. So an employee's rejection of a grooming requirement may be rooted in a very deep aspect of her conception of the good. That is the sort of interest that is vulnerable to the authority created by the employment relation, and that cannot be silenced if the workplace is to retain a cooperative character. So it calls to be balanced against the workplace reasons for greater uniformity, and potentially for reasonable accommodation.

The WJC is not supposed to produce an answer to such conflicts, but instead to remove them from the domain of conflicts of power and preference and give them a form that suits the cooperative conception of the workplace. Doing so invites reconciliation. For example, the workplace reasons that can be given for a dress code are likely to make visible what is really important from the perspective of the business, and so to make room for exceptions that can accommodate the reasonable convictions of employees.

10.5. Relational Equality without Bilateralism

The idea of workplace justification is an attempt to reconcile moral equality with the plausible assumption that workplace authority is permissible as a means of production. The basic way in which equality figures in this reconciliation is in the form of equal standing to demand justification. This is a demand that shapes the contractualist tradition, and it may be understood as a demand for equal consideration of interests rather than a demand for equal status or equal authority.

A demand for equal consideration of interests can readily be understood as egalitarian, but in what sense is it relational? What is distinctively relational is the demand that institutions and actions be justifiable *to* those who are affected by them, rather than simply justifiable. Contractualism is therefore relational because it is directed, rather than because it deals with relationships. This directedness is in turn rooted in its egalitarianism. Justification must be to those affected because they have equal standing to demand justification by their own lights.

This understanding of the relational nature of contractualist standards of justification is to be contrasted with a bilateral understanding of relational egalitarianism. Since the relational egalitarian ideal focuses our attention on the relations between people, it is tempting to think about what the ideal requires by restricting our attention to the relationship between two people.[23] But focus on bilateral interaction can be distorting. One symptom of the distortion would be a presumption that equality has nothing to say in favor of a hierarchical arrangement between two people.[24] But hierarchies can serve the equality interests of third parties, and even the equality interest of the lower-ranking member. For example, the inequality inherent in the teacher-student relationship is aimed at fostering in the student the kind of capacities (not just productive skills, but qualities of character like patience, receptiveness, and self-examination) that empower the student to relate to other members of society on equal terms.

---

[23] An example of such a framing can be found in Scheffler's suggestion that we understand equal relationships between citizens by analogy with a marriage of equal partners. Samuel Scheffler, "The Practice of Equality," in *Social Equality: On What It Means to Be Equals*, ed. Carina Fourie, Fabian Schuppert, and Ivo Wallimann-Helmer (Oxford: Oxford University Press, 2015), 21–44.

[24] This can lead to overestimating the challenge from what Kasper Lippert-Rasmussen labels "the pervasiveness problem," i.e., that many social relations seem to fall short of the ideal of relational equality. Kasper Lippert-Rasmussen, *Relational Egalitarianism* (Cambridge: Cambridge University Press, 2018), 51–53.

192 WORKING AS EQUALS

A further problem with the bilateral framing is that it neglects the question of how we may consistently conduct our relations on equal terms with all others, given the great diversity and interdependence of our various relations. Consider that one individual may relate to others both as a teacher and an employee (of the university). If we require equality in the employer-employee relation and think that this is an objection against hierarchy, we may neglect the need for the sort of workplace authority that helps to protect equality in the teacher-student relationship. A bilateral conception of equality does not prevent us from investigating the interdependence of such relations, but it does threaten to focus our attention too narrowly.

The idea of an institutional perspective provides a way to keep in view both the demands that equality makes of bilateral interactions and the fact that social institutions, and society in general, are not simply an aggregate of bilateral interactions. The requirement that a decision be justifiable to all members of an institution provides a basis for the members of the institution to see themselves as having equal standing in deliberation about what the institution requires. What is crucial in this is not the idea of bilateral equality, but rather the idea that members of the institution show up in the right way, as having equal standing in a shared space. It is the idea of standing, which goes together with the idea of claiming, that gives the view its relational character.[25] This means that deviations from the institutional perspective affect people beyond those involved in the relevant interactions. For example, a manager who decides on a whim to ban all religious symbols except those of the Christian faith may do something that is justifiable to his Christian employees, but he does not treat them as equals in the sense I have been pursuing here. In failing to adopt the perspective that requires justifiability to all his employees, he fails to treat any of them as equals in the workplace. So understood, the workplace is not a collection of individuals with competing interests who engage in bilateral interactions, but a shared enterprise.

---

[25] Joel Feinberg, "The Nature and Value of Rights," *Journal of Value Inquiry* 4 (1970): 243–260; see also Julian Jonker, "Directed Duties and Moral Repair," *Philosophers' Imprint* 20, no. 23 (2020): 1–32.

Acknowledgments

I thank Grant Rozeboom for helping me to clarify much of my thinking about the issues in this chapter. I also learned a great deal from the discussion and generous comments of R. J. Leland, Han Van Wietmarschen, and Chris Havasy. I was also helped by discussants at the Working as Equals workshop, and the Half Full Workshop held at Wharton Legal Studies and Business Ethics.

11

Relational Egalitarianism, Institutionalism, and Workplace Hierarchy

Brian Berkey

11.1. Introduction

Relational egalitarian accounts of justice have become widely accepted in recent years, and proponents have played a central role in a broader critical reaction to accounts of justice that focus primarily on distributive matters.[1] According to relational egalitarians, the fundamental value that grounds requirements of justice is egalitarian social relationships. Justice, for relational egalitarians, then, is at bottom about the terms on which individuals relate to each other. Most uncontroversially, on relational egalitarian views, justice requires that individuals do not stand in relationships to others that are characterized by domination, oppression, exploitation, marginalization, or other structurally similar features.[2] In addition, on some accounts of what egalitarian social relations require, individuals must possess certain

---

[1] The seminal contribution to the development of relational egalitarianism is Elizabeth Anderson, "What Is the Point of Equality?," *Ethics* 109, no. 2 (1999): 287–337; see also her "Expanding the Egalitarian Toolbox: Equality and Bureaucracy," *Proceedings of the Aristotelian Society*, supplementary vol. 82 (2008): 139–160; "The Fundamental Disagreement between Luck Egalitarians and Relational Egalitarians," *Canadian Journal of Philosophy*, supplementary vol. 36 (2010): 1–23; "Equality," in *The Oxford Handbook of Political Philosophy*, ed. David Estlund (Oxford: Oxford University Press, 2012). Other important contributions include Samuel Scheffler's articles, "What Is Egalitarianism," *Philosophy & Public Affairs* 31, no. 1 (2003): 5–39; "Choice, Circumstance, and the Value of Equality," *Politics, Philosophy, & Economics* 4, no. 1 (2005): 5–28; "The Practice of Equality," in *Social Equality: On What It Means to Be Equals*, ed. Carina Fourie, Fabian Schuppert, and Ivo Wallimann-Helmer (Oxford: Oxford University Press, 2015), 21–44; Kasper Lippert-Rasmussen, *Relational Egalitarianism: Living as Equals* (Cambridge: Cambridge University Press, 2018); and Christian Schemmel's "Why Relational Egalitarians Should Care about Distribution," *Social Theory and Practice* 37, no. 3 (2011): 365–390, and "Distributive and Relational Equality," *Politics, Philosophy, & Economics* 11 (2012): 123–148. Valuable overviews of the literature can be found in Rekha Nath, "Relational Egalitarianism," *Philosophy Compass* 15, no. 7 (2020): 1–12, and *Oxford Research Encyclopedias*, "Relational Egalitarianism," by Kristin Voigt, last modified June 30, 2020, https://oxfordre.com/politics/view/10.1093/acrefore/9780190228637.001.0001/acrefore-978019 0228637-e-1387.

[2] Anderson, "What Is the Point," 313; Schemmel, "Why Relational Egalitarians Should Care," 366.

Brian Berkey, *Relational Egalitarianism, Institutionalism, and Workplace Hierarchy* In: *Working as Equals*. Edited by: Julian David Jonker and Grant J. Rozeboom, Oxford University Press. © Oxford University Press 2023.
DOI: 10.1093/oso/9780197634295.003.0011

RELATIONAL EGALITARIANISM 195

egalitarian attitudes and must engage with each other in ways that reflect those attitudes.[3]

Hierarchical authority relations would appear, at least generally speaking, to be a threat to relational equality. When some people are in a position to exercise asymmetrical power over others, for example by ordering them to perform certain tasks and sanctioning them if they do not do so, or do not do so to the satisfaction of those with authority over them, there is at least an especially strong reason to suspect that the relevant relations might violate the requirements of Relational Egalitarianism.

Authority relations of this kind, however, are pervasive in our working lives.[4] Most people are subject to the authority of others in their jobs—they are expected to follow orders given to them by superiors, and are subject to sanctions being imposed by those superiors for failing to satisfy expectations. In many cases, superiors have the power to sanction those whom they supervise regardless of whether those employees have actually failed to perform their tasks well. The authority of supervisors, that is, is often largely unaccountable—when they choose to exercise it to impose sanctions, employees often have no recourse to challenge the sanctions on the grounds that they are unwarranted given the actual quality of their performance of job tasks.

Contemporary workplaces, then, would seem to be potential sites of substantial injustice for relational egalitarians. And in recent years there has been increasing discussion of the ways in which the relations among those within firms, and in workplaces more broadly, might be objectionably inegalitarian, and therefore unjust, and about what ought, as a matter of justice, to be done in response.[5] On some views, hierarchical structures within firms

---

[3] See, for example, Scheffler's "deliberative constraint," according to which each member of a society of equals must accept that "every other member's equally important interests should play an equally significant role in influencing decisions made on behalf of the society as a whole," and must have "a normally effective disposition to treat the interests of others accordingly" ("Practice of Equality," 25, 35). It seems clear that the satisfaction of this requirement involves more than merely avoiding dominating or oppressive relations.

[4] Elizabeth Anderson, *Private Government: How Employers Rule Our Lives (and Why We Don't Talk about It)* (Princeton, NJ: Princeton University Press, 2017).

[5] Important contributions include Anderson, *Private Government*; Nien-hê Hsieh, "Justice in Production," *Journal of Political Philosophy* 16, no. 1 (2008): 72–100; Sabine Tsuruda, "Working as Equal Moral Agents," *Legal Theory* 26, no. 4 (2020): 305–337. Much of the debate has focused on issues of workplace structure, and in particular workplace democracy; see, for example, Nien-hê Hsieh, "Rawlsian Justice and Workplace Republicanism," *Social Theory and Practice* 31, no. 1 (2005): 115–142; Alex Gourevitch, "Labor Republicanism and the Transformation of Work," *Political Theory* 41, no. 4 (2013): 591–617; Iñigo González-Ricoy, "Firms, States, and Democracy: A Qualified Defense of the Parallel Case Argument," *Law, Ethics, and Philosophy* 2 (2014): 32–57; Iñigo González-Ricoy, "The Republican Case for Workplace Democracy," *Social Theory and Practice*

196 WORKING AS EQUALS

ought, in effect, to be substantially limited, if not eliminated entirely, via the adoption of legally mandated workplace democracy measures, so that to the extent that some act as superiors within firms, for example by occupying a managerial role that involves delegating tasks to individuals and overseeing their performance of those tasks, they are nonetheless ultimately accountable to those over whom they exercise the authority that they have. If workers can, in principle, vote to remove a manager from a position of authority over them, then they are not, on these views, subject to domination, oppression, or exploitation, even as they follow orders given (just as citizens in a democratic society are not dominated or oppressed when they follow laws adopted by a duly elected legislature).

Even if employees within democratically governed firms would be assured of avoiding inegalitarian relations (I will offer a reason to doubt that this is necessarily the case), however, there are potential costs involved in accepting that all firms should be legally required to adopt robustly democratic internal governance structures. Perhaps most importantly, it is at least fairly widely accepted that there are substantial efficiency-based reasons that count in favor of at least some degree of hierarchical organization within firms.[6] Many relational egalitarians hope to accommodate these reasons, and therefore hold that at least certain kinds of hierarchical authority structures, including at least to some extent those widely found within firms, are not necessarily incompatible with relational equality.[7] Nonetheless, it seems undeniable that

---

40, no. 2 (2014): 232–254; Iñigo González-Ricoy, "Firm Authority and Workplace Democracy: A Reply to Jacob and Neuhäuser," *Ethical Theory and Moral Practice* 22 (2019): 679–684; Keith Breen, "Freedom, Republicanism, and Workplace Democracy," *Critical Review of International Social and Political Philosophy* 18, no. 4 (2015): 470–485; Isabelle Ferreras and Hélène Landemore, "In Defense of Workplace Democracy: Towards a Justification of the Firm-State Analogy," *Political Theory* 44, no. 1 (2016): 53–81; Daniel Jacob and Christian Neuhäuser, "Workplace Democracy, Market Competition, and Republican Self-Respect," *Ethical Theory and Moral Practice* 21 (2018): 927–944; Nicholas Vrousalis, "Workplace Democracy Implies Economic Democracy," *Journal of Social Philosophy* 50, no. 3 (2019): 259–279. For a helpful overview, see Roberto Frega, Lisa Herzog, and Christian Neuhäuser, "Workplace Democracy—the Recent Debate," *Philosophy Compass* 14, no. 4 (2019): 1–11.

[6] Anderson, *Private Government*, 67; Tyler Cowen, "Work Isn't So Bad after All," in *Private Government*, 108–116, at 115. It is important, however, not to exaggerate either the strength of these reasons or the types and degrees of hierarchical arrangements that they might support. For example, some ways of ensuring that workers have greater influence on firm policy, such as reserving a certain number of seats on the board of directors for representatives of labor, plausibly would not tend to reduce the efficiency with which firms operate. In addition, even when reasons of efficiency do favor certain forms of hierarchy, these reasons will sometimes be outweighed by competing reasons, for example, reasons of relational equality; see Anderson, "Expanding the Egalitarian Toolbox," 146–147; Anderson, *Private Government*, 52, 142–143.

[7] For the claim that hierarchical structures are sometimes compatible with relational equality, see Nath, "Relational Egalitarianism," 2; David Miller, "Equality and Justice," *Ratio* 10, no. 3

the conditions that must be met in order for individuals at different levels in a hierarchical authority structure to relate as equals must be fairly demanding. Indeed, the more hierarchical the relevant authority relations are, the more demanding it would seem these conditions are likely to be.

All of this presents us with a challenge—one that, I will argue, cannot be overcome within the constraints of the widely accepted "Institutionalist" view about the limited range of application of principles of justice. The challenge is, roughly, that the view that justice requires that individuals relate to each other as equals appears difficult to reconcile with the view that it is permissible, as a matter of justice, for firms to be organized with substantially hierarchical authority structures, and yet both claims seem independently plausible. In my view, the challenge has the apparent force that it does at least in part because many will implicitly assume that any approach to overcoming the apparent incompatibility must involve regulation by the state. This reflects the influence of the Rawlsian view that principles of justice apply to the institutions of the basic structure of society,[8] but do not apply directly to the conduct of agents within those institutions.[9] The solution that I will propose involves rejecting this view. I will claim, then, that at least some hierarchical authority relations within firms can be consistent with relational equality, so long as the individuals within those firms behave in certain ways that are not, and in at least some cases ought not to be, required by the rules of the basic structure, and so long as they adopt certain attitudes regarding both their own status and that of others within the hierarchy. The behavior and attitudes of those higher up in firms' hierarchies are, unsurprisingly, especially important if egalitarian relations are to be achieved within hierarchical organizations.

(1997): 222–237, at 232; Scheffler, "Choice, Circumstance," 17–18; Fabian Schuppert, "Being Equals: Analyzing the Nature of Social Egalitarian Relationships," in *Social Equality: On What It Means to Be Equals*, ed. Carina Fourie, Fabian Schuppert, and Ivo Wallimann-Helmer (Oxford: Oxford University Press, 2015), 107–126, at 108.

[8] On Rawls's view, the institutions of the basic structure include "the political constitution . . . the legally recognized forms of property and the structure of the economy . . . as well as the family in some form" (John Rawls, *Justice as Fairness: A Restatement*, ed. Erin Kelly [Cambridge, MA: Harvard University Press, 2001], 10). See also John Rawls, *A Theory of Justice*, rev. ed. (Cambridge, MA: Harvard University Press, 1999), 6, and John Rawls, *Political Liberalism* (New York: Columbia University Press, 1993), 258. For critical discussion of Rawls's characterization of the basic structure, see G. A. Cohen, *Rescuing Justice and Equality* (Cambridge, MA: Harvard University Press, 2008), ch. 3.

[9] See Rawls, *Theory of Justice*, 6–7, 47; Rawls, *Political Liberalism*, 257–288; Rawls, *Justice as Fairness*, 10–12.

11.2. The Trilemma

The problem, as I see it, has the structure of a trilemma—that is, there are three propositions, all of which are at least fairly widely accepted, but which cannot all be correct. The three propositions are these:

(1) Relational Egalitarianism: Justice requires that individuals relate to each other as equals, including in their interactions at work.
(2) Institutionalism about Justice (or simply Institutionalism):[10] Principles of justice apply to the institutions of the basic structure, but not directly to the conduct of agents within that structure.
(3) Workplace Hierarchy: At least some degree of hierarchical structure within firms ought to be legally permitted.

To see why these three propositions are mutually incompatible, note first that it seems clear that hierarchical authority relations are a paradigmatic threat to relational equality. This is because individuals relating as equals requires that at least one of the following two conditions are met:

(1) The institutional structures within which individuals interact ensure that there are no asymmetrical power relations that make it possible for some to dominate, oppress, exploit, or marginalize others, or to otherwise employ their power in ways that constitute or bring about inegalitarian relations between themselves and others, *or*
(2) The individuals themselves accept the equal status of all, and are committed to interacting with others in ways that clearly reflect and embody that commitment, even when they are in a position, within existing institutional structures, to exercise asymmetrical power over others.

It seems clear that the legal permissibility of hierarchical workplace structures (Workplace Hierarchy) is inconsistent with condition (1). The

---

[10] I argue against Institutionalism in a number of places; see Brian Berkey, "Double Counting, Moral Rigorism, and Cohen's Critique of Rawls: A Response to Alan Thomas," *Mind* 124, no. 495 (2015): 849–874; Brian Berkey, "Against Rawlsian Institutionalism about Justice," *Social Theory and Practice* 42, no. 4 (2016): 706–732; Brian Berkey, "Obligations of Productive Justice: Individual or Institutional," *Critical Review of International Social and Political Philosophy* 21, no. 6 (2018): 726–753; Brian Berkey, "Rawlsian Institutionalism and Business Ethics: Does It Matter Whether Corporations Are Part of the Basic Structure of Society?," *Business Ethics Quarterly* 31, no. 2 (2021): 179–209.

asymmetrical power relations that are present in hierarchically structured workplaces unavoidably provide those who are in a position to exercise power over subordinates with opportunities to do so in ways that violate the requirements of Relational Egalitarianism.[11] On the other hand, Institutionalism implies that individuals are not required, as a matter of justice, to be committed to ensuring that condition (2) is satisfied. This is because Institutionalism implies that while the institutions of the basic structure ought to be designed in the ways that will best embody and promote justice-relevant values (that is, the values underlying and embodied in the principles of justice, such as relational equality), individuals acting within the basic structure are not obligated to directly promote those values.

Consider a typical workplace in which, under present conditions, it is clear that particular individuals higher up in the hierarchy do not relate as equals to particular individuals lower in the hierarchy. Imagine that A is B's boss, and is able to exercise a great deal of control over B, at least during B's working hours. A interacts with B in ways that make it clear that A takes her interests to be more important than B's interests, and that indicate that B has an inferior status at least within the firm, if not more generally. If we think, as seems clear, that A and B do not relate as equals in this case, then there is, on relational egalitarian views, an injustice that must be remedied. And if there is an injustice that must be remedied, then there must be obligations of justice to remedy it. If one accepts Institutionalism, then the relevant remedy must be institutional, and the obligations must be obligations to bring about institutional change.[12] If, however, one is committed to Workplace Hierarchy, then there will be limits to the institutional measures that one will be willing to endorse in order to address the injustice. If entirely eliminating hierarchical structures within firms by, for example, requiring that all firms be run in radically democratic ways is not among the institutional changes one is willing

---

[11] Of course, the authority of superiors over subordinates can be, and generally is, constrained in a number of ways, and the constraints that are in place generally limit the ways in which, and the extent to which, a range of important values, including relational equality, can be undermined by the exercise of that authority. Proponents of Workplace Hierarchy can, and often do, endorse a wide range of such constraints. My claim is that even the full range of well-motivated constraints on the exercise of authority by superiors over subordinates cannot eliminate all opportunities for exercises of power that would undermine relational equality.

[12] Institutionalists generally follow Rawls in accepting that individuals are obligated to contribute to promoting the development of just institutions when such institutions are not already in place; see *A Theory of Justice*, 99–100. For criticism of the view that individuals have this obligation, but do not have an obligation to directly promote justice-relevant values, see Liam B. Murphy, "Institutions and the Demands of Justice," *Philosophy & Public Affairs* 27, no. 4 (1999): 251–291, at 270–271, 279–284; Berkey, "Against Rawlsian Institutionalism," 726–732.

200 WORKING AS EQUALS

to endorse, then, it seems to me, there is no guarantee that whatever institutional changes one might endorse as the appropriate remedy for the injustice will be sufficient to completely eliminate the inegalitarian dimensions of the relation between A and B.

Institutionalism, however, requires that there be a set of institutional measures that would be sufficient to eliminate any injustice—and so Institutionalists who accept that the relation between A and B is unjust must claim that whatever institutional measures they endorse as the appropriate response to the injustice would be sufficient to eliminate it. Institutionalist relational egalitarians, then, face pressure, I think, to accept very restrictive limitations on the legally permissible internal structures for firms. In particular, they face pressure to deny that it ought to be legally permissible for firms to be structured hierarchically, in virtually any way and to virtually any degree.

This is, at least in part, because Institutionalists are precluded from claiming that A is obligated, as a matter of justice, to exercise her authority over B within the firm differently. Because principles of justice do not apply directly to the conduct of agents within the basic structure, the obligations to eliminate the injustice cannot be obligations of individuals to be directly guided by considerations of justice in their behavior within the basic structure, including in their capacities as superiors within firms.

If, therefore, inegalitarian relations between superiors and subordinates within firms remain possible whenever hierarchical firm structures are legally permitted, then those who accept both Institutionalism and Workplace Hierarchy have no available explanation of how the inegalitarian relations could constitute an injustice. This is because they have no available account of what must be done, as a matter of justice, in order to eliminate the inegalitarian relations. Workplace Hierarchy precludes the most limiting institutional measures, which may be the only means by which egalitarian relations can be assured by institutional means. And Institutionalism precludes the view that noninstitutional means of ensuring egalitarian relations can be required as a matter of justice.

One issue that should be noted before moving on to discuss the possible approaches to resolving the trilemma is that on some accounts of what is required for individuals to relate as equals, there is a clear and direct conflict with Institutionalism that arises independent of the conflict between the conjunction of those two views and Workplace Hierarchy.[13] On these

---

[13] I am grateful to Julian Jonker and Grant Rozeboom for encouraging me to discuss this issue.

RELATIONAL EGALITARIANISM   201

accounts, individuals do not relate as equals, in the relevant sense, whenever any party to an interaction fails to possess appropriately egalitarian attitudes and commitments, and therefore fails to recognize those with whom she interacts as equals and/or to act in ways that are consistent with these attitudes and commitments.[14] Because these accounts entail that there are direct requirements, deriving from relational egalitarian principles, on the attitudes, commitments, and behavior of individuals, they are straightforwardly incompatible with Institutionalism.[15]

On other accounts of what is required for individuals to relate as equals, however, institutional arrangements can ensure that relational equality obtains regardless of the private attitudes and commitments that individuals might possess.[16] Those who are sympathetic to both Relational Egalitarianism and Institutionalism tend, unsurprisingly, to accept that just institutional arrangements would be sufficient to ensure that individuals acting within the institutional structures relate as equals in the sense that is required as a matter of justice.

My argument is, of course, directed against those who accept this second type of account of the requirements of Relational Egalitarianism, and hope to be able to combine that account with the Institutionalist view about the application of principles of justice. There are, then, two central burdens of the argument that I offer. The first is to provide grounds for thinking that there is no set of all-things-considered justified institutional arrangements that could ensure, independent of the attitudes, commitments, and behaviors of individuals within the institutional constraints, that superiors and subordinates within hierarchically structured firms relate to each other

---

[14] A somewhat narrower view that could be adopted is that individuals do not relate as equals whenever an individual in a superior position does not recognize those in inferior positions with respect to her as equals, but that relational inequality is not necessarily undermined when inferiors lack appropriately egalitarian attitudes and commitments with regard to superiors. For the purposes of my argument, this distinction is not important.

[15] Voigt suggests that despite the fact that Anderson and Scheffler are clearly influenced by Rawls, their views on the requirements of Relational Egalitarianism seem to require departing from Rawls's Institutionalism ("Relational Egalitarianism"). None, however, discuss this issue directly. Furthermore, in her discussion of what ought to be done in response to exercises of workplace authority that are incompatible with relational equality, Anderson focuses almost exclusively on institutional measures (*Private Government*, ch. 2). In addition, Scheffler has defended Institutionalism against the objections raised by Murphy and Cohen; see Samuel Scheffler and Véronique Munoz-Dardé, "The Division of Moral Labor: Egalitarian Liberalism as Moral Pluralism," *Proceedings of the Aristotelian Society, Supplementary Volumes* 79 (2005): 229–253 and 255–284; Samuel Scheffler, "Is the Basic Structure Basic?," in *The Egalitarian Conscience: Essays in Honour of G.A. Cohen*, ed. Christine Sypnowich (Oxford: Oxford University Press, 2006), 102–129.

[16] See, for example, Schemmel, "Distributive and Relational Equality," 142.

202 WORKING AS EQUALS

as equals. And the second is to offer reasons to think that, in light of this, the most plausible response is to reject Institutionalism. I have thus far offered some initial reasons in support of the first claim, which will be expanded upon as I consider the possible responses to the trilemma in the remaining sections. My central focus, however, will be to show that rejecting Institutionalism is the best option.

11.3. Option 1: Rejecting Relational Egalitarianism

If I am right that Relational Egalitarianism, Institutionalism, and Workplace Hierarchy are mutually incompatible, then we must reject at least one of these views. I suspect that, at least for most people, rejecting Relational Egalitarianism will be the least attractive option. One important reason to think this is that, in the context of this trilemma, Relational Egalitarianism need not be understood as the view that egalitarian relations are the only thing that matters, fundamentally, as a matter of justice. That view is controversial, and there are plausible grounds on which it might be rejected.[17] None of those grounds, however, would be of particular help in overcoming the trilemma, since the plausible alternatives to the view that relational equality is all that matters as a matter of justice (so that all requirements of justice are ultimately explained by reference to the value of relational equality) will nonetheless imply that A's inegalitarian relation with B is unjust. Such inegalitarian relations will, it seems to me, count as unjust on virtually any plausible view of what justice requires, and therefore the relational egalitarian component of the trilemma should not be understood as contributing to its generation only if relational equality is taken to be the (only) fundamental justice-relevant value, in terms of which all requirements and obligations of justice must be explained. It is enough, instead, if individuals relating to each other as equals is one of the requirements of justice, however the full set of requirements is ultimately grounded and explained. And I do not think that it is plausible to deny that relational equality figures into the full set of values and requirements of justice in this way.

---

[17] I argue, for example, that taking relational equality to be the value that grounds all requirements of justice requires accepting implausible explanations of why individuals possess some of the entitlements of justice that they do; see Brian Berkey, "Relational Egalitarianism and the Grounds of Entitlements to Health Care," *Ethics Forum* 13, no. 3 (2018): 85–104.

RELATIONAL EGALITARIANISM   203

In order to argue that rejecting Relational Egalitarianism is the most plausible way to resolve the trilemma, it would have to be asserted that despite the appeal of the claim that justice requires that individuals relate to each other as equals, the reasons in favor of accepting both Institutionalism and Workplace Hierarchy are stronger. Since the primary reasons that can be offered in favor of permitting hierarchical firm structure are grounded in considerations of economic efficiency, and perhaps more fundamentally in terms of the welfare improvements that greater economic efficiency can generate, it would have to be argued both that significant welfare improvements (perhaps in particular for those on the lower end of the socioeconomic ladder) are likely to be generated by permitting hierarchical firm structure, in comparison with prohibiting it; and that these welfare improvements are more important, from the perspective of justice, than ensuring egalitarian relations among superiors and subordinates within firms. Now, in principle, it does seem to me possible that the prospect of large enough welfare improvements, in particular for the worst off, could provide sufficient reason to allow certain types and degrees of inegalitarian relations to persist. But given that workplace hierarchies themselves, and the inegalitarian relations that they can generate, often have significant negative effects on the welfare of those subjected to domination, oppression, and exploitation, the burden faced by those who would press this line of argument is, I think, very difficult to meet.

It is, it seems to me, even more implausible that the reasons that are typically offered in favor of Institutionalism could be thought to outweigh, or take priority over, the reasons in favor of accepting relational equality as a requirement of justice. There are a number of grounds on which Institutionalism has been defended. Rawls offers three distinct grounds. First, he says that the basic structure is the primary subject of justice because its effects on individuals' life prospects are especially profound.[18] Second, he claims that the basic structure plays a central role in shaping individuals' characters, values, projects, and ambitions, and therefore must be the central site of application for principles of justice.[19] Last, he claims that a just basic structure is necessary to ensure "background justice."[20] Alongside this third justification, Rawls claims that if a just basic structure can be established, this would

[18] Rawls, *A Theory of Justice*, 7.
[19] Rawls, *A Theory of Justice*, 231; Rawls, *Political Liberalism*, 269.
[20] Rawls, *Political Liberalism*, 265–269; Rawls, *Justice as Fairness*, 53.

204 WORKING AS EQUALS

ensure that individuals and private associations can in good conscience take themselves to be permitted, as a matter of justice, to devote their attention and resources to the advancement of their particular goals, life plans, and conceptions of the good, since they could count on the basic structure to maintain justice regardless of the choices that private agents make within that structure.[21]

It does not seem like either the first or second ground for endorsing Institutionalism can, even in principle, provide reasons that compete with those that count in favor of endorsing relational equality as a requirement of justice. This is because these arguments are both intended to suggest that a just basic structure is the most important (and, if Institutionalism is correct, a sufficient) determinant of whether justice will be realized in a society— they do not provide grounds for favoring any particular conception of what justice requires, and do not provide grounds for rejecting a conception that cannot be guaranteed to be satisfied by a just basic structure alone.

The third line of argument can be interpreted as offering a reason in favor of Institutionalism that could, in principle, compete with the reasons in favor of accepting relational equality as a requirement of justice. In the broadest sense, this reason can be understood as at least similar to those that are appealed to in demandingness objections.[22] The thought is that an account of justice and the obligations that it generates for individuals (and private associations) is at least preferable, all else being equal, to the extent that it avoids requiring agents acting within the basic structure to be guided directly by the broadly impartialist values that are at the core of any plausible account of justice.[23] While this thought is widely regarded as appealing, it does not seem especially plausible that it could be powerful enough to justify rejecting relational equality as a requirement of justice, once we recognize the trilemma that I have described. Perhaps more importantly, I doubt that many

[21] Rawls, *Political Liberalism*, 268–269.

[22] See Brad Hooker, "The Demandingness Objection," in *The Problem of Moral Demandingness: New Philosophical Essays*, ed. Timothy Chappell (London: Palgrave Macmillan, 2009), 148–162; Fiona Woollard, "Dimensions of Demandingness," *Proceedings of the Aristotelian Society* 116, no. 1 (2016): 89–106; Brian Berkey, "The Demandingness of Morality: Toward a Reflective Equilibrium," *Philosophical Studies* 173 (2016): 3015–3035; Brian McElwee, "Demandingness Objections in Ethics," *Philosophical Quarterly* 67, no. 266 (2017): 84–105; David Sobel, "Understanding the Demandingness Objection," in *The Oxford Handbook of Consequentialism*, ed. Douglas W. Portmore (Oxford: Oxford University Press, 2020), 221–237.

[23] For discussion of the relation between Institutionalism and demandingness, see Scheffler and Munoz-Dardé, "Division of Moral Labor"; Murphy, "Institutions," 288–291; Alan Thomas, "Cohen's Critique of Rawls: A Double Counting Objection," *Mind* 120, no. 480 (2011): 1099–1141; Berkey, "Double Counting"; Berkey, "Against Rawlsian Institutionalism," 726–732.

RELATIONAL EGALITARIANISM 205

defenders of Institutionalism would endorse giving up relational equality as a requirement of justice. Rawls himself characterizes a just society as one in which everyone is committed to recognizing the free and equal status of all citizens—and while it might be argued that this requirement falls a bit short of one that requires that individuals all relate to each other as equals (perhaps, for example, all that is required to recognize everyone's free and equal status is supporting and contributing to realizing the institutional policies required by justice), it seems clear that Rawls and other recent defenders of Institutionalism are committed to accepting the more robust requirement. Resolving the trilemma by rejecting Relational Egalitarianism, then, is not a plausible option.[24]

11.4. Option 2: Rejecting Workplace Hierarchy

The second option for resolving the trilemma is to reject Workplace Hierarchy, and hold that hierarchical firm structures should not be legally permitted. This is, I think, a more plausible option than rejecting relational equality as a requirement of justice. It is clear, it seems to me, that states ought to regulate firms much more strictly than many currently do in order to limit the power that employers are able to exercise over employees. There are difficult questions about the limits of both permissible and advisable restrictions, but on the whole there are excellent grounds for thinking that those who have argued that workplaces in countries like the United States are seriously underregulated in ways that contribute to significantly unjust relations between superiors and subordinates within firms are correct.[25]

There are, however, two reasons to doubt that endorsing a legal requirement against hierarchically structured firms is either the best way, or even a sufficient way, of resolving the trilemma. The first, which challenges whether it is the best way, is that it is unclear whether we should, all things considered, endorse the type and degree of restrictions that would be necessary to either eliminate hierarchy within firms entirely, or limit it enough that it would

[24] There is much more that would need to be said here in order to make a case that ought to be compelling to those who do not already find a relational egalitarian requirement of justice at least fairly compelling. And perhaps some Institutionalists would be more open than I suggest to giving up Relational Egalitarianism in light of the trilemma that I have described. My central aim in this chapter can be understood, however, to be persuading those who are committed to Relational Egalitarianism that they must give up Institutionalism.

[25] Anderson's discussion in *Private Government*, ch. 2, makes this case quite powerfully.

not be a threat to relational equality, regardless of how individuals act within the rules. It seems plausible that, in order to ensure that relational inequality does not arise within firms, these restrictions would have to be rather severe, and this may involve trade-offs with respect to, for example, economic efficiency and enforcement costs that states would incur, such that we have reasons of justice to avoid them if possible. That is, even if very strict state restrictions on firm structure were both necessary and sufficient to ensure relational equality within firms, it is not clear that we ought to endorse all such restrictions, since there are, plausibly, other justice-relevant considerations in addition to relational equality that can take priority if they would be sufficiently negatively affected by the adoption of certain restrictions.

The second reason is, in my view, more significant, and raises a deeper challenge. This is that it is not clear that endorsing even the strictest minimally plausible set of legal requirements against hierarchically structured firms would actually allow us to maintain both Relational Egalitarianism and Institutionalism. In order to be consistent with Institutionalism, the legal requirements would have to be sufficient to ensure that relational inequality cannot obtain within firms, regardless of how individuals within them behave toward one another within the rules.

The reason to doubt that this is the case is not, of course, merely that people will inevitably be able to harbor inegalitarian attitudes and commitments, and to treat others badly, within any minimally reasonable set of institutional rules adopted by the state with respect to the structure of firms. As I have noted, on some plausible accounts of what is required for individuals to relate to each other as equals, some people's holding inegalitarian attitudes or commitments, and even treatment of one person by another that reflects these attitudes or commitments, does not necessarily amount to relational inequality within well-structured institutions. For example, within a just state, an individual with an unjustified sense of superiority and entitlement might treat some of his fellow citizens quite badly—but if he is not able to exercise any asymmetric power over those others, then it is plausible that the mere fact of his acting toward others as if he has a higher status does not, by itself, make it the case that he actually stands in inegalitarian relations to them. In fact, in my view, Institutionalist relational egalitarians are correct that institutional policies can *sometimes* ensure conditions in which, in the relevant sense, individuals will confront each other as equals, regardless of how badly one person might treat another, or the attitudes and commitments that might motivate such treatment.

When it comes to relations within firms, however, it is not clear what requirements the state could plausibly impose that would ensure that inegalitarian relations do not obtain. Consider, for example, that even under a fairly radical set of workplace democracy requirements, those elected to positions of authority within a firm would inevitably possess at least some degree of asymmetric power over others as long as they are in the position—this is just what occupying such a position involves.

Proponents of radical workplace democracy as a solution to the trilemma could claim that so long as those in positions of authority are subject to being voted out of their positions by those over whom they exercise authority, there are no inegalitarian relations of the kind that Relational Egalitarianism ought to find troubling. Importantly, however, in democracies, including workplace democracies, some people will always be outvoted by others. In many cases, there are persistent minorities, and the ability of members of such groups to relate to others as equals is not obviously fully protected by democratic procedures. In the workplace, those who are consistently outvoted may, for example, not have their interests and concerns taken as seriously by those in positions of authority as they ought to be, and they may not, by themselves, be in a position to do anything about that (because their efforts will not get the support of enough others). They may have no compelling procedural complaints about the decision-making processes and structures, and yet have substantive complaints about the ways that those elected into power regard their interests. When this is the case, it seems to me that in at least some cases relational equality may not be satisfied.[26]

This problem cannot plausibly be avoided by suggesting that the state ought to ban even democratically supported authority relations within firms. Any organization of even modest size must have some sort of authority

---

[26] I suspect that these concerns about persistent minorities within institutional structures that are as democratic as possible have more force, with respect to the ideal of relational equality, in workplaces than in states, so that even if the exercise of state authority by elected officials does not render their relations to citizens who are members of persistent minorities, and therefore oppose many of the policies implemented, unjustly inegalitarian, the exercise of managerial authority over subordinates who are members of persistent minorities is at least much more likely to render the relevant relations inegalitarian on any plausible account of what relational equality requires. This is, roughly, because of the nature and extent of the interactions that are typically involved in the exercise of managerial authority. Specifically, managers know their subordinates personally, generally interact with them on a daily basis, directly give orders and monitor the conduct of subordinates in response to those orders, and impose sanctions on subordinates directly. These factors, it seems to me, increase the risk that the relations between superiors and subordinates who are members of persistent minorities will be inegalitarian, and make it the case that what is required, either institutionally or individually (or both) in order to avoid this result will be more demanding than will typically be the case for elected officials.

208 WORKING AS EQUALS

structure in order to function reasonably well. In many organizations, including perhaps especially for-profit firms, these structures tend to be much more hierarchical and authoritarian than they need and ought to be, but few would find it reasonable to suggest that firms could operate without any authority structure that, in effect, gives some people asymmetrical power over others (even if those with that authority are subject to recall by those over whom it is exercised). If these structures are, at least to some extent, legally permitted, then there is at least significant reason to suspect that state policy alone cannot ensure that inegalitarian relations within firms will be entirely avoided.

In my view, whether they are avoided will inevitably depend, at least to some degree, on the behavior of individuals within firms, and in particular of those in positions of authority, as well as on the informal norms and expectations that exist within any particular organization.

11.5. Option 3: Rejecting Institutionalism

My view, then, is that we ought to resolve the trilemma by rejecting Institutionalism. Egalitarian relations cannot, at least within firms, be guaranteed by institutional policy alone, and therefore agents acting within the basic structure are required, as a matter of justice, to act in ways that contribute to (and in some cases partially constitute) the achievement of relational equality.

This is, of course, not to say that limiting the formal authority of superiors in workplaces is not also important. This should, in my view, be done to a much greater extent than it currently is. But it most likely ought not be done to the maximum possible extent, both for reasons of economic efficiency and, perhaps more importantly, because of the intrusiveness on behalf of the state that would be necessary to enforce requirements, as well as the costs that would be involved in enforcement.[27]

---

[27] It might be suggested that we should, perhaps for expressive reasons, endorse legal requirements that would, as a matter of publicly declared policy, be unenforced. This, however, may result in those individuals and firms that would comply with the relevant legal requirements, despite the lack of sanctions for noncompliance, facing significant competitive disadvantages. And this seems like a result that should be avoided, if possible. For the claim that there are cases in which laws should be adopted but left unenforced, see Robert C. Hughes, "Would Many People Obey Non-coercive Law?," *Jurisprudence* 9, no. 2 (2018): 361–367.

RELATIONAL EGALITARIANISM   209

One important objection to the view that we can and should resolve the trilemma by rejecting Institutionalism is that relational equality cannot in fact be achieved in virtue of those who have some degree of asymmetrical authority over others choosing to employ that authority in even the morally best ways—indeed, even if their exercise of their authority reflects a genuine commitment to the equal status of everyone within an organization. The influence of the republican tradition in political philosophy on many who are now concerned about workplace hierarchy has, I think, led many to believe that only state regulation can generate the conditions within which people can relate as equals, including within firms.[28] I have two responses to this line of objection, one less concessive, and one more so.

The less concessive response is that there seems to me to be no set of permissible state policies that could fully ensure that people relate as equals within firms, no matter, for example, how democratically they might be required by law to be structured. Inequalities of perceived social status and value within a firm (perhaps based on differences in skills, role, etc.) cannot be regulated away, and will, when combined with the unavoidable authority relations that will exist in any sufficiently large organization, tend to generate inegalitarian relations. Regulations can certainly contribute significantly to limiting perceived inequalities of status, but their elimination also requires the development of robustly egalitarian social norms and the internalization of egalitarian commitments by individuals. No matter how extensively one thinks the state is permitted to regulate the internal structure of firms in order to limit the relational inequality that often accompanies hierarchical authority structures, then, there will nevertheless be additional obligations that apply directly to individuals to contribute to making relations fully egalitarian.

The more concessive response is that even if, in principle, state policy could fully ensure relational equality, there are reasons to avoid the strictest regulations that would be necessary in order to do this, at least if relational equality can be achieved without them. In addition, it is important to note, as part of this response, that when strict regulations are not in place, and significantly hierarchical authority relations do exist within firms, the ways that

---

[28] The most influential discussion of republicanism in contemporary political philosophy is Philip Pettit, *Republicanism: A Theory of Freedom and Government* (Oxford: Oxford University Press, 1997). For discussion of republicanism and workplace issues, see Hsieh, "Rawlsian Justice"; Gourevitch, "Labor Republicanism"; González-Ricoy, "Republican Case"; Breen, "Freedom, Republicanism"; Jacob and Neuhäuser, "Workplace Democracy."

210 WORKING AS EQUALS

authority is exercised can make a difference to the degree to which relational equality is achieved.

Again, considerations of economic efficiency and the costs of enforcement provide reasons to permit at least some degree of hierarchical authority structure within firms. Where such structure can be permitted without significant damage in terms of egalitarian relations, it should be permitted (within limits). One reason to accept this is that it is plausible that some people possess what we can call "managerial skills" to a greater degree than others. These people are better than others at, for example, determining how tasks within a firm can be divided so that the firm's work will be done most efficiently. Their possessing this and perhaps related skills makes these people well suited to be in charge of delegating some tasks to others, and the work of the relevant firms will be done most efficiently if those to whom tasks are delegated are required by the rules in operation within the firms to perform them.

Importantly, nothing about the fact that one possesses such skills justifies her taking herself or her interests to be more important than those to whom she delegates tasks, and their interests. If a manager recognizes this, and interacts with those to whom she delegates accordingly, and if the firm as a whole has a culture in which all are expected to act in accordance with norms that acknowledge the equal status of all, then at the very least relational equality will be much better achieved than it is in most actual firms. This would be true, I claim, even if no changes in the legal structure of managerial authority are made. Because of this, it is implausible to deny that managers and others in positions of authority over subordinates in firms can have obligations, grounded in the value of relational equality, to exercise their authority in certain legally permitted and firm-sanctioned ways rather than others.

It might be objected that a requirement that those in positions of authority within firms exercise their authority in ways that ensure, or at the very least promote, relational equality threatens the very same values that I appealed to in order to reject the possibility of a permissible policy regime that could guarantee that individuals within a firm relate as equals.[29] For example, the deliberative burdens that such a requirement would involve for managers may pose a threat to efficiency, and might be thought to be intrusive in much the same way that state regulations aimed at ensuring relational equality within firms would be. If this is correct, then it may give us reason

---

[29] I am grateful to Julian Jonker and Grant Rozeboom for raising this objection.

RELATIONAL EGALITARIANISM 211

to reconsider the option of rejecting Relational Egalitarianism, since the very same kinds of considerations would count in favor of accepting both Workplace Hierarchy and Institutionalism.

The first thing that can be said in response is that it is simply a mistake to say that a moral requirement to act in ways that promote relational equality, and to deliberate in ways that reflect a commitment to the equal status of all, is intrusive in the same way that state regulation is intrusive.[30] It is one thing to be obligated to act and/or deliberate in certain ways, without any other agents exercising coercive power against you in order to ensure that you comply (or even being entitled, in principle, to exercise such power). It is quite another to be required, under threat of coercive enforcement and perhaps sanctions, to act in particular ways and promote particular ends. Unlike the state (or any other agent that might exercise coercive force), morality is not an agent that can, in any relevant sense, intrude on individuals' autonomy. The comparison is simply misleading.

Second, while it does seem possible that a manager's efforts to ensure that she treats her subordinates in ways that are consistent with a commitment to the equal status of all could come at some cost in terms of efficiency, this potential cost would surely be lower than what would be imposed by the regulations that would be required to promote relational equality as much as possible in the absence of egalitarian attitudes among managers. In addition, these costs would diminish over time as managers more fully internalized the egalitarian commitments that they set out to cultivate—and this is reason to think that accepting some temporary trade-off in terms of efficiency in order to promote the greater compatibility of egalitarian relations and efficient firm functioning in the long run is required.

Last, there is reason to worry that intrusive state regulation would threaten relational equality more broadly, even if it could promote it within particular firms, whereas it is clear that managers adopting more egalitarian attitudes and behaviors toward subordinates would not pose any threat to egalitarian relations more broadly.[31] One reason to worry that intrusive regulation could threaten relational equality more broadly is that it would require giving substantial powers to state officials (e.g., those who would be charged with monitoring the conduct of managers). This runs the risk of generating inegalitarian relations between such officials and those over whom they will

---

[30] See Cohen, *Rescuing Justice and Equality*, 192.
[31] My thanks to Julian Jonker and Grant Rozeboom for suggesting this point.

212   WORKING AS EQUALS

exercise authority. In addition, there could be more indirect effects on relations between, for example, superiors and subordinates in their relations outside of work—for example, having their interactions at work monitored by the state in a fairly intrusive way could undermine their ability to relate as free and equal persons more generally.

11.6. Conclusion

Let me conclude by very briefly describing what I take to be one type of noteworthy implication of my argument.

The internal changes that would have to be made when it comes to firm culture in order for relational equality to be achieved, or at least be much closer to being achieved, are, it seems to me, very extensive. For example, managerial "perks" would have to be eliminated entirely, perhaps ideally by managers themselves voluntarily giving them up and using any freed-up resources to improve things for those lower in the hierarchy. This would require that managers give up, for example, preferred parking spots and restrooms that are not made available to lower-ranked employees, as well as other benefits that are tied to positions in the hierarchy that serve primarily as indicators of status. The demands of relational equality within firms, then, require at least fairly radical changes that would have to be adopted voluntarily by those with decision-making authority, if relational equality is to be consistent with any degree of workplace hierarchy.

Acknowledgments

I am grateful to audiences at the 2021 Working as Equals Workshop, the 2021 Association for Social and Political Philosophy Conference, the 2021 Rocky Mountain Ethics Congress, the 2021 Significance of Work Conference, the 2021 MANCEPT Workshops, and the 2021 International Symposium on Rawls. Han van Wietmarschen provided very helpful comments at the Working as Equals Workshop, as did Cory Aragon at the Rocky Mountain Ethics Congress, and Lisa Herzog at the Significance of Work Conference. Dan Halliday, Chris Havasy, Julian Jonker, and Grant Rozeboom provided helpful written comments. I have also benefited from conversations with Marcus Arvan, Amy Berg, Justin Bernstein, Huub Brouwer, Barbara Bzuik,

Amanda Cawston, Chetan Cetty, Michael Cholbi, Joanne Ciulla, Rutger Claassen, Willem van der Diejl, Ned Dobos, Ryan Doody, Yvette Drissen, Micha Gläser, Phillip Hey, Nien-hê Hsieh, Chi Kwok, Katie Ebner Landy, R. J. Leland, Georgina Mills, Alex Motchoulski, Pierre-Yves Néron, Tadgh Ó Laoghaire, Eze Paez, Caleb Perl, Josh Preiss, Jahel Queralt, Tully Rector, Catherine Robb, Christian Schemmel, Andreas Schmidt, Amy Sepinwall, David Silver, Patrick Taylor Smith, Phillip Stehr, Christine Susienka, Dick Timmer, Andrew Williams, and Jonathan Wolff.

12
Good Enough for Equality

Grant J. Rozeboom

12.1. Introduction

The ideal of relating as equals is, at least in part, an ideal of persons' attitudes and dispositions toward one another. It is an ideal of a "virtue of agents"; we do not relate as equals unless we are reliably disposed to regard one another as equals.[1] But why is this, and what exactly does this virtue involve? Discussions of relational egalitarianism have focused disproportionately on its institutional implications—the laws, policies, and social structures that support social relations of equality. My aim is to better specify the foundational virtue that informs the ideal, using the workplace as an apt setting for understanding this virtue and what it entails.

Why is the workplace an apt setting? One familiar reason, which I will not take up here, concerns how workplaces figure into markets whose proper aims include, in addition to the efficient creation of wealth, enabling persons to relate as moral equals.[2] If we can assume that markets should help establish social equality, and given how workplaces support market functioning, it makes sense to think that workplace actors should be enabled to sustain and enact relational egalitarian virtue. A second reason, which I do explore further below, is that workplaces are fitting social contexts for cultivating and exercising relational egalitarian virtue. Given how workplaces bridge our personal and impersonal lives, and given how workplace authority can be circumscribed, they provide a context where all elements of relational

---

[1] Elizabeth Anderson, "The Fundamental Disagreement between Luck Egalitarians and Relational Egalitarians," *Canadian Journal of Philosophy*, supplementary vol. 36 (2010): 1–23, at 2. See also S. Stewart Braun, "The Virtue of Modesty and the Egalitarian Ethos," in *Virtue's Reasons: New Essays on Virtue, Character, and Reasons*, ed. Noell Birondo and S. Stewart Braun (New York: Routledge, 2017).

[2] This is a familiar point from the egalitarian literature on markets, stemming in part from early market thinkers such as Adam Smith; see, e.g., Debra Satz, *Why Some Things Should Not Be for Sale: The Moral Limits of Markets* (New York: Oxford University Press, 2010), ch. 1, and Elizabeth Anderson, *Private Government: How Employers Rule Our Lives (and Why We Don't Talk about It)* (Princeton, NJ: Princeton University Press, 2017), ch. 1.

Grant J. Rozeboom, *Good Enough for Equality* In: *Working as Equals.* Edited by: Julian David Jonker and Grant J. Rozeboom, Oxford University Press. © Oxford University Press 2023.
DOI: 10.1093/oso/9780197634295.003.0012

egalitarian virtue can be fully exercised. In this way, workplaces are better arenas for cultivating and exercising relational egalitarian virtue than the narrow range of democratic political contexts in which we interact simply as equal citizens.[3] This, at any rate, is what I take to follow from considering how managers can enact the autonomy-focused conception of relational egalitarian virtue I defend below.

12.2. The Importance of Virtue for Relational Egalitarianism

To begin, we should ask: why does relational egalitarianism require a virtue ethics at all—an account of the virtuous traits that "express, embody, and sustain social relations of equality"?[4] Put differently, why are character traits a central part of what relational equality requires, as opposed to merely serving as a helpful adjunct of it? And what exactly are the character traits (attitudes, practical and affective dispositions) that relational equality requires?

The first part of my answer to these questions is that relational equality requires virtue because it requires that certain social norms be established, and establishing these social norms requires certain individual dispositions and attitudes, which amount to a form of individual virtue. Let us briefly explore each of these claims in turn. Why does relational equality require establishing certain social norms? Without them, relational equality could not oppose the forms of social hierarchy it is supposed to oppose. Relational egalitarians widely agree that relational equality is centrally (perhaps by definition) opposed to (certain forms of) social hierarchy.[5] Thus, if social norms are required for opposing (the relevant forms of) social hierarchy, then they are a key piece of what relational equality involves.

A very general feature of social hierarchy—one which does not turn on any particular account of the kinds of social hierarchy that relational equality should oppose—is that it involves social norms that place some persons

---

[3] For a precursor to this point about workplaces serving as incubators of egalitarian virtue, see Cynthia Estlund, *Working Together: How Workplace Bonds Strengthen a Diverse Democracy* (Oxford: Oxford University Press, 2003), especially her argument in ch. 6 that workplaces provide a "bridging" context in society.

[4] Anderson, "Fundamental Disagreement," 2.

[5] See, e.g., Niko Kolodny, "Rule over None II: Social Equality and the Justification of Democracy," *Philosophy & Public Affairs* 42, no. 4 (2014): 287–336; Anderson, *Private Government*; Christian Schemmel, *Justice and Egalitarian Relations* (New York: Oxford University Press, 2021), ch. 6.

216   WORKING AS EQUALS

above others. That is, a social hierarchy is *social* in virtue of certain social norms being established, and it is a *hierarchy* because the pertinent social norms place some persons above others. The hierarchy norms do this in virtue of calling for attitudes of differential respect, reverence, and/or esteem by which some of the persons subject to the hierarchy norms are regarded as higher than others.[6]

We cannot eliminate the social norms that constitute social hierarchy without replacing them with nonhierarchical social norms, and given that we cannot do without social norms that call for *some* forms of respect and esteem, we thus cannot oppose social hierarchy without creating and establishing social norms that situate persons as one another's equals. These will be social norms that call for attitudes of equal respect and esteem, at least for those subject to the social norms in question.[7] Note that this is not yet to specify the relevant forms of respect and esteem.

So, moving to my second claim about virtue and social norms, why should we think that the social norms that oppose social hierarchy require some sort of individual virtue? Notice first that social norms require individuals to be committed to reliably following and enforcing them. This commitment will involve a practical disposition to apply the norm in one's reasoning, and to use it to evaluate and sanction others' behavior. Now, this practical disposition will be conditional in a distinctive way: when social norms are in place, individuals are committed to following the norms because they expect (nearly) everyone one else subject to the norms to follow them, and also because they expect that (nearly) everyone else will hold them responsible for following the norms.[8] You might think this conditionality prevents the practical disposition from constituting a virtue. I disagree, but to explain why, we first need to consider a second aspect of individual character that the social norms opposing social hierarchy involve. These norms call for attitudes of equal respect and esteem. Following the norms thus requires maintaining these attitudes—the patterns of thought, feeling, and reasoning that constitute the relevant forms of equal respect and esteem.[9] The norms are not

[6] It is a good question how to explain the "high" and "low" here—for an account of this, see Han van Wietmarschen, "What Is Social Hierarchy?," *Noûs* (2021): 1–20, https://doi.org/10.1111/nous.12387.

[7] We require *some* social norms of respect and esteem to structure our social lives, given our entrenched desire(s) for status—see, e.g., Christopher Boehm, *Hierarchy in the Forest* (Cambridge, MA: Harvard University Press, 1999).

[8] This is broadly in line with the influential account of social norms defended by Cristina Bicchieri, *The Grammar of Society* (New York: Cambridge University Press, 2006).

[9] On the idea that attitudes of respect can be directly required or commanded, see Stephen Darwall, *The Second-Person Standpoint* (Cambridge, MA: Harvard University Press, 2006), and on

GOOD ENOUGH FOR EQUALITY   217

followed simply by executing external behaviors that are symptomatic of respect and esteem.

While it is true, then, that individuals' practical disposition to follow the social norms opposing hierarchy is (or need only be) conditional, we can now see that its conditionality does not make it an instrumental commitment, and it will generally coincide with attitudes of equal respect and esteem. That is, even though our disposition to follow the norms is conditional—hinging on our expectation that others generally follow and enforce them—it does not treat following the norms as a means to some further desired end (of, e.g., appeasing others' social expectations). And it is joined with genuine attitudes of respect and esteem for others—patterns of thought, feeling, and reasoning that constitute the relevant forms of recognition, reverence, admiration, appreciation, etc. In maintaining these attitudes, one takes on a perspective internal to the social norms, in which the attitudes are sincere; one takes oneself to have good reasons to respect and esteem others in the relevant ways. This is similar to how a judge's respect for the law is sincere within the internal perspective of the legal norms that constitute the legal institution, but, still, a commitment to following the legal norms will be conditional on the norms being "efficacious."[10]

Now, you might still reply that, insofar as a disposition to respect and esteem others helps constitute moral virtue, it is not enough that this disposition is noninstrumental; it should not be conditional at all but, rather, a categorical, unconditional disposition, one which is not sensitive to others' compliance. I disagree, but we can set this issue to one side. If you wish to reserve "virtue" for unconditional normative dispositions, then we can use the term "morally desirable character trait" to cover the distinctive practical dispositions and attitudes that are required by the social norms that oppose social hierarchy.[11] What remains is a straightforward rationale for thinking

the idea of social norms directly requiring attitudes, see Han van Wietmarschen, "Attitudinal Social Norms," *Analysis* 81, no. 1 (2021): 71–79.

[10] See H. L. A. Hart, *The Concept of Law*, 3rd ed. (Oxford: Oxford University Press, 2012), 56, 104–105.

[11] A further general issue concerns what kinds of psychological states can count as virtuous (or character) states—for some recent discussion, see Nancy Snow, *Virtue as Social Intelligence: An Empirically Grounded Theory* (New York: Routledge, 2009), and Jonathan Webber, "Character, Attitude, and Disposition," *European Journal of Philosophy* 23, no. 4 (2013): 1081–1096. The dispositions I posit allow for different configurations of cognitive, practical, and affective components so long as they still support relational equality and can be realized in workplace settings, as I describe below in 12.4.

218   WORKING AS EQUALS

that relational equality requires an array of (noninstrumental) practical dispositions and attitudes that function as morally desirable character traits, which I think has been in the background of discussions of relational egalitarianism. But the specific relationship between social hierarchy, social norms, and relational egalitarian character traits has not yet been made explicit.[12]

If, then, the virtuous/character traits entailed by relational equality consist in the array of practical dispositions and attitudes entailed by the social norms that oppose social hierarchy, what exactly are these norms and the practical dispositions and attitudes they entail? Relational egalitarians have suggested they can be divided three broad categories:

(1) *Equal Authority*: regarding others as having the same basic authority as oneself and taking oneself to be accountable to them for how one exercises authority over them (where "basic" designates how the authority is held independently of more contingent or idiosyncratic roles and affiliations);[13]

(2) *Equal Consideration*: regarding others as equally deserving of certain forms of esteem, courtesy, kindness, and attention; and

(3) *Equal Importance*: giving the similar interests of others equal weight as one's own.[14]

While clarifying, this categorization ends up telling us very little until we know more about *why* and *how* the social norms and virtuous traits of relational equality fall into these three categories. Otherwise, it is difficult to know whether the norms and traits cover all three categories and, within each category, which specific forms of authority-recognition, consideration,

---

[12] This line of thought helps to account for how the virtue identified by relational egalitarianism is distinctively relational and not interchangeable with a distribution-focused or bad luck-compensating disposition—on this issue, see Kasper Lippert-Rasmussen, *Relational Egalitarianism: Living as Equals* (Cambridge: Cambridge University Press, 2018), 94*ff*, and Zoltan Miklosi, "Varieties of Relational Egalitarianism," *Oxford Studies in Political Philosophy* 4 (2018): 110–139, at 120–124.

[13] It is common to speak of power instead of authority when confronting social hierarchy. See, e.g., Boehm, *Hierarchy in the Forest*. I focus on authority because I think a concern with respect and obedience, and not just influence, is central to how relational equality opposes social hierarchy.

[14] For views that deal with all three categories, see Anderson, *Private Government*, 3–4; Kolodny, "Rule over None II"; and Sophia Moreau, *Faces of Inequality: A Theory of Wrongful Discrimination* (New York: Oxford University Press, 2020). For a view that emphasizes (elements of) Equal Consideration, see Schemmel, *Justice and Egalitarian Relations*, and for a view that emphasizes Equal Importance, see Samuel Scheffler, "The Practice of Equality," in *Social Equality: On What It Means to Be Equals*, ed. Carina Fourie, Fabian Schuppert, and Ivo Wallimann-Helmer (Oxford: Oxford University Press, 2015), 21–44.

and interest-weighing are required. We cannot just appeal to the fact that relational equality opposes social hierarchy, for there are many forms of social hierarchy, and not all of them are incompatible with the ideal of relational equality that has animated liberal moral and political thought and that seems to involve some configuration of Equal Authority, Equal Consideration, and Equal Importance.[15] To put the point differently, we can oppose many forms of social hierarchy with egalitarian norms and traits that fall short of Equal Authority, Equal Consideration, and Equal Importance.

You might think this issue can be quickly settled by appealing to our basic moral equality as persons.[16] We must oppose certain forms of social hierarchy and adopt the norms and virtues of relational equality contained in Equal Authority, Equal Consideration, and Equal Importance because we *are* moral equals. But this just pushes the bump around the rug. Our basic moral equality is itself a normative fact in need of explanation, given that the properties that putatively ground our basic moral equality are held unequally by persons (an issue to which I return below), and given that these properties do not obviously support Equal Authority, Equal Consideration, and Equal Importance. So we are still without an explanation of why the norms and character traits of relational equality involve Equal Authority, Equal Consideration, and Equal Importance, and what exactly they entail in these three categories of traits.

12.3. The Priority of Equal Authority

How, then, can we explain and justify the virtuous traits and associated social norms of relational equality? One option is to identify some underlying moral principle that is plausibly more morally fundamental than the idea that we ought to relate as equals and that explains why and how we ought to maintain character traits and associated social norms that fall under Equal Authority, Equal Consideration, and Equal Importance. One such potential principle is the equal consideration of interests, which is the focus of Equal Importance but plausibly implicates all three categories of traits. Another is equal respect for autonomy, which is the focus of Equal Authority but also

[15] Some forms of social hierarchy are aesthetic, for instance. See Lippert-Rasmussen, *Relational Egalitarianism*, 67.

[16] As suggested by Kolodny, "Rule over None II," 299–300.

220   WORKING AS EQUALS

plausibly implicates all three categories of traits. In this section, I argue in favor of an autonomy-focused conception, which I then use in the next section to begin examining how relational egalitarian virtue can be realized in workplace settings.

Let me start by explaining why an interest-focused view falls short, because this will make clearer the motivation for developing an autonomy-focused view. An interest-focused view is initially appealing because, as Samuel Scheffler points out, it seems to capture the distinctively egalitarian aspect of relational equality. It is natural to think that the equality in relational equality derives from everyone's comparable interests being given *equal* weight. As he puts it, in egalitarian relations, "Equally important interests . . . should play an equally significant role in influencing decisions."[17] Scheffler thus adopts the following conception of Equal Importance, which he calls "the egalitarian deliberative constraint": "I have a standing disposition to treat your strong interests as playing just as significant a role as mine in constraining our decisions and influencing what we will do. And you have a reciprocal disposition with regard to my interests."[18] We can readily imagine the social norms associated with this practical disposition—norms that require reciprocal consideration of one another's interests.

Now, Scheffler does not try to explain and justify the other elements of relational egalitarian virtue (Equal Authority and Equal Consideration) in terms of the equal consideration of interests. But we can envisage how he might do so, given what he says about our higher-order interest in preserving "social space" for autonomy:

> The anonymity of the relationships among the members of society sets up pressure to establish clear boundaries to those relationships and clear limits to the scope of the decisions that are thought to fall within them. The members of society will be interested in preserving social space within which they can conduct their face-to-face personal relationships and pursue their conceptions of the good life without being subject to comprehensive regulatory scrutiny from the perspective of an anonymous collectivity that lacks individualized knowledge of its members' needs, preferences, circumstances, and values.[19]

---

[17] Scheffler, "The Practice of Equality," 25.
[18] Scheffler, "The Practice of Equality," 25.
[19] Scheffler, "The Practice of Equality," 37.

GOOD ENOUGH FOR EQUALITY 221

His thought here is that an important part of giving equal weight to one another's interests is to recognize that we each have a higher-order interest in having latitude to pursue our personal interests—one way of thinking about the personal autonomy that is central to Equal Authority. This higher-order interest in autonomy stems from the "anonymity" present in many social relations. Such anonymity precludes the personal familiarity that, as Scheffler sees it, is required for sharing the "space" in which someone decides how to pursue their various personal interests. The higher-order interest in autonomy also plausibly supports various forms of consideration—courtesy, deference, etc.—by which we demarcate one another's social space, which are central to Equal Consideration. So Scheffler could plausibly extend his conception of what justifies Equal Importance to provide a comprehensive, interest-focused conception of relational egalitarian virtue (and associated social norms).

But I think Scheffler misdiagnoses the source of the pressure for preserving social space for autonomy, and seeing how reveals a more fundamental problem for the interest-focused view of relational egalitarian virtue (and its associated norms). Suppose that we could overcome the barrier of anonymity by giving everyone access to detailed information about one another's needs, preferences, and attachments. (There's an app for that!) Doing so would not seem to undercut the need for social space for autonomy. If anything, it would be even more pressing. This shows that the problem of intrusive strangers is not that their meddling is ill-informed and anonymous. The problem, I would suggest, is that it is paternalistic—that strangers rely on their assessment of one's interests without consulting and deferring to one's own understanding of them.[20]

If this is the problem that underlies the need for giving one another social space for autonomy, then the interest-focused conception falls short. For we cannot avoid the paternalistic stance—of relying on our own assessment of other's interests instead of deferring to their own—by more carefully weighing or prioritizing others' interests, so as to give more weight to their higher-order interest in autonomy. For we are then still making the mistake of approaching them from the vantage point of *our* assessment of their interests and treating their autonomy as something that can be weighed against their other interests. This means that, even if we abandon Scheffler's

---

[20] On this point, see Seanna Shiffrin, "Paternalism, Unconscionability Doctrine, and Accommodation," *Philosophy & Public Affairs* 29, no. 3 (2000): 205–250.

222 WORKING AS EQUALS

particular claim about the "pressure" for preserving autonomy (as deriving from the ill-informed anonymity of many social relations) and just assert that individuals have a higher-order interest in autonomy for pursuing their other, more particular interests, the problem of the paternalistic stance—of registering autonomy as, at most, one interest to be weighed against others— still arises.

This brings into focus an important feature of the character traits and social norms of relational equality (at least of the form that has been central to liberal moral and political thought): they are realized only among individuals who regard one another as adults, not children. Treating someone like a child—whose own judgments and decisions are subject to the discretionary guidance of a guardian—is a paradigmatic failure to relate to the person as an equal.[21] We need a conception of relational egalitarian virtue (and its associated social norms) that captures this, and that precludes the paternalistic stance in which someone's autonomy is registered merely as something to be weighed against other interests. To do this, I suggest we move away from an interest-focused conception to an autonomy-focused one.[22]

An autonomy-focused view, again, appeals to the importance of equal respect for autonomy as what explains and justifies the specific traits and associated social norms of relational egalitarian virtue. How, then, should we understand this principle of respect for autonomy? It centrally depends on what autonomy is, in the relevant sense. While there are many things that plausibly lay claim to the title of autonomy, David Enoch helpfully shows how many of them boil down to two basic forms: nonalienation and sovereignty.[23] These both concern the power to shape or author one's life. Nonalienation consists in having one's *values* shape one's life, while sovereignty consists in having one's *choices* shape one's life. Enoch argues that, in general, sovereignty derives its value from facilitating nonalienation.[24] However, in many contexts, including politics, sovereignty has

---

[21] This is not to assume that children's autonomy should not be respected at all. It is just to point out that children are not full-fledged participants in relations of equality, of the sort featured in relational egalitarianism, and this is marked, at least in part, by the fact that they are subject to interest-focused attitudes that simply weigh, rather than defer to, their own judgments.

[22] Perhaps there are more sophisticated versions of the interest-focused view that can overcome this problem, but I suspect that they will collapse into an autonomy-focused view.

[23] David Enoch, "False Consciousness for Liberals, Part I: Consent, Autonomy, and Adaptive Preferences," *Philosophical Review* 129, no. 2 (2020): 159–210, and "Hypothetical Consent and the Value(s) of Autonomy," *Ethics* 128, no. 1 (2017): 6–36.

[24] David Enoch, "Autonomy as Non-Alienation, Autonomy as Sovereignty, and Politics," Hebrew University of Jerusalem Legal Research Paper 21-18, last modified June 17, 2021.

independent significance. This is what leads us to think, for instance, that democracy, in which our choices count through voting, better respects autonomy than benevolent dictatorships, in which only our values, not our choices, count.

Which of these two forms of autonomy is most closely connected to relational equality, understood as something that is distinctively realized between adults? At a first pass, both seem relevant, given how adults grant one another wide latitude to choose careers, relationships, and projects that align with their values. We allow one another to make these choices for ourselves—realizing sovereignty—in part so that our values can shape important aspects of our lives—realizing nonalienation. But similar to what Enoch observes about political contexts, it seems that the significance we attach to the choices that we make, as adults, to shape our lives goes far beyond how these choices facilitate nonalienation. For even if some benevolent guardian could orchestrate better alignment between our values and the shape of our lives by bypassing some of our choices, doing so would seriously undermine the form of autonomy relevant to interactions between adults. It would attract the same general charge of paternalism that we considered above, in evaluating the implications of the interest-focused view. This suggests that sovereignty has central, independent significance in relations between adults. It cannot be traded off for the sake of better promoting nonalienation. Rather, the reverse is true: we allow nonalienation to be compromised for the sake of sovereignty.

Let us move forward, then, with the thought that autonomy-as-sovereignty has central significance in relations between adults. Can we conceive of the traits and associated social norms of relational egalitarian virtue as grounded in respect for such autonomy? I think so. Let us start with Equal Authority, which most directly involves respect for autonomy-as-sovereignty: in regarding others as having the same basic personal authority, we grant them standing to make decisions that shape their lives and interactions. Such a practical disposition is associated with social norms that require equal respect for personal authority and, thus, autonomy-as-sovereignty.

What about Equal Consideration? Equal respect for autonomy-as-sovereignty calls for giving others consideration on at least two fronts: first, many forms of civility serve as the expression of respect for autonomy-as-sovereignty. These will be forms of consideration that are important for signaling one's respect for others' autonomy. This will be important, in turn, for supporting the social norms that require respect for autonomy-as-sovereignty, given how, in general, social norms rest on public awareness of everyone's general

224   WORKING AS EQUALS

compliance with them.[25] Second, many forms of courtesy and esteem function as what I call the "currency" of autonomy-as-sovereignty. That is, giving others the relevant forms of courtesy and esteem—say, admiring their charisma—prompts us to take seriously their decisions about their lives and interactions and, thereby, respect their personal authority and autonomy-as-sovereignty. Garnering the relevant forms of courtesy and esteem is what "purchases" respect for one's autonomy, in this sense.[26] Thus, in order for our respect for others' autonomy-as-sovereignty to stably support social norms that call for such respect, it will need to be joined with a disposition to give others various forms of consideration.

And what about Equal Importance? To see how it functions as an important aspect of respecting autonomy-as-sovereignty, notice that a central part of how persons exercise their sovereignty is by authorizing certain of their interests for others' use in deliberation. That is, I can exercise my sovereignty by

(1) *allowing* others to consider some of my concerns, needs, and aims in deliberating about how to interact with me, and
(2) *deciding* which of my concerns, needs, and aims are most pertinent or important for their deliberation about how to interact with me.

Call interests that satisfy 1 "default authorized," and interests that satisfy (1) and (2) "willfully authorized."

Authorizing interests is an important aspect of how persons exercise authority over their lives and interactions with others. It is how they protect some aspects of their lives from unwanted scrutiny, especially in impersonal contexts where it is difficult to discern others' intentions.[27] To borrow Ian Carter's terminology, it is part of how they secure "opacity respect" in those contexts, where "opacity respect" refers to our standing to not be evaluated by others in terms of our particular inner propensities and weaknesses.[28] And

---

[25] See Sarah Buss, "Appearing Respectful: The Moral Significance of Manners," *Ethics* 109, no. 4 (1999): 795–826, and Cheshire Calhoun, "The Virtue of Civility," *Philosophy and Public Affairs* 29, no. 3 (2000): 251–275.

[26] For some empirical support of this claim, see Cameron Anderson and Gavin J. Kilduff, "The Pursuit of Status in Social Groups," *Current Directions in Psychological Science* 18, no. 5 (2009): 295–298, and Cecilia Ridgeway et al., "How Do Status Beliefs Develop? The Role of Resources and Interactional Experience," *American Sociological Review* 63, no. 3 (1998): 331–350.

[27] See Thomas Nagel, "Concealment and Exposure," *Philosophy & Public Affairs* 27, no. 1 (1998): 3–30.

[28] See Ian Carter, "Respect and the Basis of Equality," *Ethics* 121, no. 3 (2011): 538–571.

it is also how they shape the factors weighed in their joint deliberations with others. They do not simply vote on the outcome of joint deliberation; rather, by allowing and/or deciding for some of their interests to be considered as relevant, they help determine which factors are weighed and given priority.

So we can view a practical disposition of giving weight to the authorized interests (and only the authorized interests) of others as central to respecting their autonomy-as-sovereignty. This suggests that if Equal Importance consists, roughly, in being disposed to give equal weight to others' authorized interests, then we can view it as an important adjunct of Equal Authority and Equal Consideration in respecting autonomy-as-sovereignty. And, by extension, it will help support the social norms that require respect for autonomy-as-sovereignty.

We now have the (admittedly cursory) beginnings of a holistic conception of relational egalitarian virtue whose constituent traits and associated social norms are grounded in respect for autonomy-as-sovereignty. This virtue most centrally involves Equal Authority, which disposes us to accept others' equal personal authority to make decisions and judgments about their lives and interactions. It also involves Equal Consideration, which disposes us to signal our respect for others' autonomy-as-sovereignty through civil behaviors and to convey the forms of courtesy and esteem that serve as the currency of respect for autonomy (in a given context). And it involves Equal Importance, understood as the disposition to give equal weight to others' authorized interests. This is the *Authority-Centered Relational Egalitarian* virtue (ACRE).

But now we face the problem of explaining how ACRE is egalitarian. So far, Equal Authority is egalitarian only by stipulation, because is unclear whether or why autonomy-as-sovereignty entails that all persons have the *same* basic standing to make decisions about their lives and interactions. And the problem infects my depiction of Equal Consideration and Equal Importance: if it is unclear why all persons have the same personal authority that secures autonomy-as-sovereignty, then it is also unclear why they are equally deserving of the forms of consideration that express and "purchase" respect for autonomy, or why we should give the same weight to their author- ized interests, which they authorize as an exercise of their autonomy.

To solve this problem, we need an account of why, in accepting that all persons have autonomy-as-sovereignty, we must take them to have equal personal authority over their affairs and interactions. I cannot develop such an account here (although I begin doing so elsewhere).[29] But let me

---

[29] See Grant Rozeboom, "The Anti-Inflammatory Basis of Equality," *Oxford Studies in Normative Ethics* 8 (2018): 149–169. See also Carter's discussion of the importance of protecting "outward

226 WORKING AS EQUALS

briefly indicate the general kind of account that I find promising, as well as the kind that I find less so. The promising kind of account appeals to the morally important purposes of respecting autonomy-as-sovereignty, and claims that these purposes require regarding persons as having the same basic personal authority. Call this a "pragmatic" account, since it appeals to the purposes of respecting autonomy-as-sovereignty.[30] An alternative, nonpragmatic, and I think less promising kind of account appeals to the properties of persons (such as their capacities for rational agency) that putatively ground their autonomy-as-sovereignty. Call this the "property-grounded" approach. The problem with property-grounded accounts is that, for any of the properties that plausibly ground our personal authority as autonomous agents, they vary greatly across persons. They cannot provide a uniform "basis of equality."[31] Without a uniform basis for personal authority, they cannot substantiate equal respect for autonomy-as-sovereignty.

Again, my discussion of this issue must remain inconclusive here, so let me state my key claim conditionally: *if* we can establish equal respect for autonomy-as-sovereignty, *then* we can understand Equal Authority as a distinctively egalitarian disposition and, accordingly, ACRE as an egalitarian virtue. It rests on the egalitarian principle of equal respect for autonomy-as-sovereignty. This is so in the same way that Scheffler understood Equal Importance as an egalitarian disposition in virtue of responding to the equal importance of comparable interests.

---

dignity" in "Respect and the Basis of Equality," 557, although Carter's larger view is somewhat ambivalent between a pragmatic and property-grounded approach (which I discuss immediately below).

[30] Does this not just require pretending we have the same basic authority? Richard Arneson raises this pretense worry about Carter's account in "Basic Equality: Neither Acceptable nor Rejectable," in *Do All Persons Have Equal Moral Worth? On "Basic Equality" and Equal Respect and Concern*, ed. Uwe Steinhoff (Oxford: Oxford University Press, 2014), at 47. One way to solve this problem, which I defend in "The Anti-Inflammatory Basis of Equality," is to deny that our authority as sovereign agents is constituted independently of the social practice(s) by which we achieve the purpose(s) of respecting autonomy-as-sovereignty.

[31] There is an extensive debate about whether this problem for property-grounded accounts can be solved, starting with Rawls's "range property" view in *A Theory of Justice*, rev. ed. (Cambridge, MA: Harvard University Press, 1999), 444–446. I side with Arneson, "Basic Equality," and Stanislaus Husi, "Why We (Almost Certainly) Are Not Moral Equals," *Journal of Ethics* 27 (2017): 375–401, in doubting that there is a viable solution in the offing.

GOOD ENOUGH FOR EQUALITY 227

12.4. Realizing ACRE at Work

Relational egalitarians hope that the virtue of relating as equals (and concomitant social norms) can be sustained and enacted across a wide range of relational contexts.[32] But it is natural to wonder how widely or fully this is so. Perhaps relational egalitarian virtue is fully cultivated and exercised only in the narrow range of democratic political contexts where persons interact simply as equal citizens, bound only by their shared political ties and endowed with equal political rights. But when we understand this virtue as ACRE, I think it becomes clear that a wider range of social contexts, of which the workplace is a paradigm, are fitting arenas for enacting virtue.

This is because, in order to have occasion for exercising all three elements of ACRE, persons need contexts in which (for Equal Consideration) civil behavior and expressions of courtesy and esteem standardly fit within the contours of our interactions. So the contexts cannot be too personal and informal. They also need contexts wherein (for Equal Importance) they can share and account for specific interests they authorize for joint deliberations with one another; so the contexts cannot be too anonymous and impersonal. Workplaces tend to satisfy both criteria.[33] This is so even though workplaces involve extensive forms of hierarchical authority that can be abused. But as we will see, this organizational authority can be wielded with respectful restraint (for Equal Authority) compatibly with maintaining efficient production.[34]

To explain, let us start with the general structure of hierarchy in workplace settings. Managers are given wide, open-ended latitude to direct the work-related activities of employees, who are not similarly entitled to direct the activities of their managers. The precise scope of this organizational authority varies a great deal across different kinds of firms. But it standardly involves the authority to decide which projects and tasks employees are responsible for completing (within, and sometimes beyond, the broad ambit of their job description) and the schedule for completing them, laying out work-related goals and completing performance evaluations of employees in light of these

---

[32] This is clear in, e.g., Anderson, *Private Government*, and Scheffler, "The Practice of Equality."

[33] Of course, the social structure of workplaces varies a great deal across different kinds of organizations, and so the general claims I make here are bound to have many exceptions; for instance, in smaller, family-run businesses, interactions will be much more personal and less private than interactions in larger corporate settings.

[34] For a defense of this point about constrained authority and efficiency, see Anderson, *Private Government*, 130–143.

228   WORKING AS EQUALS

goals, and being able to enforce these directives by administering rewards and sanctions, up to and including termination of employment.

How could managers enact ACRE while acting as organizational superiors in this sense? Let us move through the three elements of ACRE. Equal Authority disposes us to accept that all persons have the same basic personal authority to make decisions about their lives and interactions. For managers, exercising their organizational authority over employees can coincide with accepting employees' equal personal authority if they

(1) regard the use of their managerial power as legitimated and constrained, at least in part, by their employees' agreement to work for the organization, and

(2) view themselves as morally accountable to their employees for how they use their managerial authority.

Claim (1) follows from the fact that we can legitimately share and surrender aspects of our personal authority. We can agree for others to help decide how certain segments of our lives are led and, in so agreeing, both legitimate and place constraints on the authority they thereby wield over us. This is a part of what legitimates and constrains the organizational authority that managers purport to wield over employees.[35] Recognizing this should inform how managers think and feel about their authority. They will not feel proud of themselves for wielding managerial authority, as one feels pride in an award received for meritorious performance, but rather feel respect for their employees as their authority's legitimating source. They also will be disposed to abide by the reasonable expectations about the scope and aims of their managerial authority that employees have in mind in agreeing to work for them. Doing so will preclude deciding to use their authority simply to benefit themselves, as when a manager orders an employee to perform personal chores, or meddling in employees' personal lives without good reason, as when a manager imposes a dress and hairstyle code simply for reasons of personal taste or comfort.

---

[35] Christopher McMahon, *Public Capitalism: The Political Authority of Corporate Executives* (Philadelphia: University of Pennsylvania Press, 2012), ch. 2, argues that this cannot underwrite the full extent of corporate authority over employees. I think his is an overly conservative view of legitimate corporate power—see Grant Rozeboom, "How to Evaluate Managerial Nudges," *Journal of Business Ethics* (forthcoming)—but even if he is right, my point still stands, which is simply that a necessary, even if not sufficient, component of what legitimates corporate authority is employee agreement.

GOOD ENOUGH FOR EQUALITY   229

Claim (2) points to an important clarification of my conception of ACRE, which I briefly alluded to in my initial description of Equal Authority. Accepting others' basic personal authority involves taking oneself to be accountable to them for heeding their authority.[36] This notion of mutual accountability is moral, insofar as it concerns someone's standing to blame oneself. Taking oneself to be accountable to others in this moral sense thus requires treating them in ways that enable them to determine whether one is blameworthy for what one does and, if one is, regarding them as having the standing to blame oneself and being disposed to feel remorse in response. For managers, this requires, first, exercising authority in ways that enable employees to keep track of whether they are respecting employees' equal personal authority. They will refrain from using hidden (even if effective) forms of influence, such as behavioral "nudges," that they know employees cannot readily recognize as instances of managerial interference.[37] Managers will also view their employees' blame (both in attitude and expression) as warranted when they have misused their managerial authority (and have no excuse for doing so). This, again, involves being disposed to feel remorse, to express this remorse through apology or otherwise offer some reasonable justification for a putative transgression, and to refrain from ignoring or instrumentalizing the significance of employees' blame.[38]

This is an initial picture of how Equal Authority can be sustained and enacted by managers in exercising authority over their employees. There are many details left to be filled in, but we have enough of the outlines to move on to consider how managers can enact Equal Consideration. This involves, first, being disposed to express and signal respect for employees' personal authority, which is standardly borne out in civil workplace behaviors. Managerial authority can be exercised while exhibiting such behaviors. This, again, is important for how ACRE helps support egalitarian social norms (that oppose social hierarchy), whose existence depends on public awareness that people generally comply with the norms. The expressive behaviors of civility help achieve this public awareness, including in workplaces, by making it known that people (generally) respect one another's equal personal

---

[36] On the connection between reciprocal authority and mutual accountability, see Darwall, *The Second-Person Standpoint*, ch. 4, and in connection to relating as equals, see Anderson, *Private Government*, 15ff., and Lippert-Rasmussen, *Living as Equals*, 94–97.

[37] Rozeboom, "How to Evaluate Managerial Nudges."

[38] On the relational egalitarian significance of enabling workers to express anger and indignation, see Sabine Tsuruda, "Working as Equal Moral Agents," *Legal Theory* 26, no. 4 (2020): 305–337.

230 WORKING AS EQUALS

authority and autonomy.[39] Popular discussions of workplace civility tend to take a consequentialist cast that loses sight of this deep, egalitarian significance.[40] Civil behavior may engender innovation and/or take the edge off employee motivation; either way, it remains an important piece of enacting ACRE and establishing relational equality.

We should acknowledge that the particular behaviors of workplace civility are partly determined by social convention. A behavior that counts as polite in one sociocultural context may be rude in another. But taking a particular sociocultural context as given, being disposed to manifest civil behaviors is, again, how managers express their recognition of their employees' equal personal authority. Now, a problem that the conventionality of civil behavior does pose for Equal Consideration is that civility conventions often encode sexist, racist, and otherwise unjust social relations. Does Equal Consideration dispose us to engage in civil behaviors, nonetheless? Not generally, because Equal Consideration disposes us to engage in civil behaviors just insofar as doing so conveys respect for the others' equal personal authority and autonomy-as-sovereignty. And since managers often can exercise significant influence over the socionormative ecology of their workplace settings, it may be feasible for them—in ways it is not for, e.g., strangers meeting on the street—to alter the conventions for civility behaviors within those settings.[41] They can create new practices, for instance, for how employees address one another that are more gender-inclusive and avoid sexist and transphobic language.

The second aspect of how managers enact Equal Consideration is by giving employees the forms of courtesy and esteem that function as the currency of respect for personal authority and autonomy in their context. This requires

(1) a sensitivity to which forms of courtesy and esteem serve as the currency of respect for personal authority in their workplace context, and

---

[39] This provides an alternative, but compatible, account of the significance of workplace civility's symbolic (or expressive) character to the Confucian account developed in Tae Wan Kim and Alan Strudler, "Workplace Civility: A Confucian Approach," *Business Ethics Quarterly* 22, no. 3 (2012): 557–577, at 563–567.

[40] See, e.g., the debate between Roderick Kramer, "The Great Intimidators," *Harvard Business Review*, February 2006, and Robert Sutton, *The No Asshole Rule: Building a Civilized Workplace and Surviving One That Isn't* (New York: Grand Central Publishing, 2007).

[41] Consider how, e.g., Starbucks leaders created corporate guidelines for recognizing transgender identity in the mid-2000s: Heidi Peiper, "Timeline: Starbucks History of LGBTQ+ Inclusion," Starbucks Stories and News, May 31, 2019, https://stories.starbucks.com/stories/2019/starbucks-pride-a-long-legacy-of-lgbtq-inclusion/.

GOOD ENOUGH FOR EQUALITY   231

(2) a disposition to maintain and convey these forms of courtesy and respect toward all employees.

To satisfy (1), something that managers can pay attention to is how, in general, employees try to prove they add value to their organization—what forms
of competence do employees try to exude?[42] But, turning to (2), a difficulty
is that these forms of courtesy and esteem tend to be earned along comparative measures, such that some employees will prove themselves much more
deserving of, e.g., praise for technical competence than others. What matters,
though, is that managers both sustain a minimum threshold of the relevant forms of courtesy and esteem toward all employees, which is a baseline
that corresponds to their equal basic personal authority, and overtly refrain
from granting employees who merit greater levels of courtesy and esteem
greater respect for their personal authority (and autonomy). For instance,
a manager can be careful to ensure that, even if a star employee receives far
greater accolades for her sales acumen than her coworkers, it is no easier for
her to ask and secure time off for personal matters, such as family caretaking
responsibilities, than it is for her coworkers who merit only the minimal
threshold of esteem for their sales abilities.

Finally, let us consider how managers can enact Equal Importance, which
in ACRE concerns the equal consideration of authorized interests. To enact
Equal Importance, a manager must give weight to all and only her employees'
authorized interests, and to give them as much weight as her own authorized interests. In this way, enacting Equal Importance requires the manager
not simply to be disposed to consider her employees' interests, but also to
defer to her employees' judgments about what their pertinent interests are—
the interests they authorize. (This returns us to my earlier point about how
ACRE is a distinctively antipaternalistic virtue.)

Recall that there are two forms of interest-authorization: allowing a concern, need, or desire to be considered in deliberation (default authorization),
and deciding that a concern, need, or desire is important or pertinent for deliberation (willful authorization). In thinking about how managers can enact
Equal Importance, then, what matters are determining the interests that
employees allow and/or decide are pertinent for managerial deliberation.

The interests that employees standardly allow for use in managerial deliberation and thus default-authorize will be largely determined by what

---

[42] See Anderson and Kilduff, "Pursuit of Status."

232   WORKING AS EQUALS

employees can reasonably expect that managers know about them, given commonly known corporate practices of excavating personal information about employees. Unless employees exercise an option (which they may not be given) to withhold some of this standardly collected information, they allow it to be used by their managers. In this way, workplace settings involve more default authorization of interests than purely public, impersonal settings, where we presume that our personal lives are mostly opaque to others. But this default authorization of interests will be more circumscribed and formally structured than in personal settings, where we assume that much is, by default, freely shared.

The interests that employees willfully authorize are those they intentionally disclose as relevant or important to their managers, through conversation and other conventional forms of intentional communication, such as wearing a pin that indicates solidarity with a social cause.[43] More controversial is the status of interests that employees share over social media. It is plausible that, on friend-based sites such as Facebook, employees do not take themselves to be revealing information for use by their managers, even if they know that their managers may peruse the site. They are sharing information with a community of friends and acquaintances for use in their deliberation as friends and acquaintances.[44] Which interests employees willfully authorize for managers' deliberation depends on what they voluntarily disclose *to* their managers, and not simply on what information their managers can readily discover about them. The manager who enacts Equal Importance is sensitive to this distinction.[45]

With this, we see that workplaces allow for the full exercise of ACRE. Workplace hierarchy does not preclude Equal Authority, because managers can be disposed to wield their organizational authority in ways that respect their employees' equal personal authority and autonomy—they can respect employees' equal personal authority as legitimating and constraining

---

[43] The importance of shared, conventional norms for disclosing interests overlaps with the importance of conventional norms for conveying consent, as discussed by Renée Jorgensen Bolinger, "Moral Risk and Communicating Consent," *Philosophy & Public Affairs* 47, no. 2 (2019): 179–207, 190ff.

[44] See Patricia Sanchez Abril, Avner Levin, and Alissa Del Riego, "Blurred Boundaries: Social Media Privacy and the Twenty-First-Century Employee," *American Business Law Journal* 49, no. 1 (2012): 63–124.

[45] But is it not sometimes important for managers to act on undisclosed employee interests? Consider, e.g., the employee who is reluctant to disclose extensive caretaking responsibilities. In my view, settling this issue will depend on what the manager reasonably believes about why the employee is reticent to disclose personal interests.

their organizational authority, and they can regard themselves as accountable to employees. Workplaces are not so personal as to hamper Equal Consideration, because they still involve norms of civility and engender forms of esteem that function as the currency of respect for personal authority and autonomy. And workplaces are not so impersonal as to trivialize Equal Importance, because they allow for managers to consider some of the particular authorized interests of employees. In allowing for the constrained exercise of managerial authority, and in bridging our personal and impersonal social lives, they provide an arena for fully enacting ACRE.

12.5. Toward a Holistic Account of Relational Egalitarian Virtue and Vice at Work

This is what I have tried to show, at any rate, for those occupying managerial roles. While I have not considered other kinds (or aspects) of organizational roles, my account sets the stage for doing so: We consider how, given someone's role and the corresponding organizational constraints and pressures they face, they can enact the traits specified by ACRE in their relations to other members of the organization. My account also sets the stage for reconsidering the structural constraints that relational equality places on workplaces, in two ways: it provides us with a formula for deriving constraints based on what will support and sustain the enactment of relational egalitarian virtue (understood as ACRE), rather than a formula that derives constraints with no direct concern for character traits, and it suggests that the proper constraints will make room for the exercise of virtue rather than try to establish relational equality through structural constraints alone. Finally, my account points toward a distinctive theory of vice—the character traits that directly obstruct and undermine ACRE-constituted relations of equality. In workplaces, the effects of some of these vices have been studied piecemeal—for instance, studies of uncivil work environments, or of narcissistic leaders[46]—but my view promises a more systematic framework for specifying these vicious traits and understanding their moral significance.[47]

[46] See, e.g., Lynn M. Anderson and Christine M. Pearson, "Tit for Tat? The Spiraling Effect of Incivility in the Workplace," *Academy of Management Review* 24, no. 3 (1999): 452–471; Arijit Chaterjee and Timothy Pollock, "Master of Puppets: How Narcissistic CEOs Construct Their World," *Academy of Management Review* 42, no. 4 (2017): 703–725.

[47] For a start on this project, see Grant Rozeboom, "When Vanity Is Dangerous," *Philosophy & Public Affairs* 48, no. 1 (2020): 6–39.

Acknowledgments

Many thanks to participants in the Business Ethics in the 6ix 2021 conference and the Working as Equals workshop for helpful comments and questions, and to Julian Jonker, Anne-Sophie Dubey, Alex Motchoulski, Etye Steinberg, Gopal Sreenivasan, and Federico Zuolo for incisive written comments and correspondence.

Index

For the benefit of digital users, indexed terms that span two pages (e.g., 52–53) may, on occasion, appear on only one of those pages.

accountability
  commodification of labor and, 13–14
  corporations' role as "private
    governments" and, 16
  equal authority and, 218, 229
  relational egalitarianism and, 11, 228
  upward unaccountability and, 51
  workers' interests and, 85–87, 195
aesthetics of inequality, 10, 63–65, 67,
    71–72
Affordable Care Act, 94, 95–97, 102, 111
ageism, 136–37, 148–51
alienation
  autonomy and, 108–9, 222–23
  factory work and, 20
  Holmes and, 182
  Marx's theory of, 13
  workplace hierarchy and, 34
Almond, Gabriel, 24
Amazon, 14, 29–30, 167
Anderson, Elizabeth
  on corporations as "private
    governments," 16
  on the joint production principle, 119
  on legitimacy at workplaces, 16–17,
    30–31
  on relational egalitarianism, 148–49
  on self-employment, 78–79
Aristotle, 78
Arrow, Kenneth, 56
Arum, Richard, 89–90
Augsburg Peace Treaty (1555), 103
authority
  collective authority and, 155–56,
    166–69, 172
  conservatism and, 61–62
  corporations and, 57, 60–62, 71
  joint authority and, 161–66, 172

legal authority and, 181
liberalism and, 8, 176
management and, vii, 61–62, 87, 228–33
moral authority and, 180–81
public justification constraint and, 176
republicanism and, 77–78
self-employment and, 76–78, 80–81, 84
workplace hierarchy and, 37–41, 45–47,
    232–33
workplace justification constraint and,
    175, 186–90
workplace perspective and, 181–85,
    186–88
Authority-Centered Relational Egalitarian
    virtue (ACRE), 225–33
autonomy
  feminism and, 106
  relational egalitarianism and, 9, 219–23
  reproductive autonomy and, 97–98,
    102, 109, 112
  sovereignty and, 9, 106, 223–30

Balkan, Joel, 59
Barnard, Chester, 55–56
Blattman, Christopher, 89–90
Boatright, John, 61–62
Boutmy, Émile, 64–65
Brown, Wendy, 54, 60, 67, 70
Buckley, William F., 67–68
Burke, Edmund, 68
Burwell v. Hobby Lobby Stores, Inc.
  corporations' right to withhold
    contraception coverage funding for
    religious reasons and, 94–95, 97, 98
  self-sovereignty doctrine and, 9, 95,
    102, 109–11
  Sepinwall's argument in favor of verdict
    in, 98–102

236 INDEX

Burwell v. Hobby Lobby Stores, Inc. (cont.)
    Sherbert Test and, 97
    Shiffrin's framework for understanding
      the verdict in, 101–2

Carter, Ian, 224–25
Case, Anne, 26
Chandler, Alfred, 55
Chinoy, Ely, 20
Christian Scientists, 109
Cicero, 78
Ciepley, David, 56–57
Coase, Ronald, 42, 54–55, 86–87
collective bargaining, 168–69. *See also* unions
commodification of labor
    democracy and, 10–11, 17, 19–20, 22–
      25, 28–29, 30
    dependency of workers on owners and
      managers under, 13–14, 15, 19, 24–
      25, 26–27
    human capacity development and,
      18–21, 30
    leisure and, 15, 20, 21
    Marx and, 13, 15, 19–20, 21–22
    maximization of output and, 13–14
    mechanization and, 19–20
    occupational self-direction and, 20–21,
      29–31
    quitting option for workers and, 19–20
    self-respect and, 25–27, 29–30
    Smith and, 18–19, 21–22
    specialization and, 19
    Taylorism and, 14
    unions and, 27–28
    welfare state policies and, 15–16, 27, 30
Congress of the United States, 96–97, 102
consent, 16, 45, 168, 179
conservatism
    authority and, 61–62
    aversion to change and, 62–63
    corporations and, 53, 54, 61–62, 64, 67,
      70–71, 72
    hierarchy and, 10, 58, 61–64, 66, 72
    inequality and, 62–67, 70, 72
    left-wing conservatism and, 62
    market conservatism and, 67–71, 72
    neoconservatism and, 64
    neoliberalism and, 67–71

    private power regimes and, 62–64, 67, 70
    relational egalitarianism and, 53–54, 72
    sovereign virtue hypothesis and, 65–66
    value conservatism and, 66–68, 72
contraception
    Affordable Care Act and, 94, 95–96, 97,
      102, 109
    Burwell v. Hobby Lobby Stores, Inc. and,
      94–95, 97
    religious-based objections to, 94, 96
    reproductive autonomy and, 97–98,
      102, 109, 112
cooperative paradigm of employment
    collective authority and, 155–56, 166–69,
      172
    contractualism and, 186–87, 191
    disagreement in the workplace and,
      176–78, 187
    dress codes and, 189–90
    good faith duty and, 164–66
    joint authority and, 161–66, 172
    meaningful work expectation and,
      169–71
    modification of employment terms and,
      163–64, 166–67
    occupational freedom and, 155–57,
      158–59, 161, 165–66, 167–68, 169–70,
      172
    productivity and, 170–71, 186–87
    quitting and, 159–60, 161
    societal stability and, 184
    trust and, 171
    unions and, 168–69, 171
    voluntarism and, 179–80
corporations
    authority within, 57, 60–62, 71
    conservatism and, 53, 54, 61–62, 64, 67,
      70–71, 72
    cooperation within, 57–58, 71
    efficiency and, 86–87
    hierarchy and, 54–58, 60–62, 71
    neoliberalism and, 54, 56–57
    as "private regimes of power," 61–62, 64, 67
    profit maximization and, 59–60
    religious rights of, 95, 96, 97, 99, 101,
      105, 112
    theory of the firm and, 42, 54–56, 61–62,
      71

Dahl, Robert, 16, 30
Deaton, Angus, 26
democracy
 commodification of labor and, 10–11,
  17, 19–20, 22–25, 28–29, 30
 equality and, 22, 25–26
 international declines in support for, 22
 justice and, 24
 as legitimating condition of the state,
  45–46
 meritocracy and, 64
 relational egalitarianism and, 10–11,
  227
 tempering factors and, 46
 worker-managed firms and, 22–23
 workplace democracy's underpinning
  of, 10–11
 workplace diversity and, 28–29
Dercon, Stefan, 89–90
discrimination
 actualist view of, 137–38, 141–42
 ageism and, 136–37, 148–51
 amended complex view of, 140–46,
  151–52
 commodification of labor and, 28–29
 complex view of, 139–40
 distributive justice and, 135–36
 Frankfurtian counterfactual
  intervention scenario and, 138–40,
  145
 genus misclassification objection and,
  142
 lack of relevant comparator objection
  and, 141–42
 misogynism and, 138–40, 147
 pregnancy and, 134, 141–42
 racial discrimination and, 28–29, 135–
  36, 137, 143–45, 174–75
 relational egalitarianism and, 135–36,
  146–51
 simple comparative view of, 133–34,
  135–37, 145–46, 151–52
 species misclassification objection and,
  143–44
 strong connection argument and, 135–36,
  146–47
Donaldson, Thomas, 105n.26
Dworkin, Ronald, 65–66

educational debt, 115–16
employment
 agreement, 76, 86–87, 115, 125, 129, 157,
  159, 162–63, 174–75, 179–80, 228
 contract and, 38–39, 50, 56–57, 58, 61–62,
  73–74, 78, 80, 86–87, 153, 157–60, 161,
  163, 165, 171–72
 law, 153–54, 198–200, 205–6, 207–8
 relationship, 53, 58, 74, 78, 86–87, 94–
  95, 99–101, 113–14, 118–19, 153–55,
  157–58, 161–67, 169, 171
Employment Division vs. Smith, 96–97
The Enlightenment, 4
Enoch, David, 222–23
entitlement theory of justice, 120
equality
 antihierarchy and, 4–6
 distributive, 117, 118, 120, 123–25, 127–
  28, 130–31
 markets and, 214–15
 relational, 53, 215
esteem
 autonomy and, 223–24
 commodification of labor and, 20,
  29–30
 employee interests and, 85
 equal consideration and, 218, 225, 227,
  230
 relational egalitarianism and, 2–3, 59,
  231, 232–33
 social hierarchy and, 215–17
Estlund, Cynthia, 28–29
exit. *See* quitting

feminism, 100–1, 106, 108
firms. *See* corporations
Foucault, Michel, 53, 55–56
Fourcade, Marion, 58, 60
freedom
 employment and, 47, 77–78, 80–81
 occupational freedom and, 82, 155–57,
  158–59, 161, 165–66, 167–68, 169–
  70, 172

gig workers, 29n.47, 30–31. *See also*
  self-employment
good faith, 164–66
Gourevitch, Alex, 86

238   INDEX

Hayek, Friedrich, 55–57, 62–63, 68–70
Healy, Kieran, 58, 60
Heath, Joseph, 57–58, 60, 71
hierarchy. *See also* workplace hierarchy
  conservatism and, 10, 58, 61–64, 66, 72
  corporations and, 54–58, 60–62, 71
  neoliberalism and, 55–56
  social norms and, 215–16
  the state and, 5–6
Hobby Lobby. See also *Burwell v. Hobby
    Lobby Stores, Inc.*
  Affordable Care Act's contraception
    mandate and, 94–96, 98–99, 101, 109,
    110–11, 112
  shareholders of, 94–95, 98–99, 100,
    101–2, 109–11, 112
  socially conservative Christianity and,
    94, 105
Hochschild, Arlie, 21
Hodson, Randy, 91
Holmes, Oliver Wendell, 182
human capital. *See also* human capital
    justice
  cooperation and, 123, 129–30
  definition of, 113, 117–18
  education funding and, 115–16, 125,
    129
  intellectual property and, 115–16, 125,
    129
  knowledge economy and, 114–15
  ledgers of benefits and burdens of, 117,
    121–27, 130–31
  management and, 113
  metaphysics of, 8, 117–22
  noncompete agreements and, 115–16,
    125, 129
  overall societal levels of, 116–17
  portability of, 114
  precarity of contemporary labor
    markets and, 114–15
  student debt and, 115–16
human capital justice. *See also* human
    capital
  contractualism and, 123
  distributive egalitarianism and, 117,
    118, 120, 123–25, 127–28, 130–31
  entitlement theory of justice and, 120
  equality and, 116–17, 122–23, 126–27
  individual preference and, 122–23,
    124–25, 126–27

relational egalitarianism and, vii, 117,
    127–31
  self-respect and, 126–27, 130
Hyytinen, Ari, 88

independent contractors, 30–31, 76–78,
    86–87. *See also* self-employment
Institutionalism
  arguments for rejecting, 201–2, 208–12
  individual agents' obligations under,
    198–99, 200
  institutional change and, 199–200
  justice and, 197–98, 199–202, 204–5
  relational egalitarianism, 6–8, 198–205,
    206, 208–9
  workplace hierarchy and, 197, 199–201,
    202, 206
intellectual property, 115–16, 125, 129

Jehovah's Witnesses, 109
Jonker, Julian, 134, 142–43
Julius, A. J., 38–39
justice
  contractualism and, 123
  distributive justice and, 5, 117, 118, 120,
    123–25, 127–28, 130–31, 135–36
  entitlement theory of, 120
  equality and, 116–17, 122–23, 126–27
  self-respect and, 126–27, 130

Kant, Immanuel, 4, 78, 130
Karasek, Robert, 21
Kautsky, Karl, 75–76
Kennedy, Anthony, 132–33
Kirk, Russell, 62–63
knowledge economy, 114–15
Kohn, Melvin, 20–21
Kolodny, Niko, 84–85
Kymlicka, Will, 65–66

labor
  commodification of (*see*
    commodification of labor)
  law, 153–54, 198–200, 205–6, 207–8
  organized, 27–28, 80, 168–69, 171
  power, 13–17, 19, 24–25, 28, 30–31
Lewinsohn, Jed, 38–39
liberalism
  authority and, 8, 176
  disagreement and, 176–77

INDEX 239

liberal egalitarianism and, 6, 99–100, 157, 170–71
occupational freedom and, 157
pluralism and, 5
public justification constraint and, 176
religious tolerance and, 104–5
self-employment and, 11
self-sovereignty and, 104, 112
workplace hierarchy and, 154, 172
libertarianism, 10, 53, 61–62, 63–64, 65–66, 106
Locke, John, 78
Lovett, Frank, 4–5
Lucas, J. R., 2–3

MacKenzie, Catriona, 106
Macron, Emmanuel, 70–71
Mair v. Southern Minn. Broadcasting Co, 153n.3
management
arbitrary power and, 73–75, 77, 79–81, 84–89, 91–92
authority and, vii, 61–62, 87, 228–33
business ethics and, 6
discretionary organizational power and, 7–8, 11, 227–28
efficiency and, 85, 210–11
employee interests and, 8–9, 75, 84–87, 90
employee rights and, 78–79, 85–86
higher-order decisions and, 47–48
human capital and, 113
neoliberalism and, 55–56
parallel case arguments regarding, 81–82
planning and, 55–56
relational egalitarianism and, 210–11, 212, 214–15, 228–33
republicanism and, 84–85
unions and, 86
workplace democracy and, 195–96
markets
competition and, 57–58, 71, 88–89
concentration in, 88
conservatism and, 67–71, 72
digital economy and classificatory architecture of, 58
neoliberalism and, 54, 56–57, 69, 71
self-employment and, 8–9, 88–89
social equality and, 214–15

Marx, Karl
class relations and, 47, 49
commodification of labor and, 13, 15, 19–20, 21–22
labor relations and, 5–6
on production "as human beings," 156, 169–70
Masterpiece Cakeshop v. Colorado Civil Rights Commission, 106–7
McMahon, Christopher, 228n.35
Mill, John Stuart, 5, 17, 24–25
Miller, Arthur, 13
misogyny, 138–40, 147
Moreau, Sophia, 11
Müller, Walter, 89–90

neoliberalism
conservatism and, 67–71
corporations and, 54, 56–57
"dethronement of politics" and, 70
hierarchy and, 55–56
markets and, 54, 56–57, 69, 71
New Deal, 55–56
Nietzsche, Friedrich, 68–69
noncompete agreements, 115–16, 125, 129
norms
antidiscrimination and, vii, 150, 172
business ethics and, 11
conservatism and, 63–64, 67
egalitarian social norms and, 7–8, 209–10, 229–30
employment authority and, 179, 183–84, 186
gender and, 176–77, 190
hierarchy and, 38–39, 53, 61–62, 63, 215–16
human capital and, 117, 120
markets and, 15, 56–60, 71–72
political sovereigns and, 103
recognition interests and, 99–100
relational egalitarianism and, 127–28, 215–18, 220–23, 232–33
self-sovereignty and, 112, 223–24, 225
Nozick, Robert, 29–30, 67, 120

Oakeshott, Michael, 62
O'Connor, Sarah, 14
Olsaretti, Serena, 82–83

240 INDEX

paternalism, 104, 221–23
Pettit, Philip, 4–5, 80–81, 87–88
Pickett, Kate, 60
Piketty, Thomas, 64–65
Polanyi, Karl, 31, 56
power
  arbitrary power in employment relations
    and, 73–75, 77, 79–81, 84–89, 91–92
  brute power in employment relations
    and, 73–75, 79–83, 91–92
  private regimes of, 62–64, 67, 70
  workplace hierarchy and, 38–41, 43–47,
    48–51
privacy, 38, 188–89, 190
Putnam, Robert, 28

quitting
  cooperative paradigm of employment
    and, 159–60, 161
  costs to the worker of, 49, 159–60
  as factor limiting employers' authority,
    180–81
  self-employment as a potential option
    following, 90
  welfare state policies and, 49, 159
  workers' interests and, 85–86
  workplace hierarchy and, 47–49

racial discrimination, 28–29, 135–36, 137,
  143–45, 174–75
Rawls, John
  on basic liberties and moral agential
    capacities, 170–71
  on the basic structure and background
    justice, 203–4
  difference principle and, 148–49
  distributive justice and, 5
  human capital and, 116–17, 126–27
  on human sociability and cooperative
    interdependence, 161
  on just society's institutions, 177, 197,
    204–5
  liberalism and, 5
  Original Position of, 9–10, 120–21,
    125
  relational egalitarianism and, 5
  on self-respect, 25–26
  on worker-managed firms and
    democracy, 22–23
Reagan, Ronald, 68

relational egalitarianism
  arguments for rejecting, 202–5
  authority-centered relational egalitarian
    virtue and, 225–33
  autonomy and, 9, 219–23
  conservatism and, 53–54, 72
  contractualism and, 191
  definition of, 134–35
  democracy and, 10–11, 227
  diachronic dynamics of, 150–51
  discrimination and, 135–36, 146–51
  distributional justice and, 127–28
  domination and, 5–6, 128–29, 174
  The Enlightenment and, 4
  equal authority principle and, 218–21,
    223, 225–30, 232–33
  equal consideration principle and, 8–9,
    218–21, 223–24, 225, 227, 229–31,
    232–33
  equal importance principle and, 218–21,
    224, 225–27, 231–33
  hierarchy as a paradigmatic threat to,
    198–99, 215
  human capital justice and, vii, 117,
    127–31
  Institutionalism and, 6–8, 198–205, 206,
    208–9
  interest consideration and, 8–9
  interest-focused conception of, 8–9,
    220–23
  justice and, 194–95, 198, 201–2, 204–5
  justification of, 9–11
  moral equality and, 9–10
  nonalienation and, 222–23
  republicanism and, 4–5
  social equality and, 53, 215
  social norms and, 215–18
  sovereignty and, 223–30
  state regulation of corporations and,
    205–8, 209–12
  status and, 2–3, 8–9
  virtue ethics and, 7–8, 214–18
  workplace democracy and, vii, 57
  workplace hierarchy and, 195–97, 202–3
Religious Freedom Restoration Act
  (RFRA), 96–97, 104
republicanism
  antihierarchism and, 4–5, 64–65
  authority and, 77–78
  employee work and, 78, 85

INDEX 241

independence and, 73, 77
management and, 84–85
meritocracy and, 64–65
nondomination and, 4–5
relational egalitarianism and, 4–5
self-employment and, 11, 74, 78–79
workplace hierarchy and, 209
respect
commodification of labor and, 25–27,
29–30
human capital and, 126–27, 130
rights
corporations' religious rights and, 95,
96, 97, 98–99, 101, 105, 112
employee rights and, 78–79, 85–87
Robin, Corey, 61–63, 68–69
Roemer, John, 16–17
Rottenberg, Catherine, 71
Rousseau, Jean-Jacques, 4
Ruuskanen, Olli-Pekka, 88

Sangiovanni, Andrea, 10
Scanlon, T. M., 10
Scheffler, Samuel, 60–61, 150–51, 220–22, 226
Schemmel, Christian, 129–30
Schooler, Carmi, 20–21
Scott, James C., 58–60
Scruton, Roger, 67–68, 70–71
self-employment
agency and, 80
anonymous dependence and, 87–88
arbitrary power argument in favor of,
73–75, 77, 79–81, 84–89, 91–92
authority and, 76–78, 80–81, 84
brute power argument in favor of, 73–75,
79–83, 91–92
in developing countries, 89–90
efficiency and, 79, 92
government regulations regarding, 74,
82, 90–91
hazards of, 79–80, 92
horizontal dependence and, 84, 87–89
independence and, 73–78, 79–80, 82–
83, 84, 85–86, 87–88, 89, 91–92
liberalism and, 11
market competition and, 8–9, 88–89
parallel case arguments regarding, 80–82
petty bourgeoisie and, 76
positive externalities and, 82–83
prevalence in society of, 73, 75–77

republicanism and, 11, 74, 78–79
vertical dependence and, 84, 88
wage workers and, 89–91
self-sovereignty
autonomy and, 9, 106
Burwell v. Hobby Lobby and, 9, 95, 102,
109–11
democratically approved schemes to
facilitate, 109–10, 111
egalitarianism and, 102–9
feminism and, 108
liberalism and, 104, 112
private property and, 106–7
religious tolerance and, 103, 104–5,
106–9, 111
reproductive sovereignty and, 97–98,
102, 109, 112
Sen, Amartya, 65–66, 121
Sepinwall, Amy, 96, 98–102
Sherbert Test, 96–97
Shiffrin, Seana, 101–2
Sidney, Algernon, 77
Simmons, A. John, 83
Simon, Herbert, 54–55
Skinner, Quentin, 4–5
Smith, Adam
commodification of labor and, 18–19,
21–22
on markets and equality, 6n.14
on self-employment, 78
on tradesmen and customers, 87–88
social equality
antihierarchy and, 4–6
antisectarianism and, 4–6
markets and, 214–15
relational egalitarianism and, 53, 215
socialism, 16–17, 75–76
Soper, Spencer, 14
sovereign virtue hypothesis, 65–66
Steinmetz, George, 76
Stoljar, Natalie, 106
Strauss, Leo, 68
student debt, 115–16
subordination
cooperative paradigm of employment
and, 156, 170–71
corporations and, 60, 71
discrimination and, 145
occupational freedom and, 161, 169–70,
172

242 INDEX

subordination (*cont.*)
    relational egalitarianism and, 128–29
    workplace hierarchy and, 41–42, 45–46,
        198–200, 203, 205, 210
sweatshops, 89–90

Taylor, Robert, 86
Taylorism, 14, 50
Terkel, Studs, 26–27
Thatcher, Margaret, 67–68
theory of the firm, 42, 54–56, 61–62, 71
transaction costs, 2–3, 42, 55, 58, 61–62, 180
Trump, Donald, 68–71

Uber, 30–31
unemployment benefits, 15, 27, 96–97,
    104, 159
unions, 27–28, 80, 168–69, 171
United Kingdom, 27, 115–16
utilitarianism, 53, 148–49

Van Praag, C. Mirjam, 83
Verba, Sidney, 24
Versloot, Peter H., 83
virtue
    Authority-Centered Relational
      Egalitarian virtue and, 225–33
    sovereign virtue and, 65–66
    virtue ethics and, 7–8, 214–18
voluntarism, 179–80

Walmart, 14, 30–31
Walzer, Michael, 16, 30
Wilkinson, Richard, 60
Williamson, Oliver, 55–56
Wolff, Jonathan, 65
workplace democracy
    codetermination and, vii
    efficiency and, 196–97
    management and, 195–96
    minority rights in, 207
    relational egalitarianism and, vii, 57
    workers' cooperatives and, vii
    workplace hierarchy and, 207
workplace hierarchy
    arguments for rejecting, 205–8
    authority and, 37–41, 45–47, 232–33

content limitation as tempering factor
    in, 46–49, 50
context limitation as a tempering factor
    and, 46, 48–49
duty to exclude and, 36–37, 41, 43
duty to execute and, 35–37, 41, 43
duty to treat equally and, 36–37, 41–42, 44
efficiency and, vii, 16–17, 42–43, 55, 61–
    62, 66, 170, 196–97, 203, 205–6, 210
egalitarian relationship as tempering
    factor in, 48–49
equal application as tempering factor
    in, 50–51
equal influence as tempering factor in,
    45–46, 48, 49–50, 51
escapability as tempering factor in, 47–49
favoritism and, 36, 44
higher-level equality as tempering
    factor in, 47–49
impersonal justification as tempering
    factor in, 39–50, 51
improvement complaints and, 34–35
incomplete nature of employment
    agreements and, 157
labor law and, 153–54, 198–200, 205–6,
    207–8
least discretion as tempering factor in,
    41–42, 44, 45–46, 48, 49–51
nepotism and, 35, 43
parallel-case argument regarding the
    state and, 32–33, 44–45, 48, 49–51
power relations and, 38–41, 43–47, 48–51
as "private government," 16
public interest and, 33, 35, 40, 42–43
relational egalitarianism and, 195–97,
    202–3
relations of inferiority and, 32–33, 37,
    39–40, 41, 42–43, 47
republicanism and, 209
safety standards and, 34, 38, 42–43
socialism and, 16–17
theory of the firm and, 42
transaction costs and, 2–3, 42, 55–56, 180
upward unaccountability as tempering
    factor in, 51
workplace democracy and, 207
Wright, Erik Olin, 76

Printed in the USA/Agawam, MA
May 2, 2023

809357.029